AN INTRODUCTION TO CULTURAL STUDIES

AN INTRODUCTION TO CULTURAL STUDIES

Second Edition
Revised and Updated

Pramod K. Nayar

Viva Books

New Delhi | Mumbai | Chennai | Kolkata | Bengaluru | Hyderabad | Kochi | Guwahati

Publisher's note

Every possible effort has been made to ensure that the information contained in this book is accurate at the time of going to press, and the publisher and author cannot accept responsibility for any errors or omissions, however caused. No responsibility for loss or damage occasioned to any person acting, or refraining from action, as a result of the material in this publication can be accepted by the editor, the publisher or the author.

Every effort has been made to trace the owners of copyright material used in this book. The authors and the publisher will be grateful for any omission brought to their notice for acknowledgment in the future editions of the book.

First Published 2008
Reprinted 2009, 2011, 2014, 2015
Second Edition 2016, Reprinted 2017, 2019, 2020, 2021, 2022, 2023

Viva Books Private Limited

- 4737/23, Ansari Road, Daryaganj, New Delhi 110 002
  Tel. 011-42242200, 23258325, 23283121, Email: vivadelhi@vivagroupindia.in
- 76, Service Industries, Shirvane, Sector 1, Nerul, Navi Mumbai 400 706
  Tel. 022-27721273, 27721274, Email: vivamumbai@vivagroupindia.in
- Megh Tower, Old No. 307, New No. 165, Poonamallee High Road, Maduravoyal, Chennai 600 095
  Tel. 044-23780991, 23780992, 23780994, Email: vivachennai@vivagroupindia.in
- B-103, Jindal Towers, 21/1A/3 Darga Road, Kolkata 700 017
  Tel. 033-22816713, Email: vivakolkata@vivagroupindia.in
- 194, First Floor Subbarama Chetty Road, Near Nettkallappa Circle, Basavanagudi, Bengaluru 560 004
  Tel. 080-26607409, Email: vivabangalore@vivagroupindia.in
- 101-102, Moghal Marc Apartments, 3-4-637 to 641, Narayanguda, Hyderabad 500 029
  Tel. 040-27564481, Email: vivahyderabad@vivagroupindia.in
- First Floor, Beevi Towers, SRM Road, Kaloor, Kochi 682 018
  Tel. 0484-2403055, 2403056, Email: vivakochi@vivagroupindia.in
- 232, GNB Road, Beside UCO Bank, Silpukhuri, Guwahati 781 003
  Tel. 0361-2666386, Email: vivaguwahati@vivagroupindia.in

www.vivagroupindia.com

ISBN: 978-81-309-3398-6

Published by Viva Books Private Limited, 4737/23, Ansari Road, Daryaganj, New Delhi 110 002.

Printed and bound by Anand Sons, New Delhi.

SUB-0009

Contents

Preface to the Second Edition

This second, revised edition of *An Introduction to Cultural Studies* was prepared because of the perception my editor, Sreetilak, and I had that we needed to add new domains of analysis to the existing book. Then, having decided on Selfies/Impression-management and Memory as two new domains to be added, we recognized the inevitability of having either a massive, two-volume work or dropping chapters from the earlier edition. Consequently, we retained Shopping – always the thrilling domain for Cultural Studies (CS) – and dropped Space and Communication.

The early chapter on Theories has an added section, on Posthumanism, so as to acknowledge new forms of critical thought in the world, especially those that are in the process of redefining the human. This section draws on my *Posthumanism* (Polity 2014). Given the interest in human-animal and human-machine interfaces, bioethics and xenotransplantation technologies, posthumanism is an essential component of thinking in the humanities, social sciences and the biological sciences. Posthumanism's many manifestations in popular culture, from cyborgs to X-Men, make it imperative that we familiarize ourselves with the critique.

In the age of impression management and reputation management, whether selfies are an expression of narcissistic involvement with the self or a celebritizing of the self is open to question. As a cultural phenomenon enabled by technology, the selfie is located at the intersection of impression management, informed surveillance and museumization, but also asserts a certain of agency and control over the dissemination of information about one's self. This chapter appeared in a shorter and less detailed version in *Seminar* 663 (Nov. 2014).

The digital age has transformed memory cultures in radical ways. Archiving as identity-making and self-fashioning, both individual and communitarian, is as open to hegemonic control, and hence is the domain of CS as well. The production, circulation and consumption of memory constitute us as subjects, and collective projects enable the merging of personal and collective memories. Parts of this chapter on Memory Cultures were originally written as an essay for a forthcoming volume on Cultural Studies, edited by Rana Nayar for Routledge India.

June 2015

PKN
Hyderabad

Preface to the First Edition

This book is an attempt to give a simple introduction to the various ways of understanding culture, ways that are now often collectively termed 'Cultural Studies'. It explores the meanings of everyday processes, places and acts like communication, space and shopping. It adapts Cultural Studies' emphasis and critical approaches to look at how meaning is manufactured, and ideology coded into everyday life. The emphasis is on the discursive aspect of everyday life, the construction and control of meanings of home space, of communication and shopping – that is, the *production* of cultural forms – rather than on the reception and consumption of meanings. Audience studies and reception studies are therefore not part of the work here, even though they constitute an important component of Cultural Studies work.

Both the theory and practice of Cultural Studies are introduced in this book. The two parts are organized slightly differently. The first, 'Contexts, Theories, Methods', aims to provide the student the tools of analysis. 'Sites of Culture', the second part, is a set of case studies where the cultures of communication, shopping and space are analysed. Naturally, not all the elements of the Cultural Studies approach described in Part I come into play – methods, theories and approaches are adapted and appropriated to suit the sites being studied. A thread running through the discussion of consumption, space and communication is *consumerism* and the way in which it inhabits all aspects of culture today. Hence the book has an overwhelming emphasis on consumer culture, even when discussing sites like home spaces.

There is a progressive grading in the chapters in terms of argument and method: from the more user-friendly chapter on consumption to the denser one on communication. This is intentional, in order to make the work of the student slightly more challenging.

PKN
Hyderabad
2007

Acknowledgements

First and foremost, thanks are in order to Sreetilak of Viva Books for encouraging me to write this book, waiting patiently (though he did not have to wait very long) and offering suggestions that were a fine mix of the good editor and the good businessman.

Thanks to Colin Harrison, Liverpool John Moores University, UK, for cheerfully supplying material whenever I asked for it.

It is a privilege to be able to thank:

My parents for their affection and prayers – they continue to be the support system on which I can bank,

The American Information Resource Center, Chennai, for dispatching material at short notice,

K. Narayana Chandran, whose interest in mass cultural forms (including item numbers in Hindi films), 'thing theory', space-city-de Certeau and, most of all, his attention to rhetoric makes me wonder why *I* am writing this book instead of him – thank you for the encouragement and for the references you supply with such astonishing regularity,

Anna Kurian, for reading the chapters, detailed comments, tracking down excellent journal articles, general enthusiasm for anything to do with popular culture and her enduring affection. Special thanks also for her brilliant concept-metaphor, the 'new-now' and her telling phrase 'distraction quotient' in our conversations on commodity culture,

Ibrahim, Sampath, Ajit and Panikkar, whose friendship matters so much to me, even though our lives are now led very differently.

Nandini's enthusiasm for malls, the market and popular culture has been infectious all through this project, pointing out more examples ('you must write about this') on TV, stores, magazines (and recalling with almost photographic clarity the malls in Ithaca, NY and Cambridge!) than I could have ever discussed.

Pranav, whose very pragmatic approach to commodities (toys, clothing, stationery), food and 'going out' placed a very necessary curb on my *academic* interest in these same things, deserves a special 'thank you'.

Thanks to Carolyn Wei, University of Washington, for sending me her dissertation on mobile phones.

And Narendra at Viva, for providing the tone and colour to the book with his designs: thank you.

Part I

Contexts, Theories, Methods

1

Cultural Studies: Scope, Aim, Methods

A field of academic study that finds its origins in the Birmingham Centre for Contemporary Cultural Studies (UK) and the work of critics like Raymond Williams, Richard Hoggart and later by Stuart Hall, Tony Bennett and others, Cultural Studies is a discipline between disciplines. In this chapter you will meet a few select definitions and a short history of Cultural Studies.

Cultural Studies is interested in the processes by which power relations between and within groups of human beings organize cultural artefacts (such as food habits, music, cinema, sports events and celebrity culture) and their meanings. Before we define 'Cultural Studies' we need to understand the key terms used by the discipline.

Sites, Terms, Conditions

Culture

What 'culture' has meant before:

- 'Culture' derives from 'cultura' and 'colere', meaning 'to cultivate'.
- It also meant 'to honour' and 'protect'.
- By the nineteenth century in Europe it meant the habits, customs and tastes of the upper classes (also known as the elite).

What 'culture' means now in Cultural Studies:

- 'Culture' is the mode of generating meanings and ideas.
- This 'mode' is a negotiation over which meanings are valid.
- Meanings are governed by power relations.
- Elite culture controls meanings because it control the terms of the debate.
- Non-elite views on life and art are rejected as 'tasteless', 'useless' or even stupid by the elite.
- What this implies is that certain components of culture get more visibility and significance.

Popular Culture

Cultural Studies looks at mass or popular culture and everyday life.

Popular culture is the culture of the masses. It is graffiti, comic books, mass cinema (as opposed to 'art cinema'), popular music (as opposed to classical music), the open spaces of the city (as opposed to art galleries), sports... It is the culture of the everyday life of the larger number of people.

For a very long time such forms of art were dismissed as 'inferior'. The term 'mass culture' was used pejoratively. The only 'true' culture was that of the elite members of society. The culture of the wealthy minority section of the population was projected as the 'standard' or 'true' culture. So academic studies would look at 'great works of art' or 'classical authors', ignoring the fact that the greater number of people never viewed these art forms or read these classical authors. Standards of judgement and ideas of taste were framed using these elite forms as examples. Certain authors, forms and genres were given respectability as 'culture'. That is, the very term 'culture' came to be associated with a smaller section of the population and their tastes.

What this means is that the upper classes in a society legitimized certain artefacts as 'culture'. Some objects – a painting by M.F. Hussain, the writings of Rabindranath Tagore and William Shakespeare, the films of Satyajit Ray – acquired an aura of respectability as 'culture'. Most critics did not discuss Sidney Sheldon or the films of Manmohan Desai as 'art', relegating them to the realm of 'popular culture'.

In the 1950s and 1960s a change in focus came about in cultural analysis. Scholars started taking popular culture seriously. In 1969 the Department of Popular Culture at Bowling Green University (USA) launched the *Journal of Popular Culture*. The journal carried essays on Spiderman comics, rock music, amusement parks, the detective film and other such forms of popular culture. It is in popular culture studies that Cultural Studies finds its first moments.

Cultural Studies argues that culture is about the meanings a community/society generates. This process is not easy, as those in power seek to control meanings. For this purpose certain forms of art and their meanings are treated as inferior. Reading Shakespeare or the 'great' Victorian novel is fine, but how can you be addicted to

Mills and Boon and Agatha Christie? That is, all communities quarrel over meaning. Cultural Studies argued that the objects and artefacts that are used – made sense of – by the masses must be taken seriously. Such forms of art as comic strips or the detective novel are made by the people for themselves, as Raymond Williams pointed out (1983). Popular culture is, for Cultural Studies, the set of beliefs, values and practices that are *widely* shared.

Popular culture is the set of practices, artefacts and beliefs shared by the masses, and is constituted by the everyday life of the masses: the food habits, fashion, forms of transport, the music, the reading habits, the spaces they occupy and traverse.

The Production and Consumption of Culture

Cultural Studies believes that the 'culture' of a community includes various aspects: economic, spatial, ideological, erotic and political. Cultural Studies therefore aims to include all these in its ambit. It seeks to understand how particular objects acquire meaning and value in a society or community. Culture is not a natural thing – it is produced. Cultural Studies is interested in the production and consumption of culture.

The production and consumption of culture is linked to:

- matters of class (Who decides on what is produced?)
- matters of economy (Who can afford it?)
- matters of representation (How is the artefact marketed/presented?)

Together these three coalesce into a larger theme in Cultural Studies: *the production and consumption of culture is linked to power and identity.*

The production and consumption of cultural artefacts defines one's identity. But the production and consumption of artefacts depends on the ability to do so and the ways in which these artefacts have been marketed and sold. In short, culture is a product that is:

- made
- marketed
- consumed

Power/Culture

Cultural Studies addresses questions like these:

- Why is Agatha Christie not studied in English departments when most people read Christie rather than Thomas Hardy?
- How does walking through the city streets become significant as a practice?
- What are the economic and political implications of creating special outlets and exhibitions of 'tribal culture' for elite people to purchase them in metropolises?

Each of these questions suggests a connection between culture and power. Let us see how. We can pose a series of Cultural Studies questions to the above questions:

- Who decides that Shakespeare can/must be read but not Christie?
- Who decides the spaces for the pedestrians and automobiles?
- Who gains economic profits from selling tribal artefacts?

As you can see, the decision about culture and social practices – Shakespeare, walking in the city, showcasing tribal culture – are *not simply cultural questions*. They involve politics and questions of power since each artefact or practice acquires legitimacy and value because somebody has decided they are legitimate and valued. That is, cultural issues and themes are mediated through questions of economy (profit) and politics (power). Culture is therefore about power.

Origins

Early Trends

The growth of Cultural Studies is linked to the rise in interest in popular culture in Western societies in the 1960s. More leisure time, widespread television viewing, music and other cultural 'states', especially among the youth, brought popular culture to the forefront of critical scrutiny. Within the academy cultural anthropologists, sociologists and historians were beginning to express greater interest in social history, especially those of the subordinated groups such as women, African Americans and the colonized. The work of the Birmingham school (BCCS, see below) focused on

- working class and dissident youth populations (Willis 1978; Hall and Jefferson 1976)
- television personalities
- audiences (Morley 1980)

The tone of this early version of Cultural Studies was set by students of the British New Left, especially Richard Hoggart and Raymond Williams, both of whom had working-class backgrounds. Such students with working-class backgrounds (several first-generation university students in their families) carried their own cultures into their interpretation, and found that their culture had no role in the literary studies programmes at Oxford or Cambridge. The emphasis on 'high' culture (the 'classics') meant a certain alienation for these students.

Further (in Britain), labour, union, feminist and anti-racist movements continued through the 1970s. There was some nostalgia for the student radicalism of the 1960s which had thrown up a range of new movements and cultural identities: gay, race-based, feminist, and so on. The aim was to politicize specific identities. But such radicalism had no academic attention anymore. The quest thus concretized into a study of youth subculture as the site of a new political future. Culture, especially popular culture, became the scene of struggle. Cultural Studies sought, in the tradition of subculture studies and the movements of the 1960s and 70s, to detect and theorize 'agency' among these identities (gay, woman and others).

Birmingham Centre for Contemporary Cultural Studies and Stuart Hall

The work of Raymond Williams influenced the projects and approaches of the BCCS in the 1970s. The approach was clearly Marxist, and it adapted theoretical insights from poststructuralism to develop Cultural Studies. The early approaches took the debate in the direction of textuality, where 'culture', identity, and even the nation, were seen as texts and narratives.

Between 1982 and 1987 the Open University (UK) offered a one-year interdisciplinary course, 'U203'. This U203 was a course on 'Popular Culture'. More than 5000 students took the course until it was terminated in 1987. The course was directed by Tony Bennett and evaluated by Terry Eagleton, Raymond Williams and others.

The course's stated aim was to 'interrogate critically the part that popular culture plays within your life' (Qtd. in Easthope 1991: 74). The distinction between 'high' and 'low' culture was untenable, and one needed to see this evaluative judgement as driven by the need to obtain and retain power by the dominant classes. Stuart Hall's 1980 essay, 'Cultural Studies: Two Paradigms' (reprinted in the Course reader, *Culture, Ideology and Social Process*, 1981) set the tone for the interrogation of the above concept of culture. Hall suggested that subjects were not constitutive and culturally expressive. Subjects and expression are both determined by structures of social signification. This structure is 'hegemony': the ideological structure that enables the dominant classes to legitimize, naturalize and retain power. With this U203's emphasis on the culture-power link emerges clearly, an emphasis that has been retained in the Cultural Studies approach even today.

U203 had two main assumptions about text, reader and position:

i) Textual positioning was understood as a way to answer the question: 'who does this text think you are?' Position is defined in terms of content, of 'assumptions, tastes, values'.
ii) Position is also the process by which the signifier (sign/word/image) and signified (meaning, concept) operate to constitute the subject (reader/viewer).

(Easthope 1991: 77)

This emphasis on discourse and textuality remains central to Cultural Studies. Subjects, identities, relationships are constructed out of discourse and deliver meanings only in the act of differentiation.

Stuart Hall's work has been a trendsetter in Cultural Studies and inaugurated the field in Britain. Hall's early essay, 'Encoding/Decoding' (first published in 1973) set the scene for Cultural Studies of the media (his work on ideology, cultural identity and others are discussed in subsequent chapters). The essay argued that meanings within texts – songs, paintings, television soaps – are organized through the operation of certain 'codes'. Hall argues that the apparatuses, relations and practices of production appear as symbolic vehicles within language. However, the product circulates in the discursive form. Hall uses the example of television news to illustrate. A 'raw' historical event, writes Hall, cannot be televised in that form: it must first be made into a *story* to become a communicative event. The 'message form' is the 'form of appearance' of the event. Hall is thus arguing for attention to the language norms and rules of signification which 'code' the event into a story for audiences to interpret. Hall, viewing this process as a 'circuit', marks the steps as follows:

i) The institutional structures of broadcasting with their practices and networks of production, organized relations and technical infrastructure construct the message.
ii) These structures then 'yield' encoded messages in the form of meaningful discourse. Before the message can have any effect it must be put into language, coded as meaningful discourse.
iii) The message-as-meaningful discourse now reaches the audience, which 'decodes' the message and gets the meaning of the event narrated. The decoded meanings influence people's sentiments, thinking, ideology, politics, and behaviour. That is, the message has an effect on the structures on the audience side of the circuit. However, the decoding may not be exactly symmetrical with encoding.

Hall argues that a society or culture tends to impose its classifications of the social and cultural world, which constitute a dominant cultural order.

What we have learnt so far:

- Cultural Studies focuses on mass or popular culture.
- Culture is 'produced'.
- Culture is about power.

Methods

Cultural Studies adapts methods of analysis from various disciplines: media studies, cultural anthropology, discourse analysis, popular culture studies and audience studies. Most of these methods, when appropriated by Cultural Studies, are heavily influenced and informed by the theories outlined in the later chapter. They are also geared to *political* readings of various aspects of culture, generating gender-, race-, sexuality-related interpretations that reveal the oppressive or hegemonic structures of society.

All cultural forms are linked to institutions, the market, consumers and regulatory bodies. Cultural Studies believes that we cannot 'read' cultural artefacts only within the aesthetic realm. A novel must be read not only within its generic conventions and the history of the novel but also in terms of the publishing industry and its profits, the community of reviewers, the academic field of literary criticism, the politics of awards and the hype and publicity machinery that 'sells' the book. Therefore it is not possible in a Cultural Studies project to deal with J.K. Rowling's Harry Potter books only as 'fantasy writing' (within the genre of fantasy literature) or as literature. It is now obvious that we cannot delink the literary work from the gigantic publicity machine that is in operation around the books. We do not buy a Harry Potter book, we buy an entire enterprise. We consume not just a simple growing-up story of a boy-wizard but an entire merchandise of icons, trivia, author-speak, biography and autobiography.

Cultural Studies asks:

- What does a particular artefact/event/activity *mean* to a community/nation/culture?
- *How* does a cultural artefact generate meaning in and for a community?

As an example of a Cultural Studies question: What does the tricolour or Gandhi Jayanti or a cricket match *mean* to Indians? What do they stand for? How does an audience in India react to these symbols, events and actions? What is their value

i) to Indian culture as a whole,
ii) to particular communities in India,
iii) in the age of globalization of culture when we receive cultural events and artefacts from all over the world?

The above key question is answered by Cultural Studies in two significant and related ways:

- *Interpretation*: The artefact/event/activity is seen as the *expression* of a particular community/culture. That is, the tricolour, Gandhi Jayanti and the cricket match are seen as visible *signs* or texts that are scripted/written by a particular culture/community called India.
- *Critique*: The tricolour/Gandhi Jayanti/the cricket match are seen as visible *political* signs, which carry/mask/reinforce certain ideological values in India. They are part of a *discourse that is India*. This discourse of 'national identity', territory, 'national leader', 'father of the nation' or 'India's pride' conceals questions of
    » patriarchal ideas of the nation ('*father* of the nation'),
    » nationalism (tricolour as a symbol of political independence from colonialism),
    » national identity (where cricket becomes Indian by ignoring its colonial origins, even though hockey is our acknowledged 'national game').

What Cultural Studies does is to interpret signs of culture such as the ones listed above as part of a power struggle to acquire, maintain or contest *meanings*. The 'critique' component of Cultural Studies therefore explores the political significance of such signs: what they mask or gloss, what they reinforce.

Cultural Studies thus

- studies the languages in and through which meanings are made in a particular culture
- questions how such meanings reflect the power struggle within that culture
- explores how certain meanings are privileged in that culture at the cost of others.

Cultural Studies would therefore ask a series of questions to the above question regarding tricolour, Gandhi Jayanti and cricket:

i) How was the tricolour designated the 'national' flag? Were there other flags competing for this role? If so, what negotiations enabled *this* one to be selected? Did all Indians, of various religious faiths, political ideologies and regional locations see this flag as truly Indian when it was designated as such?

ii) How does Gandhi become a 'national figure'? What is the myth/symbolism/value assigned to Gandhi? How does a Gandhi-object like the cap get appropriated by contemporary India?

iii) How does cricket attract such money and publicity? Within cricket, why or how does a Sachin Tendulkar acquire such glamour when Mithali Raj, of the woman's cricket team, never gets as much? Is cricket a *masculinized* national game? How does cricket edge out hockey as the most popular spectator sport in India, even though it was a colonial invention?

> Cultural Studies is the analysis of a culture's systems of meaning-production and consumption.

Methods, Methodology

In terms of method and methodology (contrary to accepted modes of use, these two are *not* the same) we need to elaborate the procedures of cultural analysis.

- Method is the technique employed by the researcher to frame questions, collect and organize data. Thus 'method' refers to the actual fieldwork, questionnaires, databases, identifying sources.
- Methodology refers to the political position and the interpretive strategies used by the researcher. This refers to the *epistemological* approach, and concerns the philosophical, political approach of the researcher, where s/he scrutinizes her/his own location. Methodology is the critical approach used to interpret the data collected.

For example: If you are studying representations of women in popular Hindi films, the first step in *method* would be

- to organize the questions to be asked
- to take decisions about the people to interview (age group, class composition, language)
- to prepare the questions
- to conduct the interviews

The *methodology* would include

- identifying your own ideology (Marxist, feminist)
- reflecting on your experiences before framing the questions
- interpreting the data collected based on your assumptions

Cultural Studies, as we know, is about power and studies how power informs all acts of cultural production and meaning generation. It is therefore important to realize the positions the researcher and object occupy and the power relations between them.

Cultural Studies has a set of warnings that we need to keep in mind in any analysis of culture:

- What gives us (academics, researchers) the authority to use people/communities as resource material to study their 'culture'?
- What is the relationship between knower (researcher) and the known (object of study)?
- What is the location from which the researcher is asking the questions/making the analysis?

In most cases of rigorous Cultural Studies, the researcher isolates her/his own locations and politics while analysing culture. This means, the researcher has to be conscious of the 'vantage point' from which s/he is making the observations and interpretations. This is termed 'reflexivity' in social and critical theory, where the researcher reflects on her/his own position. If, for instance, I am exploring the culture of cybertechnology in India, I need to identify my own position with regard to the 'subjects' I am observing: upper-caste, internally diasporic, metropolitan, male, middle-career academic with the humanities at an elite university with a fairly decent infrastructure (in this case, PCs, connectivity). From this position and informed by the politics of my location, I observe cybercafes, rural e-governance and a digital divide from my friends in First World universities (with exceptional connectivity, better PCs and institutional support), but who feels that the younger generation uses technology much better than I ever can! This reflexivity opens up my observation and agenda. How do I see myself as a knowledge-producer, critic or commentator in relation to and with the subjects I study? Does being an academic lend more 'authority' to what I say or ask? What is the validity of my knowledge or observations? This set of questions is central to the politics of research itself.

Cultural Studies in the Euro-American contexts, especially those from a feminist perspective, often connects empirical data and theorizing about this data with a wider feminist politics in the public realm.[1] Thus, feminist studies of film audiences link the representation of women in film media with larger issues of gender inequality in society. This is crucial because one of the basic assumptions of Cultural Studies is that cultural artefacts cannot be studied independent of the social and material contexts. Representations of women in films therefore are located in actual contexts of gender oppression, domestic violence, patriarchal family structures and economic inequalities of the genders.

Two factors have to be kept in mind:

- The study should draw upon as large a number of 'sources' (technically called 'respondents') for it to have any value. This makes the study representative of a social group.
- It should be, if possible, spread out over a period of time and context, if we need to make a generalized statement about cultural practices.

Commentators like John Fiske (1996) have argued that the old-fashioned mode of ethnography, where the researcher 'immerses' her/himself in the culture being studied is unnecessary because we mostly study *our own cultures now*. Further Cultural Studies is more interested in the way meanings are made and the discourses within which these are made. This involves a study of the processes of representation and 'texts', seeing these as instrumental in the construction of identity. That is, Cultural Studies investigates, intensively, the production of meaning rather than involving itself in extended observation. The idea is not to merely accumulate data – though such descriptions are valuable – but to ask questions of epistemology and politics of the data that has been procured.

The recording of experience is, as we shall see, the cornerstone of all Cultural Studies. Following Ann Gray (2003) three propositions can be set out here:

- Identifying what is knowable
- Identifying and acknowledging the relationship of the knower and the known
- What is the procedure for 'knowing'?

This requires formulating the structure of the 'case study'. The 'case study' is a limited bounded system which is under observation for particular phenomena.

The 'Circuit of Culture'

A sophisticated analysis of cultural artefacts requires a close examination of five basic elements, which together constitute what Paul du Gay et al have called 'the circuit of culture' (1997). These elements are:

- representation
- identity
- production
- consumption
- regulation

What these elements present is a process through which every cultural artefact, object or event must pass. The elements work in tandem, and are closely linked with each other, a process that has been called 'articulation'.

In order to illustrate the 'circuit of culture' we need to use a concrete example. Let us take a now-ubiquitous technological device: the television.

Television and Representation

What does the television represent, and how is it represented? The answers to these two related questions are basically means to discuss the centrality of representation in a culture. Television represents

- communication, information
- entertainment

Most television ads work with these three aspects, with more features and facilities.

Television and Identity

What kinds of identity does television project? What is the difference between state (that is, government) television programmes and say, STAR TV?

What kind of age group is targeted in particular kinds of promotional material? Do car and mobile phone manufacturers target youth?

What kinds of identity are given importance in television serials – Family? Young professionals? Youth? Business culture?

What does it mean to appear on television? Is the identity of a public intellectual governed by appearance on a programme?

Think of so-called 'serious' programmes on contemporary affairs like *Aaj Tak*, health and medicine or yoga. What is their target audience?

What is the Indian identity projected on television? Does the Northeast of India come into the picture? Or Dalits? If so, what is the tone of programmes that try to give representation and space to the marginalized?

As we can see the series of questions posed above are about cultural and public contexts where identities are linked to images on screen. Cultural Studies is interested in the ideologies that underlie these identity-projections.

Television and Production

The theme of production can be phrased as a series of pointed questions:

Look at the major television manufacturers. What are the policies in these companies? How is recruitment done? What welfare policies are in place for workers? How much profit does the company make?

Does the company project a democratic work culture? Does the management mix with the workers? Does the company cater to an

Indian milieu specifically? Does it project itself – as state-owned companies like Electronics Corporation of India Limited (ECIL) did – as a truly 'Indian' firm?

Television and Consumption

Who are the major buyers of television sets, black and white and colour? What are their income levels? Why would you buy a particular model? Is the choice of a particular kind dictated by fashion, taste, functionality? Do you upgrade models because you are an enthusiast and can afford to?

Television and Regulation

Consider the union government's ban on Fashion TV, ostensibly because it offends Indian cultural sentiments.

What does the government do with regard to either production or consumption? What is the role of the censor board or the Information and Broadcasting Ministry in television sales, production, programmes?

This 'circuit of culture' is perhaps the most thorough examination of any cultural artefact. As we can see it covers a range of issues and themes – from the question of media representation to the construction of identities in a culture. The 'circuit of culture' includes within it several smaller components and modes of analysis. The rest of this chapter outlines some of them.

Cultural Studies today, in most academies across the world, adopts certain key areas and methods to understand the modes of meaning-production. These are:

- language, discourse
- identity
- everyday life
- ethnography
- media studies
- reception/audience studies
- cultural intermediaries

Language, Discourse

Raymond Williams's influential definition of culture and society remains the cornerstone for much Cultural Studies even today:

> Our description of our experience comes to compose a network of relationships, and all our communication systems, including the arts, are literally parts of our social organization ... Since our way of seeing is literally our way of living, the process of communication is in fact the process of community: the offering, reception and comparison of new meanings, leading to the tensions and achievements of growth and change.
>
> (1961: 55)

Experience, as Williams's quote shows, is central to the project of Cultural Studies. Experience, especially in terms of the everyday, is a central political and analytical category itself, which we shall study later in the section on everyday life.

First, let us understand exactly why this definition is so crucial to Cultural Studies. Given below is a graded set of explanations about language and Cultural Studies.

- Studying society is about culture, and not only about economics or politics.
- Meanings and values, and their exchange or circulation, constitute a particular 'culture' or community: *communication* creates *community*.
- A society's meanings and values reflect its economic and political systems – and hence to study meanings is to study a culture.
- Culture is about the role of meanings in any society. A culture is the *sharing* of meaning.
- 'Meanings' are never fixed: they are arrived at through a process of negotiation and exchange.

Cultural Studies analyses the processes through which certain meanings are produced in a particular culture. It believes that the processes of meaning-production are connected to the structures of power in society: certain meanings acquire greater power because of their sources, other meanings become less important.

'Meanings' are processes of language. (Language here is taken to mean not just words or print but also speech, painting, photography.)

In Cultural Studies the preferred term to speak about 'meanings' is 'representation'. Representation is the process of signifying (meaning-generation), and includes the word/sign and its concept/ meaning. Representation presents the world in such a way that we can understand it. Representation can be an image, a word, a sound or a concept. It uses these 'signs' in order to generate meaning. That is, representation is the alphabet of a culture: the alphabet is used to make meaningful sentences. In short, it is language.

word + concept behind the word = meaning
word, concept, meaning, context = representation

But this language is not neutral or transparent. Language and meaning are connected to issues of class, power, ideology and the material conditions in which the speaking/painting or interpretation occurs. All expression and use of language are situated in a context. This context is *discourse.*

What discourse does is to define what can be said. That is, discourse is the context in which a culture's communication, meaning-production and interpretation occur. It is the terrain of thought and expression.

Cultural Studies examines how representations function in a particular society. No object in society can exist without its representations. That is, every object, subjectivity and identity has to have some kind of representation. This can be a name, a symbol, a word, a metaphor, a visual sign.

Activity:

Your identity as a boy or girl is made possible through a system of signs. What are these signs? Think of your name, which, in most cultures where meaning is shared, immediately identifies your gender. This is why when you hear of the names of people from other countries we cannot know right away whether they are male or female. We do not have the same kinds of names or representations as they do.

The association of a name/sign with a gender is therefore culture-specific.

Popular culture studies (within Cultural Studies) rely on such a notion of language and discourse. For Cultural Studies everything in society is language. Objects and events are also signs within a language system that can be interpreted by people who share a set of cultural codes. As an example, look at toys.

Activity:

Building on the above activity let us continue with the question of gender.

What toys are considered suitable for boys? And what toys are often purchased for girls? Ask your friends: would you gift a Barbie doll to a 4-year-old boy? Or a set of carpenter's tools to a girl? Notice that dolls are invariably considered suitable for girl children and tools/guns for boys.

The point is dolls become signs of the feminine, and therefore are given to girls. Girls and dolls become interchangeable as signs of the feminine. Just as tools and guns become signs of masculinity.

It is not that girls cannot use tools. Or that dolls are essentially feminine. It is just that the values associated with these objects govern their use. That is, the values of a particular culture decide the owner/user of dolls and tools – not the inherent quality of the objects themselves. The language of tools and dolls must therefore be read and interpreted within the context of a culture or community's notions of femininity and masculinity. 'Doll = feminine' and 'tool = masculine' is a language in that culture.

These meanings are naturalized.

Thus Cultural Studies sees culture as a *text* made of signs and generating meaning. This is an important move, for it makes use of theories from structuralism and linguistics to speak of the textuality of culture.

A text is read for the signs within itself.
A text is related to and read within the context of other texts.
A text is finally related to and read within a larger cultural text.

In the above example, we can say the *text* of tools and dolls can be read within a *discourse* through the following steps in interpretation and critique:

i) Dolls are objects given to girls; tools are given to boys.
ii) Dolls are given to girls *rather than to* boys.

iii) Girls being more 'delicate' must be given softer and harmless things. Boys being 'tougher' can be given harder objects.
iv) Dolls are harmless, soft and gentle; tools are hard and possibly dangerous.
v) Dolls are to be cared for, groomed. Tools are used to achieve certain results (repairs, construction, etc.).
vi) Grooming and care are 'feminine' qualities and jobs. Repairs and construction are male jobs and responsibilities.
vii) Dolls inculcate these feminine qualities in girls, and tools inculcate masculinity in boys.

Notice here that the interpretation looks at the language of toys and the discourse within which we interpret them. What are the discourses we can detect in the above example?

- That girls are delicate and weaker;
- That grooming and care are feminine qualities/duties.

These discourses are patriarchal and treat women as weaker, gentler and requiring protection and to be given only particular tasks. These discourses govern suitable play material because games and play are also elements within this same society. As a result the discourses decide what is suitable or not suitable for girls and boys. It then becomes natural to give dolls to girls and tools to boys. So then we can conclude our reading thus:

Text: toys
Language: meanings of these toys (dolls = feminine; tools = masculinity)
Discourse: patriarchy and gender difference

But is that all?

We discover something else from the above activity. We cannot give a doll to a girl unless we know the conventions that govern such items (i.e. unless we know the language of toys).

But we cannot define what 'feminine' means without knowing what 'masculine' means. Feminine is what is NOT masculine.

Therefore, the definition and meaning of the term 'feminine' is dependent upon its contrast with and difference from 'masculine'. In order to understand one, we need to know and understand its other or its opposite. Meaning is thus the result of difference, where the meaning of 'feminine' is only available in its difference from 'masculine'.

In short, we cannot say there is a true or complete 'feminine' because its meaning is dependent upon 'masculine'. There is no essential meaning, and all meaning is the result of this relationship with its opposite or other.

For Cultural Studies this insight – drawn from poststructuralism – is crucial. It suggests:

- All meaning is relational.
- All representation (signs and meanings) is based on difference.
- All representation is a system of negotiation where meanings contest for visibility and expression.
- This contest is situated within a discourse where (for example) dolls represent femininity in a culture. Dolls acquire meaning, *and* the term 'feminine' *becomes represented through certain signs* (dolls, care, grooming, soft/gentle qualities).

Texts and representations are therefore texts in contexts, in society. We have to move between texts and everyday life where one influences the other. Girls and boys grow up watching such images of women and toys. When they grow up they subscribe to these same values (mostly) in their everyday life, ways of thinking and social relations, and in turn produce similar texts.

As the girls and boys grow up within this system of representation where their qualities and duties are already available, they acquire an identity.

Cultural Studies is basically an exploration of specific contexts (culture, community, nation, caste, class, gender, race, sexuality) where representations produce and reinforce identities through particular modes.

What we have learnt so far:

- To study a society is to study 'culture'.
- 'Culture' is about communication and making meaning.
- Objects acquire meanings and value through negotiation, and these meanings then become naturalized.
- These meanings then create identities.

Identity

The identity of a person is, for Cultural Studies, dependent upon the roles played by that person, the signs that designate that person. Identity is constituted through experience, and representation is a significant part of experience. Experience includes the consumption of signs, the making of meaning from signs and the knowledge of meaning. However, Cultural Studies believes that experience also masks the connections between different structures in society. We do not always understand that we are not in control of our lives, and that we are subject to ideological control. That is, experience often makes us believe that we are free agents, when we are in reality victims of discursive and ideological regimes that treat us as consumers alone. We do not always have the power of choice – that is in itself an illusion generated through representation.

As we have seen, these signs are part of a discourse. Therefore, it follows that girls assimilate qualities of the 'feminine' because they are brought up within the discourse of femininity. The culture's values inculcate notions of 'femininity' and 'masculinity' in the children, where the roles they will play are clearly demarcated from childhood (care, nurture, home for girls, to continue with the above example). As adults the relation between the genders is therefore already set: women will be in charge of the home. The discourse of femininity therefore determines the power and spatial relations between genders. Identity is the consequence of representation and the effect of discourse.

Identity is based on the location within a system of relationships and discourses.

Activity:

Take your name 123 Kumar, for example.

If 1 and 2 stand for your individual name, 3 perhaps refers to your village or your family name. Notice that you as an individual are related to: (i) family (ii) father (iii) village/hometown, or perhaps all three. Your identity, as seen in the sign (your name) is the effect of the combination of all three.

So, can you be your-self without all three? Which of these three is the real

YOU?.

Identity is thus socially produced. Closely related to the theme of identity in Cultural Studies is the question of agency. Agency – the capacity and power to determine one's actions and life – is also socially produced. An individual's ability to act is limited by the contexts in which s/he lives.

For Cultural Studies this is a key debate. Who are the empowered agents in any culture? Who determines the limits of an individual's freedoms? What are the consequences of an individual's actions in any culture?

Proceeding from our discussion of identity and representation we are now in a position to explore the relations between these two and agency.

Representation is the generation of meaning and constitutes identity. Identity determines the degree of agency one possesses or does not possess. Agency is therefore the consequence of representation too. What follows from this is a crucial point.

Discourses and representations determine an individual's identity, agency and actions. Discourses, as we have seen, are structures of power that generate particular meanings/identities. In any culture therefore, it is crucial to see which classes/groups control the discourses that have such powers of determining identities and agency. In other words, we need to analyse structures of power that influence images, representation and meaning because these structures finally determine individual lives and actions.

Activity:

Let us take an instance of space and urban planning in order to understand the question of power, identity and agency.

Authorities (the Municipal Corporation, the Traffic Police) sought to ease the traffic congestion at the Secunderabad and Hyderabad Railway Stations and at Chennai Central, and buses were not allowed to go near the building. Cars, however, are allowed. What does this mean in terms of identity and agency?

It means: we are now a car-culture. When the larger numbers of people use two-wheelers, buses and autos to reach/leave the station, the authorities prohibit these very forms of transport. People now have to walk, if they are not wealthy enough to own cars, with their luggage to get transport. The space is reserved for the higher-income groups. In terms of identity, the pedestrian or the two-wheeler owning middle-class person lacks spatial privileges. The well-off have spaces delineated for free movement. The space here is demarcated, represented as car-space. It also represents some sections of the society as possessing the right to that space: they are empowered to use that space, where others are not.

Representation of space thus has very concrete, material effects on individuals and their agency.

What we have learnt so far:

- Identity is socially constructed/legitimized.
- Identity is constructed through representation.
- This identity determines the degree of agency we possess in a given social system.

Everyday Life

Contemporary Cultural Studies takes everyday life very seriously. Everyday life, especially in metropolises – and, unfortunately, Cultural Studies seems to be interested mainly in metropolitan cultures – is a site that is multi-layered and contested. Everyday life is about the practices of the routine. It is about

- lifestyle
- consumption
- social interactions/relations

The 'cultural' is constituted by and constitutes the 'social'. That is, the social realm – society – is constituted by the 'cultural' artefacts used by the people, even as the cultural artefacts are themselves produced and consumed by society. Cultural artefacts in the social realm can be studied through the analysis of everyday life.

What is crucial is that Cultural Studies analysing everyday life accounts for *subjectivity* in the people's responses, since experience is subjective. Sociological studies have often ignored the fact that people respond emotionally to things, and this is a central part of their *identity*.

A caution: everyday life is specific to locations and cultures. Everyday life in Manhattan, New York, is not the same as everyday life in Bangalore or Guwahati. Think of the differences in basic structures of everyday life in the cities – massive public transport infrastructure, no power cuts, to mention just two – and you can see that we need to ask different kinds of questions about what kinds of clothes people need to wear or whether (like New Yorkers) you can eat on the move on a public transport facility. Thus cultural artefacts/events of food or fashion are structured differently for different locations – and Cultural Studies is (or ought to) be conscious of this.

Experience is the cornerstone of everyday life. Experience is everyday life – how we experience traffic, clothing, food, social relations on public transport, the sense of community or entertainment constitute our everyday culture. Cultural Studies foregrounds experience, but sees it as the means to analyse the relations that construct reality. In order to make this shift from experience to reality (by which Cultural Studies means the class, geography, community, ideologies and discourses that constitute our reality – see the chapter on Theories to understand how discourses construct reality), Cultural Studies underscores the textual/linguistic aspect of experience.

Experience is expressed (articulated) through language: how we express what we experience, how we speak with others and how we tell our stories. When we listen to others we decode their meanings, we *mediate* their experience through the language and cultural codes they and we share. Language and representation are therefore integral to the experience and construction of reality. If experience and everyday life are central to culture, then it is important to see how these experiences of the everyday become languages, images and representations.

Cultural Studies' interest in everyday life proceeds from what Raymond Williams (1981) called 'lived cultures', where culture is produced through everyday living: the food people eat, the fashions they adopt, the entertainment they prefer or the festivals they celebrate. Cultural Studies thus believes that people leading their everyday lives produce culture. Culture is not some distinct realm produced elsewhere to be consumed by the people. It is the consequence of experiences and responses. It is in the everyday that culture is made. Cultural Studies investigates this process of making culture. This process, it believes, is linked to relationships of power. Think of two questions in particular:

i) Who has access to specific forms of culture in everyday life?
ii) What are the legitimate forms of culture acceptable in everyday life?

Lifestyle and consumption of cultural artefacts in everyday life go together. There is a consumerist ideology at work in all of us. This ideology emphasizes leisure and pleasure over duties and work. A consumerist ideology links pleasure to the consumption (of products, services). In fact, for Cultural Studies, *consumerism is itself a new form of identity*.

How does Cultural Studies document the experience of the everyday? There are two common methods of analysis of the experience.

i) It asks people to record their experience of living within particular locations (community, caste, class, geography). It then documents these autobiographical narratives as source material and evidence for a particular culture and theorizes about it. This approach is a standard component of Cultural Studies interested in the reception/audience side of culture. This assumes that the subject is not merely embedded in a context but actively produces the context, that it is the subject's experience and responses that shape the context and the meanings of cultural artefacts. This approach gives a more active role as agent to the subject/individual.
ii) Others look primarily at how structures generate representations – the *discursive* or *addresser* side of the image/text rather than the *interpretive* or *addressee* side. This assumes a degree of powerlessness where discourses and representations govern the individual and control the subject's experience. The *contexts* of representation (structures of power like gender, class, race) are given greater role in this approach.

If we want to produce a matrix for Cultural Studies' framework of everyday life, this is what we might get:

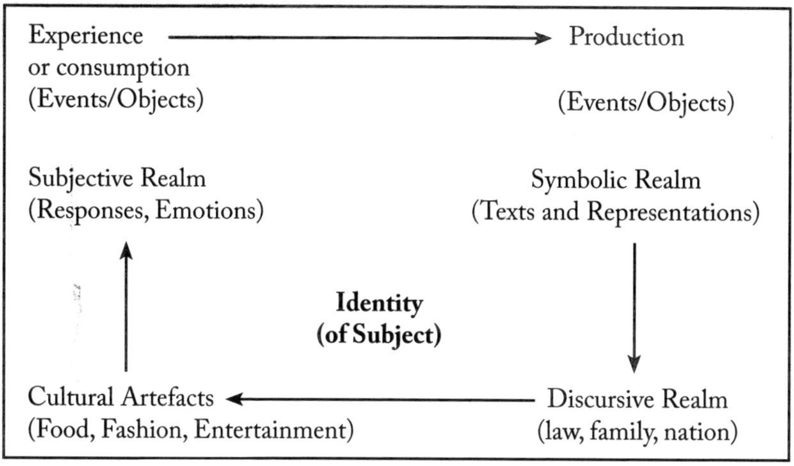

This is a version of the 'circuit of culture'. Producers make objects, whose function, style, structure are governed by discourses of the prevalent culture (family, law, religion). These objects are 'texts' with symbolic values. These are consumed by individuals, who react subjectively to the objects. Their acceptance of the cultural texts fuels further production. *Slowly the objects and events become a part of that community/nation's culture.*

The entire cycle determines the identity of the individual. The subject is an agent

- whose sense of self, experience and response are *projected onto a range of texts, images and commodities.*
- whose sense of self, experience and response are expressed through *a range of texts, images and commodities.*

The club you belong to, the cellphone you use, the clothes you wear identify you as an individual. You become part of the 'yuppie' generation of (say) software professionals with high disposable income, an MNC job, travels abroad, frequent eating out and shopping, a car and a different order of socializing. Thus what defines you as an individual is not older form of social relations (class, family, location, caste) but the lifestyle you lead and the products you use.[2]

What this means is: older forms of association and identity-structures are breaking up. As the individual moves away from such structures, she finds her identity in lifestyle. Lifestyle identity is a mode of social interaction, and bestows a degree of individualism: it is what you do/wear that identifies you, and not where you come from or your family name. Lifestyle is a matter of *individual choice*, and therefore a key component of her/his agency. The choice of lifestyle is a matter of self-realization where an individual can assert her/his own tastes, preferences, comforts as the most important factors rather than her/his family, class or other social relations. *This means lifestyle choices enable the individual to discover and create her/his own identity, no matter what her/his background.*

Thus everyday life is a place where the *individual* becomes central. The individual's subjectivity is therefore a crucial element of the Cultural Studies of everyday life.

What is important, as we shall see, is that the individual in contemporary globalized culture is an active agent. The individuals are very aware of their appropriation of global cultures, often transforming the global in their own, native contexts.

Everyday life is a site of struggle over meaning. Conflicting sources – the global and the local – battle for supremacy: should we buy *khadi* even though good *khadi* is expensive and Egyptian cotton fashions are more cheaply available because they are made in South Asian sweatshops? Should we watch only arid Doordarshan programmes when STAR offers a lot more? You cannot watch the *Indian* cricket team playing a match *in India* because Doordarshan, Prasar Bharati and other local institutions have fouled up (again), and we are forced to rely on private channels for our viewing. Is there a way of *not* using MS-Office?

These are not questions about consumerism and leisure alone. They are questions about *cultural values in everyday life*.

Everyday life generates multiple identities. One of the most significant contributions of Cultural Studies is the notion that both people and places have *multiple* identities. Places and people have become increasingly mobile, multicultural and hybridized.

What does this mean in terms of everyday life and culture? Cultural Studies sees identities in metropolises as increasingly linked to consumption and lifestyles. Today, metropolitan everyday life across the world is simultaneously local and global.

Activity:

Look at everyday lifestyles around you. Why are global names so common now?

The fabric of the shirt is Egyptian cotton, the styling is European (as the Zodiac line proudly announces) or made in China by the American company, Gap. Your sunglasses are Italian style, and your cellphone is Finnish (Nokia is a Finnish company). At home appliances are Japanese (Sony) or Korean (LG). The automobile you use is very possibly Japanese. Your American-owned MNC might order lunch for all the employees from McDonald's or Pizza Hut, or you might go out to a hotel that is partly owned by the Best Western line. Your colleagues come from various parts of India, with many having studied/trained abroad in mostly American places. Television channels that you like to watch are owned by American Rupert Murdoch (of STAR TV). The movies are, of course, Hollywood, where 7–9 mega corporations produce all the films.

And all writing is done on Microsoft Windows.

How much of what you own/do everyday is truly, purely 'Indian'?

Everyday life today is a hybrid of the local and the global. No pure local culture exists in metropolises any more: even where local ethnic chic is marketed it is part of a global consumer market. Hence everyday life gives us multiple identities, a mélange. The same applies to places, where a single street (take MG Road in Bangalore, or Banjara Hills in Hyderabad as examples) showcases all the world's leading consumer/lifestyle brands. The place also takes on multiple identities (the traffic congestion and chaos is completely local as everybody disobeys traffic rules in their foreign-produced cars!). No place has a single, coherent entity either: every place is a hybrid of the local and the global. The movement of consumer goods across the space of the globe is matched by the movement of people across the globe. London and New York, for example, are now *multicultural cosmopolises*, postcolonial and hybridized. You can hear *bhangra* as a part of the American pop music scene. Indian food is available in any city in the world today, and Tony Blair, no less, declared Indian food to be Britain's 'national cuisine'.

What we have, instead of 'local cities' with specific ethnic cultures and demography, is 'ethnoscapes': a shifting landscape of people like tourists, immigrants, refugees, exiles, guestworkers – people who are always *moving* (Appadurai 1990).

If the local was homogenous, the global is heterogeneous. Contemporary everyday life is a mix of the two, where it is difficult to see where the local culture/value ends and the global one begins. Thus both homogenization and heterogenization are central to metropolitan everyday lives today. This mix of the local and the global has been termed the 'glocal' (Robertson 1995).

> Everyday life in Cultural Studies is a fragmented, multiple space where meanings are hybridized and contested. That is, cities and identities that were once more or less homogenous in terms of ethnic identities and patterns of consumption are now completely hybrid.

What does a hybrid everyday life mean?

- It means our experiences are now not restricted to one race/culture.
- Our identities are drawn from multiple, global sources.
- Our values are themselves inspired by global cultures.

The three points lead us to yet another question: what does it mean when we say that our cultural values are inspired by global cultures?

Workplace cultures often adopt values of/from the parent company. The professionalism of the workplace in your offices, for example, will be far removed from the culture you see in, say, Government of India offices.

Everyday lifestyle cultures modify the use and meaning of global objects. For instance, the Nokia cellphone tunes are from/in local languages, and from local films. The Tommy Hilfiger T-shirt and Levi's jeans are combined with an Indian *dupatta* or a pair of Kolhapuri slippers to create a hybrid fashion system that is neither purely Western capitalist product nor Indian. Finding Chettinad chicken toppings on your Pizza Hut pizza would be a good example. McDonald's uses local tastes to modify its menu: more noodles in Japan and more fish in Scandinavian nations. In other areas too the global finds a local expression:

- the protests in India against Saddam Hussein's execution
- Indian concerns over global warming
- Indian responses to European immigration policies

These indicate local/native concerns that are informed by global developments and values.

Everyday life now adds local meanings to global cultural artefacts. The Third World individual embeds the global within the familiar local, tinges the global with a local colour, in the examples we have seen above. Thus, the local is not necessarily marginalized in the consumerist everyday life: it is emphasized.

> The global cultural artefact is indigenized, given a local flavour.

Thus, what Cultural Studies reminds is a very simple truth: We cannot say that everyday life is dominated or taken over by global cultures. Everyday life is fiercely contested where the meanings of global cultural artefacts are re-invented, re-inscribed by native cultures. The consumer is *not* a passive recipient of global cultural icons or artefacts. S/he modifies what s/he receives to suit her/his own purposes, and engages with the global cultures in a native way, often productively re-doing the global to fit in with an Indian cultural system.

> **What we have learnt so far:**
> - Global products are actively transformed and given new meanings by the local audience/consumer.
> - The consumer has a degree of power to choose the product and re-inscribe its meaning.
> - The individual is engaged in a project of self-realization and identity creation through the adoption of a lifestyle.
> - The consumer asserts agency in this process.

Postcolonialism and Cultural Studies

As noted in the previous section, globalization has a sustained engagement with and influence on local cultures. Some critics have argued that we need to address the role of globalization through the postcolonial lens. Since postcolonial studies is concerned, as the chapter on theories explores, the oppression (in the past or present) of the non-European races by European ones, Cultural Studies in a globalized age also needs to be conscious of the *racialized* nature of globalized/globalizing culture. That is, the theme of race and unequal relations has to be worked into any analysis of global cultures. For instance, we need to ask how Hollywood films circulate globally. Does the fact that audiences in Asia or Africa will be viewing these films influence the film-maker? How does a Hollywood film appear to poorer nations in these areas of the world? Think of films like *Romancing the Stone*, *Indiana Jones* and *Blood Diamond* which explore other cultures – how are these conceived by Americans and received by other parts of the world?

Simon During, noted cultural theorist, outlines a set of reasons for connecting postcolonialism with globalization studies (2000).

i) All culture now is linked with the supply of money.
ii) All cultures now have transnational subsidiaries, opponents or collaborations.
iii) Cultures are no more territorial and hence do not cohere or fuse into wholes or 'traditions'.

What this means is: culture is increasingly mediated by economic factors. Culture has increasingly little to do with traditions or territories. Global economic and media flows determine what aspects of culture are adopted or abandoned. For example, fashion changes in cultures across the world are determined less by local conditions and values than a circulation of global fashion patterns. In India, for instance, in the heavily mediated cultural context of the present, the elite/wealthy members of society can have access to Yves St. Laurent or a Chanel line because these are now available. Cultures and traditions are therefore modified not with the local culture in mind but with global patterns. Their choices are determined by the global economy.

Local cultures are linked to global economies, markets and needs, and hence any study of contemporary culture has to examine the role of a non-local market/money – which requires a postcolonial awareness of the role of racial difference, the colonial relationship between 'First World' and 'Third World' and the exploitative relationship between the two worlds even today.

Certain aspects of Cultural Studies are alert to the postcolonial perspective in global cultures. Colonialism is a kind of globalization where the European settler imposes his cultural modes on the colony, even as he adapts and appropriates local cultures. The current phase of globalization is therefore one more moment in the colonial process. MTV, CNN, Levi's and McDonald's are global companies with local presence and effects. In a sense globalization has indeed become synonymous with Americanization (a statement that has become a cliché).

Contemporary globalization is also a mode of cultural exchange, appropriation and marketing. Contemporary Cultural Studies therefore examines the role of globalizing finances and markets in the formation of cultures. Shared economies in globalization influence cultural modes, and this is what Cultural Studies is interested in.

What does such a link between postcolonial studies/theory mean for Cultural Studies in a globalizing age? This approach makes us ask certain questions:

- Are local cultural products in any way determined by the possibility of a global market?
- Are such cultural products financed by non-local moneys?
- How are such products, rooted (supposedly) in local traditions circulated and marketed globally?

As examples think of:

- Hindi films being financed by non-resident Indians.
- Hindi films and their popularity in other countries where both non-resident Indians and others watch them.
- The stage shows performed by Hindi film stars abroad, extending Bollywood culture in other ways.

What is, however, important to keep in mind is that a culture cannot be reduced to its material goods or products. The presence of American food products or clothing does not mean an extensive Americanization is on. At the same time these are not merely material products; they often carry cultural values. Thus postcolonial Cultural Studies must be conscious of:

- the material nature of any particular product/object
- the marketing and symbolic values assigned to the object

- the economic gains/losses with the arrival of a global product
- the 'share' of the local culture/economy in the production and profits of the global product
- the kind of images associated with the object (its cultural values)

Even though globalization produces 'hybrid' products and cultural values, the question of economic gain must underwrite our analysis of even these products. Thus we need to keep in mind that global material goods and products are manufactured in South and South East Asian sweatshops – where employees are paid extremely low wages – but are marketed by agencies that are both global and local, and generate profits for 'First World' companies. This analysis therefore is firmly rooted in a postcolonial perspective.

What we have learnt so far:

- Local cultural artefacts are now 'produced' keeping a global market in mind.
- This 'production' of local ('Third World') culture is often engaged in a relationship with the First World.
- The relationship between local cultures and the First World market remains, mostly, a colonial one, where the local culture is exploited or exoticized by the First World.

Cultural Intermediaries

The term 'cultural intermediaries' was introduced by the French cultural theorist Pierre Bourdieu in his work on the sociology of taste and distinction. Cultural intermediaries are those that mediate between the production of a cultural product/event and its consumer. Marketing and advertising agencies are the best examples of cultural intermediaries. These project particular images of the product at hand, suggest particular values and 'sell' it to the consumer. They constitute a link between the production and consumption of culture, and therefore a link between culture and the economy. They occur between these two realms. Their function is representation: presenting the cultural object in such a way that a desire for the same is created in the consumer, who then buys the object.

Take Hindi films again as an example. On the production side we have the film-making company, director, producer, financier and the stars. On the consumption side we have the audience. But does the audience come to the film unmediated? The answer is a clear 'no'. Today, we cannot come to any film without having *already* known something about it (especially in metropolises). How this is achieved is a question for Cultural Studies.

The marketing wing of the film, the distribution agency, puts out promotional material. Various TV channels run 'the making of ...' programmes, suggesting a large amount of 'inside' information about stars and stories. Before release there is usually the film's music that arrives first in the market and is widely publicized. Music tapes/CDs carry more promotional material. Film magazines carry stories about films due for release. Magazines also take a look at what they often call 'behind the scenes', where we are taken to the 'sets' of films under production. Newspapers also run short notices about the film. Film stars talk about their forthcoming projects.

> The creation of 'symbolic' value – that is representations – is as central to a cultural process as production and consumption.

None of these, mind you, is connected directly to the film's making/production. Neither are they linked to how the audience might respond to the film. What they achieve is a link. Advertising and marketing are key moments in the process where cultural products are 'sold'. Thus cultural intermediaries are service professions that enable the cultural product to be sold – metaphorically and literally – to the consumer.

It is also possible that cultural intermediaries have little knowledge of the actual processes of cultural production. A film magazine columnist does not need to know the processes of production. The film's advertising agency does not need to know the financial, social, structural backgrounds to the film. S/he has a product to sell, for which s/he prepares promotional material. This has little to do with any kind of expertise in the film trade. That is, the services and expertise of the cultural intermediaries have very little to do with the actual making of the product. They are experts of a different kind and order. And yet their contribution is central to the production and consumption of culture.

Even fan clubs are cultural intermediaries. They mediate between the film star and the consumer. They generate interest in the forthcoming releases of 'their' star. They perform 'extra-cultural' work when they appropriate the star for cultural programmes, philanthropic causes and political parties. They create the 'aura' around a star and this helps sell the film. And of course, they also double as consumers when they go in masses to watch 'their' star's films.

Cultural Studies is interested in the role played by such makers of representation that generate interests and markets for cultural products. We know that advertising and media are extremely profitable professions today. The cultural intermediary not only generates income for the production side, but also for itself. There is thus an economy of the in-between (since the cultural intermediary is in-between production and consumption). Cultural Studies asks:

- What exactly is the relationship of the cultural intermediary to the product being sold?
- Does the intermediary really influence audience reactions?

What we have learnt so far:

- Cultural intermediaries generate an interest in the cultural product.
- They may have an influence on consumption patterns.
- They mediate between the production and consumption of the cultural product.

Media Culture and Cultural Studies

Cultural Studies, as we have noted, is interested in the ways in which communication and community are linked. Communication is about language, discourse and representation. And, as we have seen in the preceding sections, representation is central to the production, consumption and mediation of cultural products. Therefore, it is important to look at the *structures* and *technologies* that produce these representations. In the section on cultural intermediaries we have seen how marketing and advertising generate a desire for cultural/material objects and are thus central to the production-consumption patterns of culture. Advertising, marketing and critique are all features associated with *media*. Media are technologies of communication, and therefore of meaning-production and meaning-dissemination. There can be media that is one-to-one (for example, a phone conversation between two people) or it can be a medium of mass communication (like the film). Films are often referred to as mass media or mass communication. In mass media the source is central and usually single, and the audience (or addressee) are the total number of human beings far away from the source. Thus mass media like films affect and influence a large number of people, and are therefore integral to culture.

Mass media constitute a public space. They generate debates, influence opinion and create markets. They may or may not be controlled by the state. Often, they are controlled by large corporations that generate enormous profits (think of the differences between state-owned Doordarshan and STAR TV).

Media studies and its role in the construction of cultural values, its circulation of symbolic values, and its production of desire is central to Cultural Studies today. Studying media culture is not only to focus on the *cultural* aspects of any media but also paying attention to the economics of media.

Cultural Studies of the media begins with the assumption that media culture – and here we are speaking of a wide range of media, from print to the internet – is political and ideological. Media culture reproduces existing social values, oppressions and inequalities. When, for instance, TV serials or films return us to the glorified 'perfect' family, they gloss over the gender inequalities that exist within the patriarchal family structure. When films depict the corruption of the political system and the common man's quest for justice at the hands of an equally corrupt police, they articulate issues we see every day in our own lives and read about in newspapers.

Media culture clearly reflects the multiple sides of contemporary debates and problems. It is for this reason that any reading of the media must always be a political reading.

Media culture helps reinforce the hegemony and power of specific political, cultural and economic groups. The representations in the media are

- suggestive
- provocative

This means they suggest ideologies that the audience, if not alert, imbibes. Media culture does not need to declare its position or ideology openly: it only needs to *suggest*. Showing a film star guzzling coke in a film, or using particular brands of clothing is not necessarily a marketing strategy for the product. But what it does is to *suggest* that stars wear certain kinds of clothes, and that their glamour is in part the effect of the clothes.

Media culture is *provocative* because it sometimes asks us to rethink what we know, or reinforce what we believe in. Thus the portrayal of Pakistan as a 'terrorist state' in Hindi films reinforces the political and social image of Pakistan by raising our anger-levels at the injustices of Pakistan's army (but remains silent on any human and civil rights violation by the Indian army in Kashmir).

> Cultural Studies of popular media culture seeks to bring to the surface the ideologies and political ideas hidden in mass media entertainment, in the belief that media culture transmits ideologies that reinforce oppressive structures of class, gender, sexuality and race through popular representations.

In Cultural Studies media culture is studied through an analysis of *popular media culture* like films, TV serials, advertisements rather than avowedly political programmes. The emphasis on popular media culture is because Cultural Studies, as we have seen, believes in the power of the popular cultural forms as tools of ideological and political power. It believes that a film can suggest and promote an ideological view far more effectively – because the audience sees it 'only' as entertainment and is hence less on guard for ideology and biases – than a piece of political writing.

Cultural Studies of popular media culture involves:

- an analysis of the forms of representation (symbols)

- an analysis of the political ideologies embedded in these representations (ideologies and values of the 'family', 'Indianness', 'development')
- an examination of the financial sources/sponsors of the representation (for example, propaganda advertisements by Coke after the report on pesticides in Coca Cola)
- an examination of the roles played by other objects/people in propagating ideology (for example, the choice of Aamir Khan, after 'patriotic films' like *Lagaan, Mangal Pandey* and *Rang De Basanti*, to assure people of the safety of Coca Cola)

Cultural Studies asks:

- Does the film/serial present the oppressive, unequal nature of institutions (family, education, medicine) or does it glorify them?
- Does the film tell us anything about possible resistance to such oppressive ideologies?
- Who funds these films, and therefore, who has a stake in circulating/promoting such ideologies?
- What is the audience response to such representations? What is the difference in responses?

Contemporary Cultural Studies of media culture explores what is being called 'media ecologies'. Media is the intersection of information and communications technologies (ICTs), organizational behaviour and human interaction. ICTs, as we know, constitute an *environment* of human culture today – from individuals to organizations, in metropolises across the world. An exploration of a particular technology's ecology involves looking at: marketing, 'tools' like cameras and microphones, language codes, opinion polls used to rate programmes – in short the entire universe of that particular medium. If, for instance, we are looking at the media ecology of the Hindi film, we have to look at:

- the 'star' and her/his personality
- the tools (cameras, setting, lights)
- the workers (technicians)
- the language (of the film, of instructions)

- the community (film industry, unions, star relationships)
- the audience (reception, fans)
- the marketing (publicity)
- the iconography (the posters, the appearances of the stars)
- the VJ who anchors programmes about the film on TV
- the parodies, re-mix versions of its music
- the court-cases, if any
- the role of the state (censorship)
- the reviews

And several others. That is, we are looking at the entire universe of the film, and not the film alone. We need to treat the film as an *assemblage* rather than as a unified entity.

What we have learnt so far:

- Cultural Studies focuses on media culture because it assumes that the media are very significant contributors to ideologies and political culture.
- Media culture mostly supports the hegemony of specific power groups.
- Media culture masks oppressive conditions of class and gender and often the economic angle to cultural ideologies of the family or the law.

Audience/Reception Studies

As we have noted, Cultural Studies explores the processes through which a culture produces meaning, where the meaning is the effect of communication and representation and negotiated through power relations. Communication and representations are two-way processes: the message is sent from an addresser to an addressee through a medium. Therefore it is not enough to speak of the discourses that construct meaning, objects and events. It is not enough to speak of the ways in which advertisements, media, propaganda and other cultural forms represent women, men, family or the nation. We need to examine how these representations are *received* and consumed.

Cultural Studies is interested in the ways in which audiences receive the message, how they respond to it, and the effects the message generates. A major component of Cultural Studies is therefore audience studies or reception studies. 'Audience' includes readers, listeners, viewers – consumers who consume different kinds of images and representations. Reception is the use of mediated cultural texts by the audience. That is, reception is the way in which we react to, internalize representations. This reception is not a passive process – we modify images to suit our requirements and cultural-political beliefs. Our process of interpretation, which is central to the act of reception, is based also on our cultural contexts. We function from within an 'interpretive community' (a term coined by the literary critic Stanley Fish), where exist certain conventions of reading and shared cultural codes. Thus, as Indians, we do not need an explanation for a pair of round glasses, a bald head and a walking stick. We can readily identify the image as that of Mahatma Gandhi because we are Indians, sharing a common cultural code. We interpret the symbols because we know them in advance.

When people (the audience) use and identify with particular symbols and artefacts, they express their cultural identities. When we respond readily to the tricolour or the Gandhi symbol we identify ourselves as Indians. It marks us or distinguishes us from other cultural identities. Further, our use of particular cultural codes – dress, eating habits, lifestyle – identifies us as members of particular cultural groups. We create cultural meanings through our appropriation and adaptation of cultural symbols and icons. Thus the use of *khadi* or the Gandhi cap by the politician, the use of particular kinds of technological devices set us apart from the others. Thus what we can see is that the audience creates its identities through the consumption and reception of cultural artefacts.

In Cultural Studies the survey and the questionnaire become central modes of audience studies, as we have noted in the early sections of this chapter. David Morley's path-breaking work on television audiences in Britain (1980) is an excellent example. Case studies in Cultural Studies document people's responses to television serials, films and sports.

This book undertakes all components of Cultural Studies except this last (audience/reception studies).

---

1. For a good essay on this linkage see Angela McRobbie's 'The Politics of Feminist Research: Between Talk, Text and Action', *Feminist Review* 12 (1982): 46–57.
2. However, it must be noted that one's individual sensibilities and values are not entirely free from one's family, class or caste backgrounds. To refuse the influence of these structures is to be blind to the ways in which they retain a strong hold on our thinking, emotions and behaviour, even when/after we have trained ourselves to be different. Thus even consumer individualism retains remnants of our class and family structures.

2

Theories

What is 'Theory' and why are they saying such nasty things about it? Well, most contemporary Theory – and please note the 'T' in caps – is full of jargon, incredibly diverse in its sources, playful and uses a complex methodology. But it has redeeming features, features that Cultural Studies uses quite effectively. In fact, contemporary Cultural Studies draws most of its analytical rigour from a range of theories that it has assimilated and modified for its own purposes.

Let me first provide a few key themes that Cultural Studies uses from 'Theory'. These 'themes' are distilled from multiple sources – from deconstruction to postcolonial race studies – and are common to Cultural Studies world-wide.

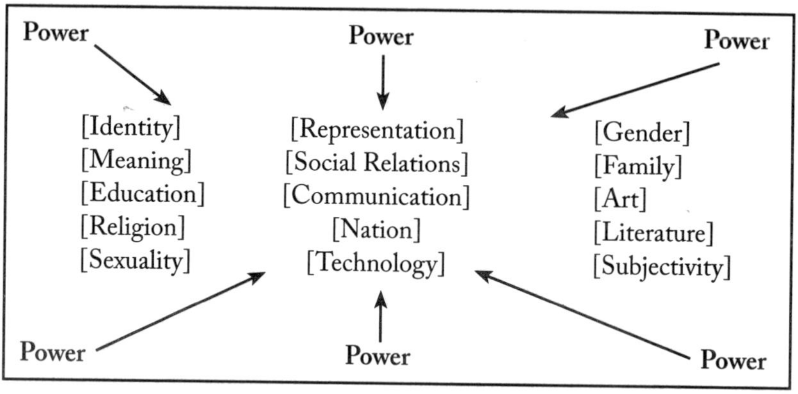

Now why is Power in the four corners of the box and why are the other terms in square brackets?

The answer is: for Cultural Studies, all aspects of society and culture are related to and embedded in power relations. Each term is 'bounded', restricted, and conditioned. What restricts, bounds and conditions each of these is POWER. Power is what frames cultural artefacts, identities, sexuality, forms of representation, subjectivity, communication, social relations and institutions like the family, religion, educational systems and the law.

As the opening moments of Chapter 1 showed, Cultural Studies argues that meaning, identity, social relations and art are about negotiations for power. This can be power relations between

- genders
- classes

- races
- nations
- ethnicities

What Cultural Studies does is to use aspects of contemporary literary and cultural theory to analyse power and its manifestations in the cultural domain.

Structuralism

In his *A Course in General Linguistics* (1916) Ferdinand de Saussure outlined three fundamental assumptions:

a) **Arbitrariness:** The meanings we attribute to words are entirely arbitrary, and prescribed through usage and convention only. There is no inherent or 'natural' connection between the word and the meaning. The word has no quality that suggests the meaning (except perhaps in onomatopoeic words like 'hiss', 'grr' or 'cuckoo'), nor does meaning 'reside' in the word. Therefore language cannot be said to stand for, or reflect, reality or the world: language is *a system in itself*. Language refers only to itself, since all words lead to other words. To phrase it in its proper terminology, the relation between the *signifier* (the word) and *signified* (meaning) is purely arbitrary.

b) **Relational:** Every word makes sense (has meaning) because it is *different* from other words in the organizational chain. Thus 'cat ' means cat only because of its difference from 'cap' or 'hat'.

c) **Systematic:** Language constitutes our world, and our very existence. We need to analyse how meaning is produced through the acts of language. We need to understand the set of structures *in* language that enable us to speak and make sense. In short, we need to study signs and sign systems.

Language constructs the very nature of our perception of reality. Thus literary/visual/musical texts are structured like a language, or what they call its 'grammar'. Art is a system within and in relation to other systems in a particular culture, all of which are based upon the linguistic model.

Structuralism seeks the processes of meaning-production, that is, *how* the text constructs meaning. Anything that generates meaning through certain forms of representation is a 'text'. Here the notion of 'text' suggests more than the printed word, and is taken to include all forms of communication – visual, gestural, verbal, aural. The TV soap opera, sports, wrestling, the novel, politicians' speeches, music videos, our identities are all *texts* constructed in language through a process of relationality (in relation with other things) and difference (our difference from others that generates our unique identity we can call 'our meaning').

Activity:

How does a sports event function as a text or system of meanings?

Take cricket, for instance. There is a formal arrangement of players, infrastructure (wickets, boundary markers, crease lines on the pitch and other people). We separate the players from (i) the umpires, (ii) the audience. We separate the players among themselves (batsmen, bowlers, fielders, wicket-keeper). We identify the players as belonging to two distinct sides. We identify the processes of the game: bowling, batting, fielding and the rules they follow. We note the arrangement of the players in particular locations. The movement along the processes of the game is important: one side bats, the other bowls and fields, the umpires referee. Then, after one side is bowled out, the other bats and tries to exceed the total number of runs raised by the first side. This is the progression of events within the context of the game.

All these things put together constitute the text of the game: where meaning (winner/loser) is decided through the process of difference, logical movement and our understanding of what is going on out there in the field. Remember, the meaning generated depends on our understanding of the rules (the language, formula, structure) and sequence of what is happening. Thus the text of a cricket match may be analysed at three levels:

a) as a system in itself with its own constitutive elements and laws (the grammar of player arrangements, its rules)

b) as one element within the sporting system as a whole. That is, the generic contexts of a cricket match within the system of other sports (its difference from football and its rules)

c) as it relates to 'culture' as a whole (the Indian obsession with cricket, the money involved)

And now ask: is there a language at work in a game?

Cultural systems work in pairs – or what structuralists call 'binary oppositions'. Thus 'cat' and 'hat' are pairs that define each other in terms of their *differences* ('cat' is not 'hat'). That is, just like language works through a system of relations and differences, culture works through a series of relations and oppositions.

Roland Barthes's work in *Mythologies* (1972) has provided exceptionally useful for Cultural Studies. In his study of fashion, Barthes analyses the rhetoric of fashion writing. We have the *fashion signifier* where meaning derives from the object (e.g. cap), its support (the head) and the variant (caps/hats). The *fashion signified* is the external context of the fashion object, a context shared by a society ('woollen equals winter'). Thus the meaning of the advertisement-text is available to us because:

- we understand that caps or hats are to be worn on the head (the grammar or rules of the text of clothing)
- we understand the larger contexts in which certain kinds of clothing are needed and worn

Meaning is a *combination* of the two – the grammar of the text and the grammar of the cultural context.

A cap is worn on the head *as opposed to* a shoe which is worn on the foot; cotton clothing is worn in summer *as opposed to* woollens which are worn in winter. Notice here that the binaries are between items of clothing and between seasons and cultural contexts. There is clearly a structure at work.

> Structuralism in Cultural Studies asks us to look at the rules that govern meaning formation through a system of differences and relations between signs and their contexts.

Dick Hebdige's work built brilliantly on Barthesian semiology and set a trend for Cultural Studies. For Hebdige style is a signifying (that is meaning-making) practice. This style is attained through the transformation of signs of commodities, through 'bricolage' into new meanings in fresh, sometimes unexpected contexts. Analysing punk, Hebdige argues that it was a dramatization of British economic and social decline that had erupted into frustration and anger among the youth. It thus used objects of sexual fetishes (leather, chains and bondage gear) in wardrobe styles, noise and 'obscene' lyrics in music, unruly/jerky dance movements and so on. What punk did was to use language in such a radically different way that notions of 'taste' in music, 'beauty' in looks/appearances and 'appropriateness' in dancing or behaviour were questioned and subverted. Thus, the powerlessness of the punksters inspires them to evolve a new grammar of fashion and a new politics of culture. They used their bodies to generate art and music because they could not afford the expensive halls and theatres where 'high' art forms like the opera were held. Punk is thus a mass cultural form.

What we have learnt so far:

- Meaning is arbitrary.
- A text is a collection of signs that depend on each other.
- Texts have an internal grammar that can be decoded.
- The grammar or meaning of a text can be deciphered in conjunction with other larger texts (often called 'culture').

Poststructuralism and Deconstruction

Associated mainly with the work of the French philosopher Jacques Derrida, deconstruction and poststructuralism provided a radically new approach to language, narratives, and interpretation.

Derrida and Différance

For poststructuralism language is never stable. Meaning is the result of difference, and this process of differentiation is *endless*. Meaning is never *present* in the sign, simply because the sign refers to (yet) another sign which is *not here*. For example, in order to understand the term 'cat' we need more words like 'animal' or 'four-legged' or 'organism'. Then, we need to understand 'animal', 'organism' using words like 'living' or 'non-human', which in turn requires an explanation and understanding of 'human' and 'life'. Notice how each term can be explained only through newer terms. Meaning is never available in one term alone – it always implies and demands *more* terms.

Thus reading or interpretation is the movement through the chain of signs, seeking a temporary meaning from/at each halt. This suggests that every signifier (word/sign) leads not to a stable end-signified, but to more signifiers. This implies that meaning is never fully graspable, and the final meaning is always postponed (deferred).

A sign may be reproduced any time any place (the *iterability* or repeatability of the sign). Thus it can be made to mean differently each time it repeats in a different context. It is never *absolutely* the same sign that we encounter at each moment of its repetition. It follows that if meaning is never fully *present* then human identity – which is the result and product of language – is also never stable or unified. The 'presence' of identities or meaning is an illusion, for all presence is tainted with the impurity of the absent and the excluded. The very term 'structure' presupposes a unity, a centre and margins. There is never a centre without a margin. In fact, if we did not have margins, we cannot locate a centre. This means the existence of the centre is never definite and unified: it depends on the existence of the margin. The centre is identified in its *difference* from the margin. And, in order to explain/understand the centre, we need to refer to the margin. That is, the meaning of the term 'centre' is *deferred* (postponed) until we explain the term 'margin'.

Activity:

Think of defining the inside of your house, of delimiting the boundaries of the house. Can you define it without referring to the outside world, the road outside or the next house? Can you draw the boundaries of your house without also marking the boundaries of what is not inside your 'territory'?

And now ask: how are we to distinguish between inside and outside? Are inside and outside mutually dependent?

Hence meaning is available only through *difference* and *deference.* To suggest the togetherness of these two features of the sign and meaning Derrida coins the term *différance* (to say both differ and defer).

For Derrida the entire field of signs is 'writing', or *ecriture*. Here writing is *not* restricted to the graphic sense of the word, but refers to the *figural* sense: writing is the term used to denote any system that is based on difference and deference (*différance*). The study of such writing, Derrida terms 'grammatology', the very science of 'difference'.

What we have learnt so far:

- Identity and meaning are based on difference.
- Identity and meaning are never stable or unified.
- Identity and meaning always depend on some other term or concept which is not present in this term.
- There is no final meaning because each time you arrive at a set of 'key terms' or meanings, you discover that you need to move on to more words.

Michel Foucault and Power/Knowledge

Foucault was interested in the way power structures depend upon structures of knowledge (arts, science, medicine, demographics) and how, once they acquire knowledge, create subjects to be controlled.

Foucault's methodology seeks to understand how some sections of the population have been classified as criminals or insane. That is, he is interested in understanding the processes of classification that helped exclude some people from society. Foucault argues that certain authorities who possess power in society produce knowledge about those who lack power. Such a system of knowledge is called 'discourse'. The arts, religion, science and the law are discourses that 'produce' particular subjects.

Let us look at a concept-map of designations of deviance and their remedies in history as produced by specific 'authorities'.

Category	Discourse	Authority	'Corrective'
Immorality	Religion	Priest	Penitence
Vagrancy	Economics	Economist/Social commentator	Forced employment
Criminal	Law	Police/Jury	Imprisonment
Insane	Psychiatry	Psychiatrist/Psychoanalyst	Asylum
Sick	Medicine	Physician	Hospital

The last column, 'corrective' marks the actual enforcement of power or process/act, where the 'authorities' ensure that the deviance is rectified *according to what they think is right.*

Discourse and knowledge produce certain categories of 'subjects' (people) who are then treated in particular ways: the immoral are 'remedied' by priests, criminals are jailed by the law, the sick are treated by doctors, and the insane shut away in asylums by psychiatrists. What happens, therefore, is that the production of knowledge about those who lack power leads to very effective *practices* of power on the part of the authorities. Knowledge and classification systems such as medicine, the law or religion are therefore modes of social control.

Power and knowledge help identify and classify individual subjects as mad or ill. The task is to analyse the working of power and knowledge within a social set-up. These can be at the level of the family unit or at the level of the nation-state. There is, therefore, no such thing as neutral or objective knowledge because knowledge is always used to serve the interests of the dominant groups.

Now, after Foucault we know that discourses produce particular subjects, who are *subject to* control. People who lack the power to determine their lives and futures are said to lack *agency*. They are called 'subalterns'. Every social formation (contexts such as class, nation) has its own subalterns. The dominant groups in social structures that construct subalterns also use particular modes to ensure that the subalterns remain powerless. One such means of keeping the power relation in favour of the dominant category is ideology. Ideology is a system of beliefs and ideas that permeates social formations. Ideology justifies oppression and social inequalities by suggesting that the lower classes have always been inferior and persuades them of the validity of this belief. That is, ideology circulates as a system of representation and images that 'naturalizes' oppression and creates the illusion that oppression is natural.

Gayatri Spivak and the Subaltern

A distinguished literary and cultural critic Gayatri Spivak utilizes methods and approaches from Marxism, feminism and deconstruction. Her work in postcolonial studies has great relevance to Cultural Studies, especially those dealing with formerly colonized nations.

The 'subaltern' is a term Spivak borrows from the Italian Marxist Antonio Gramsci to signify the oppressed class. Spivak's well-known (and controversial) argument is that the subaltern cannot speak for him/herself because the very *structure* of colonial power (it must be noted that Spivak is speaking of the context of colonialism) prevents the speaking. For the colonised *woman* speaking is even more impossible because both colonialism and patriarchy ensure that she keeps quiet. The subaltern cannot, therefore, represent herself. Spivak argues that the work of intellectuals is to make visible the position of the marginalized. The subaltern must be 'spoken for' (that is, represented). Spivak points out that during colonialism the British assumed the authority and prerogative to speak for the oppressed native woman. The construction of the oppressed native woman was necessary to justify the presence of the modernizing, saviour Britisher. The native woman apparently 'called out' for liberation – which the white colonial master was supposed to provide. The nationalists also resurrected the voice of the native woman for their own ends, but, as Spivak points out, the voice of the woman is effaced in the discourse of both nationalism and colonialism: she is only spoken for.

Building on this notion of the subaltern a new mode of writing history, the Subaltern Studies project, was launched in 1982, under the leadership of Ranajit Guha. This project argued that traditional historiography only celebrated the actions of the elite. Thus the 'freedom struggle', in traditional history, was represented as the story of the actions of select leaders like Gandhi, Nehru and Tilak. It ignored the peasant and tribal rebellions that preceded the formation of the Indian National Congress. That is, such an elitist history ignored or marginalized certain kinds of revolt against the British in favour of the dominant (upper caste, upper class, metropolitan) movement. The project therefore, explored and recorded smaller rebellions and tried to redress this balance. It gave a voice to the subalterns within the freedom struggle.

Activity:

You will remember that when cellphones were first introduced there were debates about how they can cause brain cancer. Then, all of a sudden such reports stopped. Can you explain why there was such total silence on the issue until recently, when several reports appeared disproving the earlier theory: cellphones, they say, are now perfectly safe? The question poststructuralism, especially of the Foucault type, poses is: is the knowledge about the safety of cellphones generated by a 'neutral' science? Who funded the research? It asks us to distrust even scientific studies because science is a discourse partly dependent on capital.

And now ask: How many billions of dollars would be lost in cellphone sales if scientific experiments proved cellphones unsafe? Is it possible for science to be neutral when what is at stake is such huge amounts of money?

Let us look at another concept-map of the various kinds of social formations (contexts) and the subalterns they construct:

Social Formation	Subaltern	Dominant Group	Ideology
Class	Working classes	Capitalist-bourgeois	Capitalism
Empire	Natives	Europeans	Colonialism
Patriarchy	Women	Men	Gender
Nation	Ethnic minorities	Majority	Homogenization and nationalism

In a capitalist society the capitalist holds the power. The working class, toiling to generate profits for the capitalist, lacks any agency, but is made to believe it is happy because capitalism as an ideology spreads the illusion that the exploitative capitalist system is actually a generous, benevolent and caring patron of the working class.

In a patriarchal society the woman is assigned particular roles – as wife, as mother, as daughter, all of which make her dependent upon the male, and reduce her identity to her relationship with men. The ideology of gender is such that the woman is trained, right from childhood, to believe that motherhood and wifely roles are the goals to aspire to. It naturalizes the unequal relationship between the genders.

In a nation-state, the minorities are asked to believe in the ideal of the nation even when the nation does not respect their cultural rights, or solve their problems. Any attempt to seek cultural rights or protection or recognition is seen and treated as a threat to the nation itself. Further, the nation is supposedly unified – an ideology that ignores through a process of homogenization, all cultural, ethnic and regional differences.

Poststructuralism in Cultural Studies proposes difference as intrinsic to identity, the contingency of meaning, and the linkage of all knowledge with the exercise of power where the dominant group generates knowledge and meaning in order to keep sections of people under control through ideology's system of representations.

What we have learnt so far:

- Knowledge and power are linked.
- Power is based on assumptions, information and analysis of people and events.
- Thus power is about a cultural condition – of knowledge.
- People who possess power employ knowledge to discriminate against, imprison or even kill those who lack power.
- Those who lack power – the subalterns – are oppressed and marginalized.
- This marginalization is rendered natural through a system of commonly circulated beliefs called ideology.

Marxism

Marxist cultural theory originates in the work of Karl Marx and Friedrich Engels in the nineteenth century. The Marx–Engels analysis of society and the conditions of production spilled over into an analysis of culture.

Activity:

Look at contemporary advertisements for various consumer objects. Note how they carefully suggest that the acquisition of an object marks a certain lifestyle (the nuclear family, the working woman). Therefore, you do not simply buy an object/product – you buy a lifestyle that locates you in a particular class. This mode of selling objects is the ideology of consumerism.

> *Thus taking certain kinds of holidays, buying certain products and wearing certain clothes identify you as a member of a certain class. Thus the Chocolat model of the LG cellphones suggests that in its presence, everything else – from buildings to clothes – looks ancient and backward. Clearly what it is suggesting is that if you want to be 'in' and modern, you must acquire this model. Now the ideology is very simple: modernity and 'development' can be reduced to a consumer product, a technological device. What is not mentioned is that you are being sold (i) this idea of modernity, (ii) the object that concretizes the idea, (iii) selling you this idea and product generates profits.*
>
> *Another example would be the way families are represented in soap operas and families: the image of the caring wife/mother often masks the fact that she has little economic independence, works extremely hard (without pay) and is often exploited. On TV and on the big screen such a mother/wife is projected as the ideal woman. Even when she has another job, she cannot afford to 'neglect' her 'family duties'.*
>
> *And now ask: why is a consumer product linked to your identity? Why does a restaurant designate separate spaces as 'family rooms'?*

i) The capitalist mode of production justified and naturalized itself through certain patterns of thought. The exploitative *economic* relations of the factory are carried over into the *social* realm. The *economic base* influences the *social superstructure.*

ii) *Classes* are the basic units in social conflict. Class membership is defined by the ownership or lack of ownership of the means of production. The working class is made up of those who sell their labour power, the capitalist class of those that purchase labour power.

iii) The oppressed classes, however, believe this inequality as 'natural' or 'preordained', and do not even recognize that they are oppressed. The system of thought and representation that helps legitimize inequality and oppression is termed *ideology.* Ideology is a *false consciousness* that prevents the recognition of oppression by the oppressed.

iv) Ideology is sustained and reproduced through cultural forms such as art. Culture must be understood in relation to the economic conditions of the age. There is a correlation between the socio-economic conditions and the kind of cultural works produced.

v) The capitalist economy creates illusions about itself. The workers are under the illusion that they are free and unexploited, that the capitalist has a legitimate right to the surplus, and that the commodities, money, and capital have properties and powers of their own. This is fetishism, where properties are assigned to objects.

vi) Antonio Gramsci emphasizes the institutional and cultural bases of ideology. Ideology may be in any form: political propaganda, sermons, folklore and popular songs. Ideology is not false consciousness, simply because for Gramsci popular songs and superstitions are themselves *material forces*. He develops the concept of hegemony to demonstrate how ideology works. Hegemony is the *nexus of material and ideological instruments through which the dominant classes maintain their power*. Hegemony thus *mediates* between the ruling ideas and the subjects. The hegemony of the ruling/dominant class is maintained through *coercion* and *consent*. The ideas of the dominant class are institutionalized in the civil society: the law courts, the bureaucracy, the religious and educational systems. The coercive apparatus is the *state* with its army and police apparatuses. A more subtle form of control is to employ intellectuals to naturalize the present (oppressive order). The ruled must be made to accept things as they are, i.e. accept and *consent* to oppression of their own volition.

vii) Ideology for Louis Althusser constructs the individuals as *subjects* of the system. It gives them the identity necessary to the functioning of the existing state of affairs, while making them feel *as if they are free agents* – what Althusser terms 'interpellation'. It is a system of *representations* (images, myths, ideas or concepts).

viii) State power is maintained through *Repressive State Apparatuses* (RSAs) like the police, the army, law courts and prisons that operate through actual or threats of *coercive* force/violence. But power is also maintained through the active *consent* of the subjects. This is achieved through *Ideological State Apparatuses* (ISAs) of State control: the political groups, the media, the education system, religion and art.

ix) Culture is the expression of class conflict and social relations that are structured by and through power relations.

Marxism sees culture as the masking of real social and economic conditions where cultural artifacts conceal exploitative labour and ideology (a system of representations) convinces people that everything is alright. Thus the boom in employment for young graduates at call centers – projected as a great advance – masks the real economic condition that they are paid far less than their American counterparts.

What we have learnt so far:

- Economic conditions determine social and cultural formations.
- Ideology that reinforces class differences and power relations functions through culture.
- Culture is often a mode of concealing economic conditions, where images and representations make us believe that these conditions are 'natural'.

Postmodernism

Postmodernism, especially in terms of its use for Cultural Studies, rejects the opposition between 'high' or elite culture and 'low' or mass culture. It questions the criteria by which certain forms/texts/assumptions are projected as 'good taste', 'classics', permanent ('for all time to come') and universal. Postmodernism is closely aligned with Cultural Studies in its rejection of the 'high/low' distinction between cultures, and its focus on the modes by which certain cultural artefacts come to occupy higher status.

It interrogates any notion, philosophy or ideal of a general, universal and overarching nature. It rejects the claim of any universal or totalizing theory (such as the Marxist idea of the ultimate emancipation of all mankind, the idea of science as the creator of truth for all humans). It celebrates plurality, heterogeneity, and the small, local, innovative, marginalized and unfinished narratives that respect differences and specificities of cultures, individuals and regions. Meaning is seen as differential (see poststructuralism above), contingent and purely arbitrary. The process of representation seeks not to offer any insights into reality or Truth. Rather, it only calls attention to itself. That is, it is *self-referential.*

In literature it collapses the distinctions between genres and conventions. The thriller format becomes part of the 'serious' novel. Comic elements and absurdity mark the author's attitude to tragic events like death, suffering, the Holocaust (Joseph Heller's *Catch 22*, the fiction of Kurt Vonnegut, Jr). Myths, fairy tales, legends and contemporary realities merge (Donald Barthelme, Salman Rushdie and Gabriel García Márquez). Historical figures jostle with contemporary people (for instance, the use of Goethe and Hemingway as characters by Milan Kundera). It becomes impossible to distinguish between reality and illusion, for both the characters and the reader (Pynchon's *The Crying of Lot 49*, for instance). The distinction between 'real' history and 'mere' fiction is called into question (Graham Swift's *Waterland*). The narrator continually undermines his own apparently 'reliable' narrative and we are left wondering: can we trust this story at all?

Postmodernism suggests that power relations structure all social truths, approaches and even conceptions of reality.

Jean-François Lyotard and the Postmodern Condition

Jean-François Lyotard characterizes the postmodern as a disbelief in and resistance to metanarratives (narratives that seek to explain and address universal conditions while assuming that these explanations suit all contexts and locations).

i) The disbelief towards metanarratives is the disillusionment with *totalizing* explanations of reality. This includes the narrative of science, philosophy and religion. For instance, the Marxist ideal of an emancipatory agenda and aim for communism or the Christian narrative of redemption are totalizing narratives because they ignore differences and variations at local, individual and regional levels in favour of an overarching universal programme or explanation.
ii) These knowledges and explanations are therefore tyrannical and oppressive because they ignore differences in order to impose

a false unity on knowledge and reality. These knowledges also conceal beneath an apparent objectivity, their tactics of 'terror'. Lyotard suggests that scientists and scientific discourses are not employed to disseminate Truth but to augment power. That is, scientific discourses seek to *legitimize* certain kinds of knowledges and actually *suppress* oppositional knowledges in order to retain their stranglehold.

iii) Postmodernism acknowledges that all knowledge is fragmentary, partial and incomplete. One can only utilize local knowledge to know a *part* of the truth. Thus the individual's experience, knowledge and voice is to be retrieved as a resistance and *delegitimation* towards grand narratives that simply pass off *one* version of knowledge and reality as universal.

Activity:

Think of Subhash Ghai's films where he makes small, cameo appearances. Now, we all know Subhash Ghai is the director and/or producer of the film we are watching. We are aware that it is a fictional world up there on the screen where real life people (flesh-and-blood actors) pretend to be something else (the roles they play, as hero/ines). But when Ghai appears on screen, he complicates matters. Is he there as an actor? Or is he the director now? What the appearance does is to merge screen life with true life messily, making it difficult for us to see him either as only an actor or only as the director. He draws attention to the fact that it is a film that he is directing and which we are watching. It is self-reflexive and relies on undecidability.

And now ask: Is it possible for us to watch a film where we are not aware of the off-screen persona of the hero/heroine? Do you think the public discussions in film magazines about film stars – the hero's drinking or the heroine's origins – influence how we view them on screen?

Jean Baudrillard and the Hyperreal

Baudrillard's central argument is that in the age of perfect reproduction (the photocopy, the digital copy) and endless repetition of images, the distinction between the real and the illusory, between original and 'copy', between superficiality and depth has broken down. What we now have is a culture of 'hyperreality'.

i) Baudrillard suggests that a sign merely refers to other signs. The entire system is constituted by such signs that are ultimately empty because they only refer to other similar signs rather than 'Truth'. 'Truth' is thus a *simulacrum* of the real in a process he calls 'simulation'. Simulation is when the image/model becomes more real than real. It is the generation of copies and models of the real without origin or reality, or what is called the 'hyperreal'.
ii) Virtual reality, global communications, the infinite reproductions of data banks and holograms are examples of the redundancy of the distinction between real and imagined, between 'true' and copy.
iii) In a consumer society objects are not simply consumed. They signify a *status* rather than satisfy a need. In a consumer society objects become *signs* and what we consume are not objects but signs where the objects have value for us *as signs*. Therefore we consume *images*, and the exchange value is transformed into *sign-value*.
iv) For Baudrillard, then, the postmodern is characterized by the hyperreal, by the collapse of distinction between the private and the public (home, office, and now homeoffice). This is the 'implosion' of meaning in the media: where signs without referents enchant us.

Activity:

On several occasions MTV makes fun of itself in its advertisements. It suggests that MTV is not to be taken seriously. Now: do you think this self-mockery enhances your interest in viewing MTV or does it cause you to stop viewing it? That is, will you take MTV's self-mockery seriously and say 'okay: they themselves say their programmes are meaningless, so let me stop watching'? The point is, the rhetoric here draws your attention to the programmes, even as it proposes the meaninglessness of the activity. This is a very postmodern move, where the work of art or culture mocks itself. The mockery is a part of the programme.

And now ask: is it possible to separate MTV's 'serious' advertisements from their self-mocking ones? Are both 'art'?

Postmodern Arts

In Cultural Studies, postmodern visual art, sculpture, plastic art and designs may be seen as possessing the following features:

i) Incompatible styles are a favourite device. Classical 'clean' images and the fragmented modern aesthetic style are used simultaneously.

ii) The use of the vernacular and slang in art. This rejects the distinction between high/elite and low/popular art when the artists adopt the style and language of the masses. Thus we have 'ethnic chic', where very space-age kind of fashion also uses local, ethnic styles, fabric or designs: mixing the very contemporary and the older. The recycling of traditional styles, songs, folk tunes, other-cultural forms are combined (fusion music, where eastern and Western styles mix). Rap, rock 'n' roll, beat, progressive rock are styles that have developed and held sway in this category of popular music.

iii) A conscious and excessive use of ornamentation, often mixing geometric and non-geometric shapes.

iv) An increased use of the technological media (videos, digital images) and electronics.

v) The emphasis on privacy and individual use of goods rather than products for the masses (especially in furniture and cutlery/crockery). Perhaps the stress and demand for the 'exclusive' is part of the postmodern redefinition of necessity and fashion.

vi) The use of 'schlock' – trivia serving as memorabilia in our lives. The schlock item has rarely any *functional* use. The toy dog hanging in the car, the stickers in the car window, the toy models, the wood/plastic/metal artefacts that constitute much gift exchange today all classify as schlock.

Subcultures, Popular Culture and Postmodernism

The arrival of rock music, MTV, films such as Ridley Scott's *Blade Runner* (based on Philip Dick's 1968 novel *Do Androids Dream of Electric Sheep*?) have created a whole postmodern popular culture. Dick Hebdige terms these new forms of cultures, produced by marginalized groups, 'subcultures'. These subcultures evade the hegemony imposed by the 'high' cultural forms and alter power structures and social formations, leaving the society and art forms in a state of permanent evolution and change where no form/style occupies any privileged position.

A good example of a postmodern art form that exhibits several of the concepts and themes discussed above is cyberpunk. The writings of William Gibson, Bruce Sterling, Melissa Scott, Pat Cadigan, Neal Stephenson and others consciously craft texts that defy classification (science fiction, fantasy, contemporary realism) and reflect a growing concern with the constructed nature of truth, culture and knowledge.

> Postmodernism in Cultural Studies celebrates the fragmented, the plural, the contingent and the local while rejecting universals and totalities, even as it sees representation as an end in itself, calls into question the notion of a TRUTH behind signs/words/images and collapses the distinction between original and copy.

Paul Virilio and Hypermodernism

Paul Virilio's work on dromology (the 'science of speed') is an exciting reading of late twentieth century cyberculture.

i) Virilio argues that histories of socio-political institutions such as the military or even cultural movements demonstrate the need for speed rather than commerce. Virilio argues that politics' relationship with speed is as important as its relationship with the accumulation of wealth. Virilio argues that higher speeds belong to the upper reaches of society and the slower ones to the bottom. It is a world increasingly governed by speed – of the transmission of information, money transfer, arming of nations, 'first strike' and transportation.

ii) For Virilio the concept of 'pure' war is actually the weaponry of new information and communications technology because it is the weapons of the military-industrial complex that cause 'integral accidents' such as the 1987 world stock market crash – brought on by the failure of automated program trading.

iii) Virilio suggests that hypermodern vision and the hypermodern city are both products of military power and time-based cinematic technologies of disappearance. Discontinuous and interrupted images rule our visual life: we get, literally, only a 'bit' at a time, but we compose the whole out of these disappeared bits.

iv) Military technologies and the technocratic system controls every aspect of our life. The faith in nuclear deterrence, submission to a system of mass destruction (appropriately termed, in military rhetoric, MAD, or 'mutually assured destruction'), and societies preparing for the perpetual possibility of war are all aspects of Virilio's pure war.

v) Speed and technology replace democratic participation, and undermine politics. Effective media politics diminishes the space of democratic political participation. Instantaneous communication actually reduces the time for detailed discussions, deliberations and consensus-building.

vi) Virilio suggests that there has been, with contemporary technology, the replacement of 'local time' with one single 'global time'. Virilio argues that time has 'telescoped', where every city will be in the same place – in time, cities that have telescoped in time. That is, geographical distances become irrelevant. For Virilio the new world order is a manifestation of what he terms 'globalitarianism'. The single market, the convergence of time towards a single time (which dominates local time), the telecommunications conglomerates and cyberspace all suggest a 'totalitarianism of totalitarianism'. Where totalitarianism was once localized and singular (as in the Soviet Union), with the advent of globalization, one can be under surveillance anywhere.

What we have learnt so far:

- Postmodernism rejects any totality – of knowledge, ideology or philosophy.
- It believes in the contingency of values and the very local nature of truth.
- It collapses the boundaries between high/mass culture.

- It is self-reflexive – refers to itself, parodies itself self-consciously.
- In the contemporary world the distinction between original and copy, reality and illusion break down.
- It argues that we live in a world of signs, where the signs are ends in themselves and need not refer to any reality, and we cannot, therefore, know the difference between original and image, reality and illusion.
- Postmodern art and culture deliberately evoke older forms to parody and subvert the hierarchy of elite/mass culture.
- It believes that with the advent of more technology and media, our lives are under constant surveillance.

Feminisms and Post-feminisms

Feminism can be defined as a political, cultural, pedagogic and theoretical response to the patriarchal structures of power that seek to subordinate women's lives, interests, bodies and sexualities. It argues that these structures create and enforce all relationships between men and women. The Women's Movement became a major political force in Europe and America in the 1960s and 70s. The movement took various issues for the gender-debate – science, politics, economics, culture, epistemology. In the literary arts the feminist critics exposed the patriarchal ideology that informed the construction of the 'Eng. Lit' canon in the first place, and which made male-centred writing possible. During the 1970s 'feminist theory' emerged with works such as Kate Millett's *Sexual Politics*, Shulamith Firestone's *The Dialectic of Sex* and others. With the 1980s and 1990s, we have a post-feminist phase that also addresses questions of technology.

Activity:

Ask yourself what the woman, or more appropriately the woman as a body, is doing trying to sell cars or cellphones in most advertisements. There seems to be an implicit connection between two commodities: the consumer product (car/cellphone) and the woman. Both are: (i) objects, (ii) objects that can be acquired, (iii) objects that can be acquired to add to the status of the male buyer. In advertisements designed to attract the female consumer, the ideology and politics is even worse. Think of the Fair and Lovely ad, which also stars K. Srikanth, the former cricketer. Ask yourself: does the woman in that ad get the job because she is good, or because her complexion has improved through the use of cosmetics? And notice that Srikanth seems to acknowledge her as a 'presentable' woman – thus emphasizing the importance of her looks rather than her talent.

And now ask yourself: is it necessary to use a woman to sell a product?

i) Feminism looks at all the representational strategies in popular and other cultural forms, drawing attention to the masculinist/patriarchal constructions of women within these representations, and acquiring a political platform from which such an agenda can be articulated and justice fought for.

ii) Literary and cultural texts operate on the lines of power struggle: that between men and women. The 'text' (meaning, cinema, poetry, theatre, advertisements) naturalizes the oppression of women through its stereotypical representation of women as weak/vulnerable, seductress, obstacle, sexual object of the male's desire, a procreating device and so on. That is, such 'texts' reproduce patriarchal social biases that see the woman as only the 'Other' of the male. Religion, social conditions and cultural traditions perceive the woman as an adjunct to the male. This means that the woman's identity is never separate, but is subsumed under that of the male.

iii) Sexuality becomes a tool through which stereotyping of the female – as prostitutes, virgins, unchaste women – achieves patriarchal domination.

iv) The woman is typecast as 'Mother Nature', thus reducing her to the role of the perpetual 'giver'. Religious doctrines aid these representations. Language makes it appear permanent and 'natural' through the use of patriarchal terms like Mother Earth and Mother Nature.

v) *Sex*, argue feminists, is biological, while *gender* is socially constructed. There is no necessary link between gender and biological sex. Masculinity and femininity are essentially coercive categories that ensure that men and women behave in certain ways. The socialization of woman renders her a woman with certain apparently 'inherent' qualities – weakness, feeble-mindedness, patience and so on. Notions of morality or sensibility are used by males to argue that women need to be confined to the home (being weak), protected (being vulnerable), and controlled (being naïve, unpredictable and unstable). Feminists suggest that inequality of sexes does not have a biological basis or origin, it originates in the cultural constructions of gender difference. *Gendering* is a practice of power, where masculinity is always associated with authority. Further, authoritarian discourses such as those of law or science are based on certain assumptions and binary thinking about women, sexuality and 'welfare'.

vi) In terms of language and epistemology the feminists seek to formulate either a gender-neutral language which will reject patriarchal terms like *his*tory and *man*kind, or a specifically female language which will help create an alternative system of knowledge (epistemology) itself – one based on female subjectivity, identity and experience. This is what Elaine Showalter termed 'gynocriticism'.

vii) Capitalism produced a massive spilt between the public and private spheres. The family became the 'retreat', away from the factory. For the women, within the family, 'work' and 'life' had collapsed into one another. Housewives had the responsibility of maintaining the emotional and psychological realm of personal relations, and of preserving the morality and tradition of the family.[1]

viii) Luce Irigaray argues against the 'logic of sameness'. Irigaray shows how Freud's theory of sexuality is basically premised on one sex – the male. There is the male and there is the absence which is the female. The male is the paradigm of all sexuality – physical changes.

ix) Irigaray suggests a specifically feminine writing practice. Her own writing is unique with puns, word plays, syntactic experiments and new arrangements. Reading and writing then must favour the images and metaphors of fluidity, dynamism, polysemy and plurality (all feminine) rather than those of unity, monologism, stability and fixity.

x) Postfeminism seeks multiplicities and varieties rather than singular and unified subject positions. Contemporary feminism moves away from the Eurocentric and heterosexual biases of early feminism and develops into Black feminism, 'Third World' or postcolonial feminism, and lesbian feminism. A good example would be from feminist science studies. Sandra Harding's *Is Science Multicultural?* (1998) looks specifically at the women (and men) whose lives are affected by technologies, but who have no role in the knowledge-processes that *create* these technologies. Standpoint epistemology identifies the Eurocentric and male-centric elements in the conceptual frameworks used to analyse scientific and technological change. Thus tribal and local knowledge must be incorporated into development projects and programmes.

xi) *Cyberfeminism*: This is the age of heavily media-driven, technologized and globalized network society. Feminist studies of the relationship of gender and technology looked at technological artefacts, technological practices, systems of knowledge, institutions and competencies. Cyberfeminists see cyberculture as a revolutionary social experiment with the potential to create new identities, relationships and cultures. Cyberfeminisms seek ways to link feminism with contemporary feminist projects and networks both on and off the Net. The work of the cyberfeminist group, the VNS Matrix aims to employ specifically and graphically female arts for the construction of libidinal pleasures in a feminized and postfeminist erotics of technocultural production. It appropriates paternal organs, spermatic metaphors, and metaphors of viral infection as well as those references on female genitals and bodily processes.

Feminism in Cultural Studies focuses on the ways in which the woman and her body is represented as a commodity, an adjunct to the man in a society whose cultural, economic and political contexts enforce this unequal division, and where gender is socially constructed and imposed. In Cultural Studies feminist theory examines the gendered use of media and rhetoric to reinforce patriarchy. In general practice – which is Cultural Studies' larger goal of 'praxis' – feminism seeks empowerment for the woman over the modes of representation advertisements or in medicine, changes in the role of technology, religion, politics and economics control the women's lives even as it theorizes about media, culture, medicine, the law and the general forms of cultural control exerted by men over women.

What we have learnt so far:

- Feminism argues that gender inequalities in society are 'naturalized' through systems of representation in media and culture, where the woman is always a secondary figure, an object.
- Cultural artefacts are, therefore, modes of social control, and must be examined for their gender prejudices.
- It suggests a more just system where women discover means of writing their true selves, representing themselves and having greater control over their lives and bodies.
- It proposes using resources as diverse as local spiritual beliefs, the ballot and cybertechnology for the empowerment of women.

Queer Theory

Queer studies is an attempt to redefine sexual identities. It seeks a cultural/political space where the homosexual is no more the 'perverted', 'sick' Other of heterosexuality. Queer Theory is a significant contributor to Cultural Studies and is closely aligned with political and social movements and activism. In 1969 police raided the Stonewall Tavern in New York City. Many gays, lesbians, transvestites fought back. The subsequent battles and riots received wide publicity. The first meeting of the British Gay Liberation Front took place at the London School of Economics on 13 November 1970, and the first Annual Gay Pride march on 1 April 1972. Since then the gay liberation movement has sought to fight social, legal, medical and religious oppression and tried to locate a whole new cultural space for the thus far marginalized community.

Activity:

Watching even recent Hindi films, notice the ways in which queer sexuality becomes the subject of comedy and satire (in Dil Se and Kal Ho Na Ho, both, incidentally, starring Shah Rukh Khan). How is it different from making the disabled man or woman a subject of humour?

Is an alternate sexual preference evil? Look at newspaper debates on the subject, some of which take recourse to myth and religion to 'prove' that homosexuality is sinful.

In the West you will rarely see two men holding hands in public because they would be immediately identified as gay. Now in India, it is a common sight. The Lonely Planet warns the Western traveller that this is a common practice in India, and they should on no account assume that the men are gay.

And now ask: is there a cultural difference in the way we perceive men, sexuality and women?

i) Gay and lesbian theory assumes that sexuality and sexual preferences/orientations play a prominent role in the construction of social identity. Sexual orientation is the fundamental category of analysis and understanding. Gay and lesbian studies (now called 'queer studies') suggests that the patriarchy which feminism contests is actually 'heteropatriarchy'. Kinship and marriage are deemed to be completely heterosexual (gay marriages are current controversies across the world, if you have been reading the newspapers). Sexual practices and relationships that are outside the purview of a law that recognizes only heterosexual marriages are deemed to be untenable. Thus heterosexuality is taken as a given and natural.
ii) Queer theory argues, following Michel Foucault, that the homosexual as a social category emerges essentially in the

post-Renaissance period. In the late nineteenth century several legal and medical texts speak of the homosexual as a deviant or a criminal, and homosexuality as a perversion and/or sickness. Homosexuality was projected as the dark Other of heterosexuality. Thus it is not so much the sexuality of the homo/hetero individual than the political and cultural contexts in which these sexualities are lived that need to be studied. For Cultural Studies this is crucial, for it suggests that sexuality, like gender, is primarily a socially constructed and enacted aspect of life and individuality.

iii) The use of poststructuralism by queer theorists like Judith Butler, Lee Edelman and Diana Fuss enables gay/lesbian theory to debate issues of identity, marginality, authenticity and epistemology. There is an emphasis on the social context of identity. Queer theory rejects an 'essentialism' of identity politics, and the binary opposition of heterosexual/homosexual in favour of a more fluid, and impermanent nature of the same.

iv) Lesbian theorists argue that even heterosexual women exhibit a certain fear (homophobia) of lesbianism. That is, even the feminist critiques of patriarchy are informed by an acceptance of heterosexuality as the standard, and homosexuality/lesbianism as a deviation (summed up in Adrienne Rich's well-known 1979 essay 'Compulsory Heterosexuality and Lesbian Existence'). Lesbians were seen as monsters or unnatural. The argument of the lesbian feminists is that the feminist movement so far has assumed heterosexuality to be the universal condition of *all* women. Moreover, the experience of the white, middle-class, urban woman was the 'standard' subject of analysis. Lesbian feminists thus emphasize the need for accommodation of differences within a feminist practice: the difference of class, race, culture and sexual orientation.

v) Some lesbian studies have suggested that the woman-woman bond need not always be sexual. The concept of the 'lesbian continuum' (Adrienne Rich: 1979) is a term that seeks to incorporate within itself the whole range of woman-woman relations: mutual help networks, camaraderie, woman's institutions, female friendships that are not necessarily sexual in nature.

vi) Queer theory suggests the possibilities of political change, where gay/lesbian identities find a voice. Gay/lesbian theories are sensitive to racial and class categories within sexuality. The assumption here is that gay/lesbian individuals of, say, the economically disadvantaged working class Asian-immigrant population, are *doubly marginalized*: by the white race for being the racial Other, and within their own community for being not-heterosexual.

Queer theory in Cultural Studies looks at various cultural constructions of the gay/lesbian as deviant, sick or criminal, and asks us to interrogate the ways in which an entire range of sexuality has been excluded through the politics of identity, a politics that informs and governs popular cultural representations of the queer.

vii) In addition to framing a homosexual canon (writers who were gay or lesbian, but whose works have been marginalized), queer theorists detect a veiled homosexual thematic in apparently heterosexual works. 'Woman's friendship' (the title of a book by Janet Todd) and male bonding are located within classics such as *Jane Eyre*. As an extension they also detect the homophobic tendencies in classic literary works.

viii) Queer theory emphasizes the liminal nature of identity. They stress the gay/lesbian identity as a 'crossing-over'. The work of Judith Butler is crucial here because it offers a new way of dealing with the problem of identity. Butler begins with the assumption that identity is not a stable entity. Gender identity is 'performed', and is performed repeatedly. Butler argues that feminism has presupposed the category of woman as a stable and unitary subject. Feminism, by treating the very fact of being a woman as the defining factor of identity, ignores other equally crucial factors of identity such as class, race or sexuality. Butler is suggesting that even feminist theory cannot assume that being 'female' or 'male' creates certain kinds of identities.

ix) Identity is a switching of roles. Identity is not closed, stable or unitary thing which is separate from an Other. The Self and the Other are not mutually distinct species. The Other is thus installed in the Self to attain a self-identity: the Self thus contains the Other within it. The citation/repetition of queer identity may be used to destabilize the very discourse of heterosexuality.

x) Queer theory interrogates the modes by which sexual boundaries of the inside and outside are constructed, sexual identities assigned and sexual politics formulated. Language and law regulate the establishment of heterosexuality as both a practice and as a system. It is the language of defence and protection: heterosexuality secures itself against the intrusion of the homosexual contaminant. The homosexual is the excluded.

xi) Contemporary Cultural Studies of gay and lesbian sexualities speak of a 'situational homosexuality', same sex practices that result from circumstances – imprisonment and the barracks, for instance. This is supposed to be different from 'true' homosexuality, which is supposed to have a psychic or somatic origin. The idea of 'situational homosexuality' brings up the issue of cultural and social factors in matters of sexuality and sexual preference. There is a marked reluctance on the part of even social constructivists and historians of same-sex desire to analyse the historical conditions of situational homosexuality. This somehow renders it 'timeless' and therefore in the realm of nature rather than culture. What is required is a study of how social scientists effectively foreclose the discussion of situational homosexuality in order to understand how even so-called cultural historians fall prey to methods they claim to eschew or reject (Kunzel 2002: 253–70).

What we have learnt so far:

- Queer theory demonstrates how heterosexuality has been considered the norm and homosexuality as deviance.
- It argues that identity is secured only through performance, and repetition.
- Homosexuality is a social construction – the result of power relations between the 'dominant' sexual types (heterosexuals) – and how such a construction delegitimizes gays and lesbians as deviants, criminals and immoral.
- AIDS has added to the criminalization of the queer.
- What is needed is a study of the queer canon, a battle for political power and social acceptance, while theorists argue for a fine-tuning of race and gender studies to address queer sexuality among blacks and postcolonial societies.

Postcolonial Theory

Colonialism has been an integral part of the history of numerous nations in Asia, Africa and South America. European nations controlled much of the world's resources and populations from the seventeenth century, well into the twentieth.

Postcolonial theory looks at the ways in which the non-white races have been subject to oppression and exploitation during colonial rule. It foregrounds questions of race in discussions about the West and the West's interaction (both past and present) with the East. It also looks at how the present age of globalization brings back memories of colonialism, albeit in a new frame and with newer rhetoric and modes of exploitation.

Activity:

Think of the number of times we have seen the WTC bombings on our TV screens. Now, write and ask your friends and/or relations in the USA or Europe if they have seen as many visuals of (i) the Bhopal gas tragedy, (ii) the Latur earthquake on American TV (The first has left behind an enduring legacy of disease, the second, of poverty). The imbalance in the numbers reflects a global condition: disaster news isn't news unless it happens in Euro-American territory or affects Euro-American populations (one extensively covered Daniel Pearl death [a major motion picture starring Brad Pitt], versus the number of Indian students found mysteriously dead in American, Australian and other First World nations). This imbalance is the politics of representation driven by a global cultural condition where non-white deaths and disasters do not matter so much.

Think also of the ways in which non-white ethnic objects (from jewellery to Bhangra music) get commodified and marketed in the west).

And now ask: Is the TV coverage of disasters in Asian or African nations (while they are almost always about poverty or civil war) influenced by ideas of race?

i) In postcolonial studies, the basic task is to see how colonial systems of knowledge – medical, legal, literary – enabled oppression. It seeks to explore the modes of representation through which colonial writings and culture justified exploitation and oppression.

Postcolonial theory in Cultural Studies looks at the global circulation of Euro-American culture, which uses products created out of exploited Third World labour, the question of race and gender in economic and cultural policies (from Walt Disney's representation of the non-white races in cartoons to IMF policies), the centrality of techniques of representation to the cultural imperialism of the Euro-American nations.

ii) The category of 'Man', argue postcolonialists, means only 'white man' because the non-white is rendered less than human within colonialism. Eventually, through western education and 'acculturation' the native also comes to believe in this stereotype of the white man as superior and himself as inferior. Postcolonial critics are thus very interested in literary and cultural representations of the non-white races by Europeans because they argue such representations are extremely powerful.

iii) Other thinkers like Homi Bhabha argue that the stereotype actually reflects the flaws and anxieties within colonialism – where the stereotype is an attempt to maintain stability.

Colonialism for Bhabha is ambivalent because on the one hand it wants to 'improve' the native into being more like the white man, but on the other does not want to lose its status of being uniquely white.

iv) Contemporary postcolonial studies looks at the ways in which globalization works on the same principles of earlier colonialism. The free trade agreements and treaties benefit the West even as they exploit the Asian nations. Global immigration policies suit particular skills alone, and not the lower working classes.

v) The global circulation of Hollywood, for critics like Simon During (2000), is a colonizing phenomenon where cultural and material icons and actions (from Britney Spears and Barbie to McDonald's) are sold by a First World corporation in Asian markets and ease out local, ethnic products.

vi) Global culture is facilitated by technological developments – where, again, the intellectual resources of Third World academics, software engineers and others are used to further the profits of First World corporations.

vii) Globalization and its dissolution of the nation-state damage the chances of the deprived in Asian and African nations because internal economic policies for the emancipation of these classes are regulated by global, transnational bodies like the IMF and the World Bank.

viii) Racism is not completely dead even in the politically correct age. The differential salary-wage structures that enable Medical Transcription or BPO work involves, in postcolonial studies, questions of race (statistics will reveal that Indian call centre workers are paid far lower than the US basic minimum wage).

ix) Further, globalizing culture means that McDonald's appropriates native spaces and cultural systems in order to sell its products. This works because the products utilize a representational technique where the consumption of that product is projected as a status symbol for the (metropolitan) individual or class. Thus desire is first created through representation and then commerce fulfils the desire.

What we have learnt so far:

- Postcolonialism emphasizes the race question in politics and culture.
- It demonstrates how colonialism relies on representation to convince the native (non-white) to accept, indeed welcome, colonial rule.
- Postcolonial theory asks us to pay attention to the politics of representation of non-white races in white-race-controlled media.
- It suggests that exploitative mechanisms that drove colonialism continue to exist in newer forms today.

Technoculture and Risk

Contemporary critical theory has had to negotiate with massive environmental disaster, industrial disaster, 9/11 and other cataclysmic events. Much contemporary social theory examines the role such events play in culture. One of the most influential of such theories is that of the risk society.

Activity:

Take the home PC as a device that provides solutions to numerous problems of communication, writing and information-access. This technological device, however, is not free of risks. List for yourself all the risks involved in using a PC with access to the www (and not only bad posture at the PC!).

You will discover that this very PC gives you information on all the risks involved in using it: virus, 'illegal operation', repeated striking of the shift key, corruption of the hard drive and so on. Finally, it also offers solutions: contact the help centre, download anti-virus, update your PC, and so on. Notice that both risk and solution are embedded in the same system. The more you use the PC/device the greater information you need and acquire about all that can possibly go wrong with it. It creates a sense of anxiety to the non-professional user about the loss of data and system collapse, but does not stop her/him from working on.

And now ask: do you understand (i) the degree of risk involved (ii) the kinds of risk involved (iii) the solutions to the impending disaster? Do you see the use of technology as risky, and that same technology asks you to buy more protection to avoid risks?

Ulrich Beck propounded the influential 'risk society' thesis in *Risk Society: Towards a New Modernity* (1992) and later works (1995, 1997). Risk, Beck inform us, is not real, risks are about 'becoming-real'. As soon as risks become real, they cease being risks, and become, instead, disasters. (If one may engage in an aside for the purpose of illustration, India's famed batting line-up, all way to number six, always carries the *risk* of collapse. When it happens on the *field*, then it is not risk any more: it is a national catastrophe.) Risks then get displaced to other 'sites': future disasters. Thus risks are *potential* disasters. While it is not necessary to run the entire debate about risk society here, it may be useful to pay attention to one particular arena where the risk thesis appears most relevant: technoculture. We live in an increasingly technologized world. Global capitalism – the immediate geopolitical context of our nation-states – runs on the engines of information and communications technologies. Our everyday life – from shopping to education – depends heavily on technology, with greater or lesser degrees of both efficiency and necessity. Further, as 9/11 and its aftermath demonstrated so clearly, everyday life is vulnerable to technological threats, and these threats – real or imagined, such as Weapons of Mass Destruction (WMD) – are 'solved' using more technological systems and machines (smart bombs, electronic surveillance systems), which in turn generate more threats/risks ('Hey! Are you authorized to enter that room with the codes to the smart bombs?')... and so the long tale spins on.

i) Beck begins by suggesting that technoscience in industrial society has generated numerous dangers. Industrial society is based on the production and distribution of goods – which are required to fill the 'scarcity' within society. Beck suggests that a society based on scarcity and the removal of scarcity can handle goods and needs only when they actualize, as 'visible'. Such a system cannot handle the risks and hazards of industrial production and distribution. But as long as risk is secondary to scarcity or needs industrial society has no problems. This is the feature of industrial modernity – the production of goods to overcome scarcity envisaged and imaged as 'needs'. Which implies that risk is seen as an obstacle to be overcome, but also the side-effects of the very attempt to overcome. In other words, risk generates solutions which generate more risk.

ii) Individualized beings experience newer forms of insecurity and anxieties. We have here a culture of warnings – in banks, railway coaches, malls, in fact any place you go you discover warnings against all sorts of dangers and risks: whether to use a condom, wear a seatbelt, talk to a stranger, handle this object, eat this particular food item. This has something to do with the excessive amount of technological/technologized and mediated information being made available to us about the potential of risk from *every* object – casual sex, car crashes, molestation/kidnapping/exploitation, infection, food poisoning (the risks correlated with the above list of items). Van Loon argues that this risk information is not only produced by science and governance, but also by commerce (Van Loon 2002). Each of the above objects/events can be made safe, and the 'safety' lies in acquiring newer merchandized products. Thus the Aqua-Guard and the range of water filters that ensure your safety from contaminated water, the numerous cleaning fluids for the floor and the bathrooms that ensure a bacteria-free home, the variety of safety devices (anti-skid brakes, reinforced chassis, air balloon) in automobiles. The very technological systems geared towards greater security and safety, instil greater *risk sensibilities*: we become increasingly anxious about potential threats to our health and safety precisely when we are fed information from technologies. The McAfee anti- virus scanning software that runs with 'hotmail' warns us: 'Don't become a statistic', and tells us exactly what could go wrong with virus infection of our PCs. We are made aware of the risks involved in using email or the www by a technology that seeks to ensure that we do not incur such risks.

iii) With increasing and easier access to information and the risk of releasing confidential information (credit cards numbers and residential addresses by children via the Internet) have both increased considerably. Moral panics about children accessing porn, or allowing themselves to be cyberstalked (and eventually persuaded to meet in real time) have been common for some time now. Such technologies engender risks while simultaneously providing solutions to such risks. Risk thus generates commerce via a surfeit of information about risk.

iv) Thus, when technoscience reveals the risk involved in contamination and other newer problems which were previously unknown, it also delivers information about these risks (what are the possible effects/dangers of certain objects/events such as bacteria or genetic defects). Then it reproduces the risks by making us aware of these risks. It is, as Van Loon notes, a circular arrangement: to deal with the individualized responsibility of risk, the consumer needs more information. But the information comes from the very technoscience that revealed/generated the risk.

Risk theory for Cultural Studies reveals the extent that society/culture thrives on risk, providing information about risk potential, possible solutions and so on. Risk theory reflects on the psycho-social impact of technoculture where cultural responses to new devices are based upon an awareness that they create new risks.

v) Beck's solution to the autopoietic risk culture (where a system generates risk and its possible solution *within* itself) is to find political potential *outside* government. We need to open up intrasystemic closures. Politics must be about being able to communicate between systems – something that is becoming increasingly impossible today. Thus the complete indifference of the government to any criticism – witness the ease with which governments get out of such accusations by appointing, with a complete lack of transparency, a commission of inquiry, or simply refusing comment in India – is a mark of the autopoiesis of the political system. The representatives of the people are no more accountable to the people. They refer only to *each other* in debates that are increasingly disconnected from the opinions/criticisms/demands of the people. It is this autopoiesis that causes people to withdraw from politics as a system that has 'closed' itself.

What we have learnt so far:

- Risk is integral to technoculture.
- Risk involves the acquisition of newer and greater amounts of information about what could possibly go wrong.
- Risk entails resolution, which in turn creates newer risks.
- Most systems – social, political and technological – are now self-referential: they generate risks and provide solutions; they talk only within the system and rarely to the 'outside'.

Posthumanism and the Reinvention of the Human

In popular culture, the instances where humans are no longer 'pure' humans are numerous, from *Terminator* to *X-Men*, *Terminal Man* to *Gattaca*. Cyborgs (human-machine interfaces), humanimals (human-animal interfaces) are common today where tissues and organs from animals, computer chips and such are woven into the very fabric of the human body and mind. Since the late 1990s, therefore, these 'models' of the human have redefined the very idea of what it means to be human.

Posthumanism, especially its critical variety, argues that it is impossible to think of the human as a cogent, autonomous, self-bounded entity. Noting the work of evolutionary biologists and cognitive scientists, posthumanism argues that the human evolved in conjunction with other forms of life, inanimate objects and the environment. It acquired its present form through the evolutionary cooperation (not competition) wherein other forms of life, such as bacteria, enabled biological processes like digestion and energy generation. Biology now tells us that the mitochondria, that generates the power of the cell, was originally bacteria that the human absorbed. Bacteria in the stomach enable our digestive processes, and we learn to use our appendages in conjunction with inanimate objects. Posthumanism therefore proposes that we redefine the human.

One strand of posthumanism studies cultural representations, power relations and *discourses* that have historically situated the human above other life forms. Thus, the superiority of the human is a discursive and cultural construction rather than 'natural'. It calls into question the idea generated from the European Enlightenment in particular, that man is the centre of the universe. Its more philosophical strand examines the nature of the human in the age of technological modification, hybridized life forms and new discoveries about the sociality of animals. Critical posthumanism, as this second strand is called, argues that the human incorporates difference in the form of other DNA, species and forms of life: it might no longer be considered unique.

Critical posthumanism's origins are diverse: feminism, technoscience studies, evolutionary biology, animal studies, poststructuralism, critical race studies among others.

> Posthumanism calls for a radical rethinking of the very idea of the human by demonstrating how the idea of the human as a coherent, self-contained entity is a social construction. It proposes that the human has co-evolved with other forms of life and even inanimate matter and so we need to reconfigure the human-animal or human-plant relations as not of hierarchy (human/plant or human/animal) but as companion species, mutually dependent and equally vulnerable.

i) Critical posthumanism argues the very idea of 'human nature' is socially constructed.
ii) Critical posthumanism proposes that the human co-evolved with other life forms. The human shared ecosystems, life processes, genetic material, with animals and other life forms. In other words, we need to rethink the human as emerging out of a network, dependant on other forms of life and even inanimate matter.
iii) It argues that technology is not a mere prosthesis to human identity but is integral to how we have evolved.
iv) Critical posthumanism draws the connections between traditional (European) humanism's exclusionary strategy and women, races or ethnic groups, but also animals, being kept out as slaves, monsters or mere providers of meat, entertainment or labour. It has also excluded from the very category of the 'human' people with different anatomies, skin colour or physiologies. Thus, when European humanism defined the

human as white, male and singular, it enabled the founding of ideologies of sexism, racism and other exclusionary practices wherein other forms of life were condemned to be lower than the human male.

v) It proposes that if we recognize humans to be networked with and dependant on other forms of life, we also recognize that all forms of life are *precarious*, similar in their vulnerability.
vi) Posthumanism suggests that if we see this shared vulnerability and mutual dependence, we begin to recognize other species as 'companion species'.

Critical posthumanism is an ethical project that calls attention to the processes by which cultural texts – films, comics, soap operas, songs, scientific writings, literature – arc built around thc human/non-human, human/animal or human/machine binary where the human is always the superior component of this pairing. Critical posthumanism as a critical strategy is a key component of contemporary CS when it reads superhero comics, science fiction and utopian narratives about the human. It is also an ethical approach within CS to animal rights, representations of non-human life forms and the environment.

What this Unit has Demonstrated

Culture is a mode of enforcing identities and constructing 'subjects'. These subjects are *subject to* control by the dominant classes, a process that makes use of representations and images. These representations 'naturalize' differences and exploitative mechanisms, and suggest that these social structures have always been so. Patriarchy, capitalism, colonialism and consumerism are ideologies that construct particular forms of social control through such representations. 'Meaning', generated by the grammar of cultural artifacts like the soap opera, the fashion system or poetry, is an effect of the negotiations between classes and ideologies where the dominant class seeks to control meaning. Meaning for CS is therefore about power – who controls the meaning-production in culture, what are the politics of interpretation and representation, and what possible means are available to ensure that meaning does not become a tool of oppression. Theory reveals the ideological basis of cultural representations, of images that we have 'consumed' without being conscious of what they conceal (gender oppression, racial inequalities, colonial exploitation, caste and class discrimination). CS makes use of theory to reveal how meaning is always a series of negotiations, impermanent, local and the effect of power relations being contested and fought over. Theory suggests that identity is not 'natural', science is not objective, history is not universal – that each of these achieves some degree of uniformity because they suppress other histories, stories and knowledges. CS seeks to reveal how this process takes place, and Theory serves a useful function for this praxis.

Further Reading

Structuralism

Jonathan Culler. *Structuralist Poetics: Structuralism, Linguistics and the Study of Literature.* London: Routledge, 1994 (1975).

Terence Hawkes. *Structuralism and Semiotics.* London: Methuen, 1977.

Poststructuralism

Christopher Norris. *Deconstruction: Theory and Practice.* London: Methuen, 1982.

Barry Smart. *Foucault.* London: Routledge, 1985.

Feminism

Toril Moi. *Sexual/Textual Politics: Feminist Literary Theory.* London and New York: Methuen, 1985.

Marxism

David Hawkes. *Ideology.* London: Routledge, 1996.

Terry Eagleton. *Marxism and Literary Criticism.* London: Methuen, 1976.

Postmodernism

Linda Hutcheon. *A Poetics of Postmodernism: History, Theory, Fiction.* London: Routledge, 1995.

Angela McRobbie. *Postmodernism and Popular Culture*. London: Routledge, 1994.

Postcolonialism

Ania Loomba. *Colonialism/Postcolonialism*. London: Routledge, 1998.
Leela Gandhi. *Postcolonial Theory: A Critical Introduction*. Delhi: Oxford UP, 1999.

Queer Theory

Diana Fuss. Ed. *Inside/Out: Lesbian Theories, Gay Theories*. New York and London: Routledge, 1991.
Sally Munt. Ed. *New Lesbian Criticism: Literary and Cultural Readings*. London: Harvester, 1992.

Posthumanism

Cary Wolfe. *What is Posthumanism?* Minneapolis and London: University of Minnesota Press, 2010.
Rosi Braidotti. *The Posthuman*. Cambridge: Polity, 2013.

---

1. A theme we see often in Hindi films, where the woman is described as the 'ghar ki izzat' (the prestige of the house). It assumes that the morality and prestige of the family/house depends only on the woman's behaviour. Therefore, she is called upon to sacrifice her desires, needs and ambitions and regulate her life in order to protect the family's prestige.

3

Locations

This chapter looks at the conditions in which a critique of culture has emerged in the late twentieth century: modernity, postmodernity, globalization and neo-colonialism, and the new social movements.

Modernity

The term 'modernity' was used to distinguish the Christian present from the so-called 'pagan' past. 'Modern' is most often associated with the European Enlightenment in the seventeenth and eighteenth centuries.

Modernity and the Enlightenment mark a decisive shift in ways of thinking because they enshrined 'Reason' and empiricism over sentiment and faith. 'The Age of Reason' as the eighteenth century is often called – in fact periodization of literary history in 'Eng. Lit' courses continue to refer to this period, exemplified in the works of Alexander Pope, Jonathan Swift and others, by this epithet – was marked by a belief that Reason could ensure human progress. In the nineteenth century modernity was increasingly associated with industrialization and the spread of the capitalist mode of production. As a result, modernity today is frequently referred to as 'capitalist' or 'industrial' modernity.

Modernity is characterized by differentiation. Labour becomes more specialized and divided along specific lines of expertise and tasks. Work, home, religion and leisure become separate spheres. With the twentieth century families become smaller ('nuclear'). Activities once performed by the Church (in Western societies) such as educational instruction or health care are now allocated to schools, hospitals and such specialized institutions. Consumption increases with the massive increase in production of commodities.

The process of regulating work and other spheres of life through rules and norms becomes a hallmark of modernity's 'rationalization' process. Precision, which was central to the production process in industrial modernity and science, becomes a much sought-after quality. Bureaucracy and administration also get 'rationalized'. Automation of household functions, coordination of timings, regulation of movement are all part of the process of rationalization. From this it follows that anything classified as 'deviant' or 'inefficient' becomes excluded from the process/system. It is thus important to note that modernity's rise is linked to the rise of massive surveillance and regulatory technologies. The prison, the old-age home, the hospital, the asylum were indisputably sites of regulation of the 'criminal', the economically non-productive old, the sick and the insane, even if they were created as efforts at humanitarian concerns. What these structures of power did was to generate a set of ideas and beliefs about age, sickness, and sanity – ideas that are concomitant with the rise of modernity itself (as the work of Michel Foucault demonstrates).

The rise of the modern city is closely linked to modernity. The city becomes the industrial and commercial 'logos' of the nation-state. Increasingly, the city also becomes the cultural centre, where leisure, recreation and cultural life are concentrated. The city itself becomes a massive structure of regulation. Pavements are the designated spaces for walking. Lines divide the road for drivers. Signals regulate the movement of the vehicles. Spaces are allocated for parking. Sites are demarcated for shops, gardens, and schools. Regulations in India – for instance, the rule that prohibits bars and wine shops within a 50-yard area of schools – are meant to control space and spatial behaviour. This 'spacing of public space' is a disciplinary regime that seeks to prevent randomness (and the correlative, chaos). Walking, shopping, vehicular transport, leisure are all circumscribed within certain areas. In addition, there is the 'ghettoization' of cities, which are, in most cases, sharply distinguishable as 'poor' and 'posh'. Recently, discussing two such areas of Hyderabad – one of India's fastest growing metropolises with the IT revolution – with a colleague, a senior professor of English, and who is, incidentally, committed to Marxian 'social reform', I discovered the cultural antagonism that prevails in such an urbanization process. In response to my comment that Jubilee Hills – the site of the 'Hi-Tech' city and 'Cyberabad' – was 'old money' (I meant that the lands there had been acquired decades ago, when it was a mere wasteland), the colleague responded: 'No, Jubilee Hills is *new* money' – meaning the money that has arrived with post-1991 economic liberalization, software companies, and yuppie culture. The same person, who resides in an area that is surely 'old money' in a property worth a few crores – went on to mourn the fact that their neighbouring house was being continually built and *re*-built by a man who was obviously 'new money', and had no idea of what he wanted as 'new'. The wealth of contempt in my respondent's voice and comment indicated the elitism that marks the clash of 'modernities'. The nostalgia for what-was-once-modern-and-radical-but-has-now-been-displaced by the generation of 'moderns' refers to the continuous process of modernization itself, a process that goes with ghettoization. The antagonism that such a ghettoization engenders is also marked by the creation of desire for the mobility from the 'poor' to the 'posh', a desire that is closely aligned, in contemporary Indian cities, with the culture of consumption.

Consumerism and the enormous range of commodities, which flood contemporary societies, are central to capitalism. This culture of consumption frequently conceals from visibility the exploitative structures that enable the commodities to be available in the first place. Thus cheap and unorganized labour in Asian and African nations produces brand products for American multinational firms. Lifestyles that define identities today are the façades for global capitalism.

Modernity is marked by an uprooting from tradition. Ties of family, kinship, neighbourhood and community began to disappear. Increasing mobility meant people moved away from their parents and communities, shifted jobs and employer-loyalties, thus rendering them far more unstable, without moorings or strong local ties. This anomic condition of the increasingly rootless individual divided the social life into spheres without traditional rules. Systems became self-referential, isolated from other systems (see section on risk society).

In the twentieth century, in the post-1945 period, mass production and consumption was the hallmark of economic practice. The production process was 'rationalized' in the name of efficiency. Henry Ford introduced the assembly system of production, where tasks were broken down into their component parts, labour allocated, and the whole process carefully monitored and regulated. This is what is known as 'fordism', a condition best satirized brilliantly by Charlie Chaplin in his classic, *Modern Times*. Such a fordist approach standardized products and commodities, and undertook mass production on a scale never encountered in human history. Mass production, the use of standardized parts, protected national markets, highly hierarchic work-organization and a close link between mass production and consumption characterized the fordist model.

Postmodernity

Postmodernity is the condition commonly taken to refer to highly industrialized Western societies of the late twentieth century. Postmodernity is actually a condition that is constituted by a range of social, political, economic, technological and cultural practices. It is the postmodern condition that becomes the immediate context for Cultural Studies as it evolved from the 1970s and 1980s. This discussion of postmodernity maps the spectrum of issues and structures that constitute the immediate backdrop to the work of Stuart Hall and others.

Modernity was characterized by the dominant role of machinery in production (coal driven, electrical). Postmodernity – associated with the post-industrial scenario – is marked by a concern with the generation and control of information.

Postindustrialism and the New Production/Consumption

In the 1970s the fordist model began to face a crisis. The mass production of goods flooded the markets with commodities, and the markets were saturated. That is, the crisis was one of overproduction. Further, the economies of Japan, Korea, Singapore and China began to pose serious threats to Euro-American monopoly over the world market. Slowly, an alternative model emerged. Instead of mass production, the system evolved to small batch customization. Instead of uniformity, the focus was on flexibility and niche marketing. Products were manufactured and delivered only on demand (what came to be called JIT, or Just-in-Time stock management). Labour was more multi-skilled and job demarcations began to collapse. Daniel Bell's *The Coming of Post-Industrial Society* (1973) argued that the post-industrial society emerged from changes in the social sector only. Bell sees the economy and occupational structure as influential here, but does not see politics or culture as significant factors in the change. Bell suggests that the following changes occur in the shift from industrial to post-industrial societies:

- reduction in industrial labour
- increase in industrial output despite reduction in labour due to increased mechanization
- increase in wealth due to higher productivity, and inducing newer needs of leisure and other services (entertainment, holidays)
- new job opportunities in the service industry

With the shift from factory-industrial to service-industry, the battle (or the 'game', as Bell terms it) is between people (as opposed to that between people and nature in the pre-industrial, and between people and fabricated nature in the industrial). What is involved in this game between people is information. Service work – whether banking, holidays or therapy – is based on information about clientele, the client's needs, paying capacity and demands. In such a society professionals in research, health and education become the 'new intelligentsia' (Bell's terms) because the information needs of the post-industrial society increase considerably.

Information and Communications Technology (ICTs) have transformed production processes. Finance capital is now global, with the interlinking of the world's major stock exchanges and banks. This means that agents and governments can now deal with exchanges across national boundaries. Large amounts of money are represented only as numbers on a screen. That is, *cash flows* are now *information flows*, and money is data.

There is no geographical specificity or 'localization' of finance-sources, labour, sources of raw material, or the factory-site any more. In contrast, contemporary production processes are fragmented. The factory is frequently located in so-called Third World countries because of a perennial supply of cheap labour. Finances today are controlled by offices and banks headquartered in countries in an entirely different continent. This is a form of 'disorganized capitalism' with its de-concentration of capital through globalized production, financing and distribution. In addition to this globalization of production processes, contemporary consumer culture also has the splitting of production through subsidiaries. Thus Tommy Hilfiger commissions all its products from other companies. Pepe Jeans London makes Hilfiger jeans, Oxford Industries makes Tommy shirts, the Stride Rite Corporation makes its footwear. All Tommy Hilfiger does is to put his signature to the products.

Manuel Castells identifies four forms of labour in contemporary informational production systems: the producers of high value, based on informational labour; the producers of high volume, based on low-cost labour; the producers of raw materials, based on natural endowments; and the redundant producers, based on devalued labour. Castell's central emphasis here is that these forms of labour are not restricted to geo-political sites. Any country can contain all four types in varying quantities. What is important is that these types are connected *globally*, where one MNC can coordinate all four types all over the globe (Castells 1996).

Niche marketing breaks up the market into increasingly smaller groups. Eventually every individual can, at least in theory, find a commodity to suit her/his exact specifications. This is feasible because of the information economy where with each visit to the store the individual 's data is recorded for future use. Information feedback into the production system and the product *with the specifications of that individual fulfilled*, arrives at the store. Evidently such particularization can occur only through ever-faster information flows in cyberspace. In a sense, the user/consumer is herself/himself producing the technology: users are now active participants in (technological) innovation. The fact that supermarkets record individual purchases simply means that they possess exact details of a customer's preferences and needs.

To summarize the post-industrial scene:

- The rise and expansion of a service economy, where more people are employed in services such as banking rather than in factories or manufacturing units.
- The formation of knowledge-elites – especially technical elites in universities, research institutions, governments and economic enterprises. The elites constitute the 'white-collar' occupations. This goes with new hierarchies of technical labour.

- The rise of New Social Movements.
- Information becomes a product and a process.
- Information networks and wired societies (see section below on the 'information society').
- Centralized control but decentralized production units where finance and administrative control is located in, say, Western metropolises and manufacturing units in the 'developing' nations.
- Uneven global development, where industrial mass production occurs at the 'periphery ' and knowledge production occurs in the Western 'centre'.

The Information Society

Frank Webster (1995) suggests that the 'information society' can be defined in five ways.

A. **Technological:** This view suggests that developments in information processing, storage and transmission have led to the large-scale and ever-increasing application of IT in everyday life. This view sees the convergence of telecommunications and computing, and increasing linkage between banks, homes, offices, factories, shops and educational institutions. This is the 'networked society', where the information grid links these various sites, just as electrical or water-supply lines did once.

B. **Economic:** The new information-based society is an 'information economy' where economic values can be easily placed on information.

C. **Occupational:** This is a fairly straight-forward definition of the information society. It pays attention to the change in nature of occupation, with larger numbers of people being involved in information work (when clerks, teachers, lawyers and entertainers outnumber engineers and technicians). This shift in occupations from industrial labour to desk-bound information dealers is what Daniel Bell famously described as the rise of the 'white collar society'.

D. **Spatial:** The emphasis here is on 'networks' that mark the information society. John Goddard (Webster: 18) and Manuel

Castells, for instance, speak of 'flows' of information that link towns, regions, and nations. Transborder movements of information – from research data to speculative capital – along electronic information highways radically alter notions of territory. Further, aligned with the information flow is the dispersion of business corporations, where the financial centre and the production unit can be in different continents but wired together (the multinational/transnational corporation).

E. **Cultural:** This emphasizes the extraordinary predominance of information in everyday life: movies, radio, television and now the Internet. The process of information-exchange is an end in itself. Signs and images do not refer to anything or any 'reality' outside themselves: they are 'self-referential'. Therefore, in the media-driven culture of today, we get a surfeit of signs. This is what the philosopher Jean Baudrillard terms 'hyper-reality' – a world of signs, but not much meaning (see Chapter 2, for theories of postmodernism).

An interesting example of how (fictional?) images and projections of reality influence the way in which we perceive and interpret actual events is the response to 9/11. Kakoudaki reports people's response to watching the collapse of the WTC twin towers: '"I thought it was an ad for a new blockbuster movie"' or '"I thought I was in a disaster film"' or '"This was just like *Independence Day*"' (See Kakoudaki 2002). Thus real events now seem to echo, reflect and extend pre-existing fantasies. The sign(s) of disaster precede the event of the disaster, and we are unable, anymore, to distinguish between the two.

Globalization

Globalization is a term frequently used with an astonishing lack of specificity. It has been used to refer to everything from worker migration to global warming, from Microsoft's presence in every PC in the Third World to fundamentalism.

The essential features of globalization as it occurs in the twentieth century (though it has been going on for a long period in human history) can be summed up as follows:

- The expansion of trade in terms of trading relationships and movement of capital.
- The development of transnational and global communication networks.
- The diminished role of the nation state even within its territorial space.
- The rise of transnational cultural, economic, political networks (such as the IMF, Greenpeace and Amnesty).
- The increased presence of Western consumer products and cultural artefacts (from Levi's to Microsoft), a 'McDonaldization' of the world.

David Harvey is a geographer whose 1989 account of global postmodern culture has become an extremely influential thesis today. Harvey argues that the Enlightenment certainty about space and time has disappeared. With increased capital circulation across the world this 'space-time compression' – which, for Harvey, is the cornerstone of postmodernity – has become a feature of contemporary society. This space-time compression is a description that applies readily to globalization, where global transport and communications and circulation of capital has literally shrunk the world.

David Held et al in their *Global Transformations* (1999) argue that while globalization may unite the world physically (through mass communication networks, for instance), it does not necessarily inculcate a sense of global community and citizenship. The question they ask is this: 'what is the proper realm of jurisdiction for developing and implementing policy with respect to health issues such as AIDS, narcotics, the management of nuclear waste, military security and eco-hazards?' (446) The question has larger implications for Cultural Studies because it specifically addresses a politics of globalization. The question is not simply one of organizational structure or the juridical extent of the UN's powers. It addresses the issue of autonomy of nation-states in decision-making when dealing with issues of dumping, terrorism, refugees or financial and market laws. Thus Cultural Studies with its emphasis on the specificity of local practices within a larger political and cultural framework, finds the question useful in formulating its own critical practice in the phase of contemporary globalization.

Globalization has several aspects that come in for critical scrutiny in Cultural Studies. Some of these are discussed briefly below.

Global Culture

A questionable effect of globalization is global culture. Global culture already exists, in a sense. The most self-evident forms of cultural globalization are the products of Western media: television, Western pop and Hollywood icons such as Britney Spears or Arnold Schwarzenneger, and products such as a Lee or Coca Cola. Stuart Hall argues that as yet there is not globalized equivalent of local cultures (by which he takes to mean the corpus of myths, legends, icons and stories embedded within a national consciousness). Hall argues that local cultures have a strong emotional appeal for people, while global culture may have an ethnic 'appeal' without the emotional content (Hall 1999 [1992]: 304–9). Mike Featherstone suggests that whereas local culture is closely tied to place and time, global culture is 'disconnected' and 'de-territorialized', existing outside the usual reference to geographical territory (1995).

Numerous commentators argue that global culture is increasingly global consumer culture. Anita Roddick, the founder of The Body Shop writing in her autobiography, captures the contours of the 'New British Empire' beautifully:

> I wanted to be Christobel Columbus, going into little villages in Mexico or Guatemala or Nepal and seeing what they had to trade instead of going to those boring old trade fairs where everyone buys the same mediocre products year after year.
>
> (Qtd. in Brabazon 2001: 189)

The commodification of ethnic products is essential to a global consumer culture.

David Held et al identify the following as the principal agents of cultural globalization: pop music, television, cinema, and tourism. In the early years of the twenty-first century we need to add global telecommunications technology and the Internet as factors that affect and effect cultural globalization. Held et al see three responses to cultural globalization:

i) those who see cultural homogenization as an outcome of the impact of Western media and consumerism (what they call 'hyperglobalizers'),
ii) those who see the impact of global culture as superficial (the 'sceptics') and,
iii) those who predict the emergence of new global cultural networks and hybrids (the 'transformationists').

(1999)

However, globalization cannot be seen as a one-way effect of Western culture on local ones. While admittedly the impact of Coca Cola and Levi-Strauss on India and Mexico is an important feature, the reverse is also true of cultural globalization. Local products such as Indian cuisine and ethnic wear have now reached global markets. When the 'curry' is declared UK's 'national dish', we have a very globalized local product. African music and Italian pizza are now as much global as Coca Cola. Further, migration of software and communications workers into all parts of the world has altered demographic, and therefore cultural, constitution of various countries in Europe.

Rustom Bharucha, following Richard Schechner, uses the term 'interculturalism' to refer to the cultural exchanges that are facilitated by globalization. Interculturalism emphasizes that the exchange among cultures, done by individuals or by non-official groups, without obeying national boundaries (Bharucha 2001: 5).

Ashis Nandy's argument (1998) on inter-Asian civilizational dialogue seeks a new cosmopolitanism that can fight the cultural hegemony of the West. While we need to recover the 'disowned' or 'subjugated' West (which now enters public domain in 'pathological' forms as fundamentalisms and ethnic chauvinism), and make it our ally in the fight against the hyper-modernizing West. In this dialogue of civilizations, there will have to be the following methodological principles:

i) Demand for the participating cultures' equal rights to interpretation.
ii) Jettisoning the nineteenth century legacy of comparative studies which offsets the practices of one civilization against

the philosophical or normative concerns of another. We need a 'cultural conversation of equals'.

iii) A conversation of cultures resists the idea of a culturally integrated world.

(147–8)

Glocalization

Roland Robertson defines glocalization as 'the creation and incorporation of locality, processes which themselves largely shape, in turn, the compression of the world as a whole' (1995: 40).

Resistance to globalization is also local. In India the Mumbai Resistance (which held parallel sessions opposite the World Social Forum, Mumbai, January 2004) and the Seattle protest marches are clear acts of local resistance.

An interesting variant of such a process is the way in which metropolitan-based cultural artefacts affect folk and local traditions in India. The spread of mass-mediated music genres, especially film music, has significantly effected the decline and even extinction of folk genres in India. Collectively performed music has been replaced by mass-media music. The individuals who once performed collectively as a community (in folk theatre, for example), and the very idea of a community has been changed. With declining personal interaction – as a result of the minimal community performance – there is a decline in community social life rooted in folk drama and music, tea-stall culture and festivities. Instead of such collective 'acts' we now have atomized families passively consuming the impersonal media of video, TV, cinema or radio (Manuel 2001). In a sense, such mass-media entertainment functions as unifying entities, promoting a consensus of values and taste (Shah Rukh Khan in rural India, and films with specifically rural settings, such as the high-profile *Lagaan* or *Swades*).

Globalization can be resisted through a recourse to a 'national imaginary'. That is, the 'glocal' cannot entirely do away with the nation state as a concept or as entity. The national facilitates an oppositional discourse to the global. However, this does not mean that the national is homogenous. Bharucha's national imaginary, for instance, argues that 'the right to criticize the official agendas of the state is eminently possible within the seeming constraints of a national imaginary, *along with new articulations of cultural representation* relating to women, dalits, tribal communities, and other minorities' (2001: 32, emphasis added). While it engages with the hegemonic practices of the global using a national imaginary, it also argues for a further reification of the national itself. It actively supports an extension of the local and the 'alternate' into the national. By suggesting that 'new articulations' by/of women and dalits must be worked into the national, Bharucha is seeking to remedy the obvious defect where the national is itself hegemonic.

Cultural Hybridization

Cultural hybridization is also known as 'creolization'. This is a process where foreign cultural artefacts and systems are assigned fresh values within and by the receiving culture. The consumer of an imported foreign style imparts fresh meaning to it, occasionally involving a radical redefinition. World music, a participation (via the global media) in Oscar ceremonies, exotic holidays (usually in Third World nations by First Worlders) are examples. Cultural hybridization is a mode of dealing with cultural difference.

Cyber-Counterculture

Globalization is closely aligned with the digital transformation and the rise of the Information Society. This cyberculture of high-power business, increasing corporate control over daily lives, the division of the world into domains by corporations rather than nation-states has generated its own counter-culture.

John Perry Barlow's Electronic Frontier Foundation set up in 1990 is an example of a counter-cultural movement within cyberculture. This organization (abbreviated wickedly but suitably as EFF) is dedicated to the preservation of free speech on the Internet and the complete democracy of cyberspace.

In an important move for Cultural Studies and university-level research Arjun Appadurai (2000) suggests numerous possible issues in the globalized world. Appadurai begins by suggesting that there is a double apartheid evolving around globalization. The first form of the apartheid is the separation of academic debates (especially in the United States) and the vernacular discourses about how to protect cultural autonomy and economic survival in the local/regional/national sphere. The second form of apartheid is that the poor and their advocates find themselves as far from the anxieties of their own national discourses about globalization as they do from the intricacies of the debates in global policy discourses (2–3).

Appadurai argues that there is an increasing disjuncture between the 'globalization of knowledge and the knowledge of globalization'. There is an inherent temporal lag between the processes of globalization and the efforts to contain them conceptually. Finally the uneven economic process of globalization means that there is an uneven distribution of those resources for learning, teaching and cultural criticism that are most vital for the formation of democratic research communities that could produce a global view of globalization (3–4).

Research is not just about any kind of knowledge: it is about knowledge that meets certain criteria, a community assessment is required before it is acceptable as knowledge. Thus reliable new knowledge cannot be the direct result of intuition or revelation, but the effect of legitimation, argumentation, replicability, and ratiocination (9–11).

In the globalized world, actors in different regions have elaborate interests and capabilities in constructing world pictures whose very interaction affects global resources. Area studies must deliberate upon this relationship between regions. This deliberation requires a new research ethic, which Appadurai characterizes as follows:

- a commitment to the routinized production of certain kinds of new knowledge
- a special sense of the systematics for the production of such knowledge
- a quite particular idea of the shelf life of research results
- a definite sense of the specialized community of experts who precede and follow any specific piece of research
- a distinct positive valuation of the need to detach morality and political interest from properly scholarly research

(13–14)

Thus scholars from other societies and traditions of inquiry should be able to bring to the debate their own ideas about what counts as new knowledge and what communities of judgement and accountability they might judge to be central in the pursuit of such knowledge (14).

We need to pay attention to the vocabulary of the grassroots globalization, to their modes of inquiry, and formulate new protocols of inquiry that have thus far rejected any mode other than Western as unacceptable (Appadurai 2000: 17–18).

It calls into question so-called 'established' forms of inquiry, the hierarchization of knowledge, the exclusionary principle on which 'research' has been institutionalized and so on. The return to the vernacular, the parochial, and the local is the attempt to 'de-gentrify' research and cultural criticism. The institutionalization of Cultural Studies – through the co-optation of forms of critique such as queer theory or postcolonial studies into the academy, a process of legitimizing it – is therefore, itself a subject of inquiry.

The Nation-State

Nation-states are primarily predicated upon control mechanisms for an equitable distribution of resources. If this function, and the power over political economy are taken over by transnational corporate offices, then an important role of the nation-state will end. However, governments in the new order will serve other purposes, such as decision-making about external investment or the development of the local telematics infrastructure.

The image of a globalized, 'postnational' constellation induces feelings of helplessness. Jürgen Habermas argues that we need to start thinking of forms of the democratic process beyond the nation-state (2001). With globalization, the nation-state loses the fiscal basis for social policies, and its capacity to steer the economy. Nationality as a way of life and the homogenous basis of civil solidarity are diminished. These make it difficult for nation-states to meet the need for self-legitimation.

The interdependency of world society challenges the basic premise that national politics is enough to address the problems of individual nation-states. Habermas therefore suggests that there is a need to bring global economic networks under political control. A democratic order need not be rooted in the nation. Habermas detects two problems for nation-states in this age: how can we envision the democratic legitimation of decisions beyond the schema of the nation-state? And what are the conditions to ensure that states and supranational regimes see themselves as members of a community who need to consider one another's and general interests? Habermas offers two answers to the above problems:

(a) Democratic procedure is legitimized by the general accessibility to the decision-making process. A functioning *public sphere*, discussion, and accessibility free democratic legitimacy from the established forms of state organization. Habermas suggests institutional participation of non-governmental organizations in decision-making process at national levels.
(b) Global powers may have to involve themselves in the institutionalized procedures of transnational-will formation. They have to willingly broaden their definitions of 'national interest' into a viewpoint of global governance, marking a change from 'international relations to a global domestic policy' (Habermas 2001).

The important challenge to the nation-state is from the ethnic and other minorities. A subaltern resistance to the hierarchic, oppressive upper class/caste state is clearly visible now. Subaltern historiography in India, for example (exemplified in the *Subaltern Studies* series), draws attention to the way the Indian nation has been constructed through a process of exclusion and marginalization of the Dalitbahujan, of women and of the working classes. Kancha Ilaiah argues that since the 1990s Hindu politicians and writers have sought to portray the Dalitbahujan as Hindus. The irony, Ilaiah notes, is that when the Dalitbahujan had tried to be accepted as Hindus, they had been kept apart as 'others'. However, this process of co-optation is not entirely honest: for socially, and culturally (and even physically), the Hindus want Dalits to remain their 'other' (1996). Ilaiah argues that the exclusivity of the Indian nation state – which he clearly indicates was Hindu – meant that throughout (Indian) history Dalitbahujan voices have been silenced, though their hands and bodies have been working. The Hindu (Brahmin) culture of learning alienated them from the Dalitbahujan culture of work and kept Dalits away from learning. Ilaiah suggests that Dalit histories must be based on their own epistemology, their own selfhood.

The nation-state must therefore be interrogated for the ways in which it concentrates power – and therefore culture – in the hands of a few. The women's, queer, Dalitbahujan and working class movements/ counter-narratives seek to recast the nation-state by revealing its elitist biases and exclusionary structures.

In the Third World, the task of a nation-state is to induce social mobilizations in order to create a national society. For this the social and political elites of the country seek to create a supra-cultural entity through the discourse of nationalism. This meant that the nation-state sought to 'integrate' ethnic minorities into a national society through educational, cultural and social policies. It is this forced homogenization – to which Ilaiah is referring when he speaks of the Hindu Brahminical India – that has created a feeling of minoritization and marginalization.

It is in this context of minoritization and secession that popular cultural forms such as Hindi cinema must be read. Tejaswini Niranjana's work on *Roja* (1994) and Ravi Vasudevan on *Bombay* (2001) locate the significance of a Tamizh filmmaker's success at a *national* level at a time when – after the Rajiv Gandhi assassination – Tamizh peoples' popularity was rather low.

Dipankar Gupta (1999) suggests that we should stop thinking in terms of stable minorities and majorities. What we need to pay attention to is the process of minoritization. Secularism sees the world as incapable of bigotry now that religion has been privatized, or it sees the world in terms of fixed expressions of bigotry (50–1). New minorities emerge and communities are picked on for persecution by the majority: the South Indians of Bombay in the 1960s, the Sikhs after 1984, Tamizhs after 1991 (52–3). Minority listings, believes Gupta, do not hit out at minoritizing sentiments. Official minorities continue to be viewed by the majority as suspect members within the nation-state. Thus SCs and STs in India – once described as minorities by the Constituent Assembly – are no longer considered to be so. This happens because the majority accepts the fact that they have no loyalties outside the Indian nation-state (56). Muslims and Christians continue to be treated as minorities for this very reason. What we need is greater protection of the identity as citizen rather than as minority or majority (56). In order to see citizenship as a protecting device in the public sphere, we need to have a degree of homogeneity – literacy, political interest, capability – among the people. Such a homogenization cannot be achieved *except through affirmative action* (such as reservations) for those who have had little role to play in the process of secularization. But Gupta does not address the fact that the very process of secularization is determined, run, and administered by an elite citizenry. Secularization as a process – and Gupta points to the dynamics of capitalism here – is unequal and uneven: it does not guarantee the same privileges or protection to every citizen. What we need to understand is that just as there is an *ideology of secularism* that minoritizes, there is a *process of secularization* that minoritizes too. And it is here that the pedagogic, cultural, social and ultimately political interventions into the public discourses become significant. Contemporary Cultural Studies must address the very process by which citizenship is defined within the modes of secularization.

Duncan Ivison's (2002) 'postcolonial liberalism' proposes a 'form of mutually acceptable coexistence between indigenous and non-indigenous peoples' (30). A postcolonial liberal state is committed to rights and dignity. We need to focus on the conditions of the struggles for both recognition and particular forms of distribution. In an age where both the governmental and the democratic have been dispersed through globalization, modes of restriction and resistance also cut across national borders. This is both challenge and opportunity for indigenous peoples. The challenge includes contesting the legitimacy of the state (in India, state-sponsored violence against the tribals in Kerala in 2003, the state-sponsored sale of agricultural and other lands in Bengal in 2006–7 and other places resulting in loss of arable land and tribal lands are examples of the causes and justification for interrogating the legitimacy of the state) and normative concepts of justice, equality and freedom. Normative concepts and ideals of equal citizenship have been used – in countries such as Australia – to justify forms of coercive assimilation.

Ivison outlines five features of a postcolonial liberalism:

i) The idea of a basic but contestable threshold: A threshold identifies those basic human capabilities central to living a life that is recognizably human. Such a list of capabilities is no doubt controversial, but it can be done through actual deliberations between indigenous and non-indigenous people.
ii) Multiple realizability and normative flexibility: Although the central capabilities denote the relevant space for interpersonal comparison between all citizens, the approach allows for 'multiple realizability' of those capabilities according to local beliefs and circumstances. Implementation of basic capabilities is thus left to *local* institutions.
iii) A norm-suffused and contextual theory of rights: Rights derive from beliefs. The capabilities approach ties its list of human capabilities to a conception of the good, but one that admits of potentially enough variability and local specification so as to be amenable to many different cultures and contexts.
iv) Socialization of capabilities: Internal capabilities (the developed states of the person that are sufficient conditions for the exercise of the requisite functions) require favourable *external* circumstances. We can evaluate the asymmetries of social arrangements – such as alternative modes of power, production modes – to ensure that citizens' freedom and equality are unaffected. With the socialization thesis we look not at the legitimacy or otherwise of entitlements but at the social arrangements that enable or disable the fulfilment of those entitlements.
v) A practice-dependent conception of freedom: The assumption here is that to act freely is to have the material and institutional means to convert opportunities into achievements, but also to question those norms of recognition and distribution that govern access to those various means.

(Ivison: 129–33)

Ivison, Nandy and Ilaiah all offer visions of social arrangements and structures built upon notions of local rights/beliefs and the freedom, opportunity, and means of fulfilling these. Their more egalitarian view seeks to underscore the illegitimacies that have informed even liberal nation-states.

New Social Movements

Social movements have been integral to human history, especially with modernity. The Luddites in nineteenth century England, for instance, smashed machinery in factories. Similar movements, pursuing a variety of aims have occurred the world over. In a sense the Freedom movement in India was a social movement. Greenpeace is an important social movement in contemporary times. What is interesting and relevant to understanding contemporary culture is the increasing political influence of such movements. Greenpeace, for instance, has a significant role to play in world politics, even getting into Parliaments in some countries. Before examining the role of social movements we need to explore specific aspects of these movements.

A term that is frequently used in connection with social movements is 'protest'. Protest – either social or political – refers to the questioning and/or challenging of established cultural, social, political practices. Protest can be by individuals or by groups. In this case, we shall look at group protests, where movements have resisted authorities in power.

A social movement is a collective, organized and mostly non-institutionalized challenge to authorities and established social/cultural practices. Social movements blur the line between collective action and institutionalized action. They are formal organizations – Greenpeace or the World Social Forum – and frequently develop a system of hierarchy and cultural/social practices. *Revolutions* differ from social movements principally in their aims: they seek to overthrow the government or state. A social movement is a set of opinions which represents preferences and demands for change in some elements of the social structure (McCarthy and Zald 2003).

New Social Movements are characterized by:

- anti-authoritarian stance
- democratic and activist nature

- flexibility
- a more participatory nature

Frequently, social movements are about identity. The American Civil Rights Movement, the Women's movement, and the Gay and Lesbian movements have essentially been 'identity movements'. These are movements that assert radical racial, gender or sexual identities in order to build communities and challenge hegemonic cultural norms that have consistently refused certain identities. Identity movements are based on characteristics such as ethnicity, gender or sexual preference.

Fundamentalism

While the term 'fundamentalism' is most often used to refer to *religious fundamentalism*, it applies to any chauvinistic rejection of an alternate form of thinking. Such fundamentalisms have always existed, from the beginning of human life on earth, rising with the divergence of civilizations and cultures, and the recognition of different faiths. The Crusades, the European wars of religion or the Spanish Inquisition are the better known, and more spectacular, instances of fundamentalism. However, for Cultural Studies in the twentieth century, dealing as it does with everyday life and modes of meaning generation, fundamentalism is an important context and location. The term 'fundamental' comes into popular lexicon with the twentieth century. The sociologist T.N. Madan (1997) in his analysis of fundamentalism and secularism focuses on spiritual authority exercised by religious functionaries. Madan's emphasis is particularly useful in its shift of focus to issues of *power* from mere analysis of any religion's *doctrines* and beliefs.

The Hindu fundamentalism of 1990s India is a community-centric one, since it seeks social cohesion and power based on a particular belief system (see Katju 2003). Fundamentalism is a movement that responds to modernization by seeking a social obedience to the scripture(s) or tradition. Further, it seeks political power which can impose this 'renewed' tradition. Fundamentalism can thus be defined as a defence of a way of life that was being rapidly superseded, and as being rooted in revivalism and pietism.

Fundamentalisms claim that some source of ideas, usually a text classified and revered as 'scripture', is beyond error and complete. Thus Protestants believe that the Bible is the actual word of God. Islamic fundamentalists see the Qur'an as God's word and the Hadith as the true record of the Prophet's sayings and actions. The Rama Rajya of Hindutva is based on the chief figure of the ancient text, the *Ramayana*. However, monotheistic religions such as Judaism, Christianity and Islam are much more amenable to fundamentalist 'versions' than Hinduism or Buddhism. Thus fundamentalists believe that the original sources provide a perfect guide to living and society. Steve Bruce points out that such beliefs about the authenticity of the texts are basically matters of hermeneutics, and arise with the print culture in the West. In the Middle Ages most people saw the Bible as a special and magical book. In the nineteenth century scholars began to differ over what the original texts/authors meant. Thus questions such as which translation of the Bible was more faithful, is a correct interpretation possible, began to be raised.

Fundamentalism advocates a return to true religion in order to reclaim that golden age. Fundamentalisms are also radical revisions of the past provoked by changes in the community. Such changes are perceived as threats to the continuity of the past, and the very tradition itself. The goal is therefore to aggressively return to the past, to 'hold on' more grimly to it in order to resist change.

Modernization has been seen as the major cause of fundamentalisms in the Western world. With increasing fragmentation of the community and family, and a progressively minimal role of religion in economic and other social activities – what is called secularization – the power of the Church and the priestly class eroded. With differentiation and societalization the plausibility of a single overarching moral and religious system declined, and was displaced by competing concepts of the divine. Finally, with rationalization and science several beliefs – about the cosmos, for example – were called into question and eventually rejected. Modernization also caused demographic shifts, and new groups were brought into the nation-state. Religious diversity, therefore, became a norm of the new nation-states.

In Asian nations modernization has been traumatic for many social groups. In the monarchic Middle East there has been little scope for popular political participation. The Western modernization 'project' has been about extending political participation (racism and gender biases not withstanding). Social institutions could not keep pace with the changes being wrought in Asian societies. The Nehruvian socialist model of modernization, Structural Adjustment Programmes with economic liberalization, the IT revolution, and now disinvestments have produced changes in demographic patterns and changes in things such as the family. The injunctions on compulsory purdah for women by Islamic fundamentalists in Kashmir and Afghanistan under the Taliban, the BJP–ABVP's objections to Western dress codes on Indian women and their objections to Valentine's Day can be explained as the fundamentalists' need for control. Further, it shows how everyday dress and clothing possess different meanings for different people. Jeans and T-shirts (especially on women) *mean* evil Westernization for the right wing (of Hindu or Islamic variety). Native Indian dress codes like the saree or the salwar-kameez (with all its variations across India) mean 'Indianness'.

Fundamentalism is not the ideology of the marginalized. It develops in situations where social, cultural, economic and political power is up for grabs.[1]

Ideological cohesion – such as Hindutva – is a feature that emerges from the interaction of the belief system with the environment. Thus Hindu fundamentalism emerges when Hindus are asked to pay attention to their sense of identity. External pressure from a source – in this case, Muslims – is presented as anti-Hindu to promote a common identity. Hindus then see themselves as sharing a common culture/belief system that is under threat from the 'outsider' (the 'anti-national' or foreigner is a Muslim, invariably). Thus fundamentalists are concerned about boundaries: of identity, of beliefs, of territoriality, of political power. Karen McCarthy Brown has argued that in groups led by men whose identity is constructed through an us/them binary, there is a need to control the 'other' in their own group. In most cases this becomes the attempt to control its women, under the guise of 'protection' (1994).

Twentieth century fundamentalisms, with their origins (in the West and in the East) in various reactionary moments and movements can therefore be described as follows:

i) Espouses belief in the authenticity, infallibility and final authority of scriptures.
ii) Is often a reaction to perceived threat or crisis.
iii Shows a strong intolerance of dissent, implying monopoly over truth.
iv) Embodies a cultural critique, implying that all is not well with society.
v) Appeals to tradition in a selective manner that establishes a meaningful relationship between past and present, and inventing tradition in the process.
vi) Seeks capture of political power and remodelling the state for the achievement of stated objectives.
vii) Marked by a charismatic leadership.

(Madan 1997: 27–8)

These are some of the key 'locations' in which Cultural Studies originated and grew as a 'discipline'.

---

1. Sati, which saw a brief attempt at revival in post-independence India, was supported by right-wing Hindu fundamentalists. This actually had nothing to do with religious beliefs. John S. Hawley quotes reports which mention that Roop Kanwar's in-laws collected Rs. 950,000 by 12 December 1987 – Kanwar 'committed' Sati on 4 September 1987 – as offerings from people (Hawley 1994: 84, 105)

Part II

Sites of Culture

4

Cultures of Consumption

The twentieth century, especially in the metropolises, can be described as a century of consumption.

A set of terms and concepts has evolved to describe the phenomenon of consumer societies in metropolises across the world. Even though these concepts have been used to describe cities like London and New York, the globalization of urban spaces in New Delhi, Hyderabad, Bangalore and other cities in India has ensured that most of them apply equally well, with minor variations, to these too.

In this chapter we focus on the discourses of shopping, the organization of the shopping experience, and the ideologies of consumption.

- It must be understood that the arguments are focused almost entirely on *metropolitan* India, and centres case studies in Hyderabad city.
- It focuses entirely on the discursive, narrative and spatial organization of consumption rather than on *practices* of shopping and mall-trawling.

It also *excludes* other kinds of shopping experience such as the now-burgeoning tele-shopping, online shopping and the older retail outlet shopping.[1]

Sites, Terms, Conditions

What does Cultural Studies have to do with shopping and consumer trends? Let us recall: Cultural Studies is interested in everyday life, and everyday life has three major components:

- lifestyle
- consumption
- social interactions/relations

It is important to ground a study of shopping in specific contexts of economy and spending.

Economic liberalization, from the early 1990s, could very well be treated as the opening moments of India's new consumption patterns and cultural globalization. Economic liberalization, which included reduction of import duties, the entry of private industry into what used to be state-controlled domains, the modification of the banking sector, entry of foreign products and companies and the rise of newer service sector were some of the main economic dimensions of the liberalization policy.

India's fast moving consumer goods (FMCG) sector is the fourth largest sector in the economy with a total market size in excess of US$13.1 billion. India topped the 2006 AT Kearney Global Retail Development Index, indicating a sharp rise in spending on consumer durables, apparel, entertainment, vacations and lifestyle products. To use just one instance, Indians are spending 30 per cent more on vacations now than in 2002.

According to the highly respected AC Nielsen Consumer Confidence and Opinions Survey (the October–November 2006 one was conducted with over 25,000 respondents from 45 countries, including 15 from the Asia-Pacific region) India is at the top of the consumer confidence index for the fourth time in a row. The survey states in its news report: 'By markets, consumers most likely to go on a spending spree in the next 12 months continue to hail from the world's most optimistic countries of Denmark (71%), India (61%) and Norway (66%)' (<http://www.acnielsen.co.in/news/20061219.shtml>).

The India directory at www.mapsofindia.com describes India as a 'shopper's paradise' and declares: 'the whole country is a shopping mall' (<http://www.mapsofindia.com/travel/treasure-house.html> 15 March 2007).[2]

While these are not foolproof modes of gauging consumer behaviour, they certainly provide some idea of the increasing significance of shopping and consumption for Indians.

We will be looking at the theme of lifestyle as linked to consumption in some detail because it plays such a crucial role in everyday life. While consumption cannot be reduced to shopping, shopping does constitute a significant component of consumption.

Consumption is a process but also a product, a consequence of:

- discourses (about lifestyle, media advertisements, the pleasure of shopping, etc.)

- practice (the actual act of shopping, visiting malls, etc.)
- imagination (the fantasy, desire and imagination of particular objects)

This chapter focuses on the discourses and organization of the shopping experience. It does *not* look at actual consumer movement or conduct an ethnographic study of the use of malls. Proceeding from the premise that the shopping experience is *constructed* and *controlled* discursively and in practice (the organization of space in the mall, for example), it looks at the production of consumption and consumer culture rather than the assimilation or subversion of the same (this latter would include the audience-research part).

Ideally, such a study should be sharply focused categorizing the consumers such as urban youth. Indeed it could be argued that the best way to study consumption and globalization would be to study youth culture (Motorola's Marketing Manager, Pramit Bhargava, stated: 'We see the youth as a core consumer'). *Time Magazine* announced a 'new breed of consumer in India – young, increasingly wealthy and willing to spend on everything from mobile phones to speakers to French fries' (Michael Schuman, 'Hey Big Spenders', 25 August 2003). Kurt Salmon Associates' *Consumer Outlook 2004*, which studied consumer shopping and buying behaviour, opened its report with a visual that showed people in the age group 7–35. The visual was accompanied by a tag line: 'India is young…' (<http://www.ksa-technopak.com> 1 April 2007). Examples of youth marketing are all round: the average age of the shopper represented in promotional material, magazines like *Seventeen*, the 'Elle 18' line of cosmetics or HBO's Generation Me programme is 20–30 years. In the terms of Reed Larson, 'adolescents around the world are learning to aspire to consumption and ownership of brand names such as Nike, Nestlé, Coca Cola, and Levi Strauss, which are recognized all over the world, even by street children' (Larson 2002: 13). Youth culture, consumption and cultural globalization can thus be 'read' together as part of a process and located on the same continuum.

Statistics show that the median age of the Indian consumer is 24 years and that India had a booming 'young consumer' market. Thus studies of the culture of consumption dovetail into studies of youth culture, and analyses of shopping ought to locate discourses within practices through observation and data from actual young people who shop.

This chapter, however, is a more general outline of how a study of consumption can be done, without focusing on particular demographic groups.

Lifestyle

Hyderabad city hosts an annual 'The Hindu-Eenadu Lifestyle Show'. *The Hindu* carried special features on the event. Billed, according to *The Hindu*, as the 'largest consumer exhibition' of its kind, the write-ups smoothly merged lifestyle with shopping. *The Hindu* essay (28 September 2006) – opening with a collage showing a poised ballet dancer, a plasma TV, drawing and dining room furniture, a dressing table, music system and a wall painting – was titled 'Hyderabad's greatest shopping extravaganza'. The article focuses entirely on consumer goods, consumers and retailers.

What we see here is a coding of lifestyle – that actually includes other aspects such as the work ethic, attitudes and social relations – as consumption alone.

What is lifestyle? How is lifestyle connected to (i) commodities (ii) identity? Why should Cultural Studies be interested in lifestyle?

Lifestyle is the distinctive style of life of particular social groups in a given age. It is now used to describe the construction of individuality through a specific process. Lifestyle is an individual's preference in clothing, food, leisure activities, automobile and housing. The individual's choice of clothing, food or leisure activity is taken to be expressions of his or her individual taste and sense of style. That is, the choice asserted by an individual is a symbol of her or his individual identity.

Taste, of course, is a marker of difference as Pierre Bourdieu has demonstrated (1989). Taste is 'manifested preferences' (Bourdieu 56). It refuses other tastes by positing one's own as the standard. Taste becomes a mode of exclusion because it governs the consumption of certain kinds of goods and a certain lifestyle. Thus taste, choice and their effect – lifestyle – become the new modes of identity-making.

But why is this so important? We have seen that early meanings of the term 'lifestyle' indicated a community or social group's way of life. Today there are few such 'groups' where individuals share a lifestyle. What we have is individual ways of life acquired through the use of particular *commodities* and *services*. And there is more attention paid to lifestyle today than ever before (Zukin 1998).

Lifestyle is the expression and construction of an individual's identity through the choice of particular commodities and behaviour in terms of clothing, housing, leisure activity, speech, automobile and food.

People who acquire certain products or who use certain services are linked through these rather than class or caste affiliations. That is, the consumption of goods and services enables and informs social relations. It *empowers* the users. Further, consumption and lifestyle make certain goods and services more valuable. When users acquire certain products, they invest that product with more value and meaning. Thus, lifestyle is about cultural values of artefacts and services.

Thus all other social, community, ethnic identities are erased in a kind of democratization. Instead of these earlier forms of identity, consumer culture creates just one: the *consumer citizen*. What the culture of consumption does is to

- *universalize* the consumer – the rhetoric appeals to you as an individual (as it appeals to all individuals), without reference to your class, caste, ethnic identity or religion,
- present an identity based entirely on what you buy or wear, irrespective of other markers of identity,
- link you to others through the act of consumption (of particular brands or lifestyle).
- brings you into the ambit of a group of users and consumers not only when you buy and use a product but also when you send in user-feedback, suggestions and advice (these last three being key features of online shopping).

The paradox is that consumer culture projects identity and happiness as the result of *individual* likings/taste but also as the values and ideals (represented in the objects consumed) that are recognized and validated by the *community*. That is, consumer culture

- posits the individual as one who has specific tastes and therefore adopts a certain lifestyle and buys certain products,
- links this individual's tastes to others' tastes, thereby building a *community of people with similar tastes* (for example the discussion boards on eBay constitute a community and a constituency).

Activity:

Look at the number of internet service providers, cellphone services and telecom companies that emphasize instant connectivity, entertainment and information (phone, music, the internet). Why is it now that connectivity is so important?

Increasingly mobile lifestyles, where people travel a lot in their jobs, means that they need to stay connected with their offices and homes. A professional travelling, say 10 days a month, requires some form of communication that enables her or him to stay connected.

Do you think such a lifestyle gives greater importance to quick and easy communication technology?

Does a mobile lifestyle therefore help the sale of mobile phones or wireless-enabled laptops (for internet access) for easy and instant communication?

Cultural Studies is interested in lifestyle because:

- lifestyle is about everyday life
- lifestyle defines identity
- lifestyle influences social relations
- lifestyle bestows meaning and value to artefacts in a culture
- The organization of lifestyle, in terms of self-help and advice columns, product biographies and user feedback but also consumer satisfaction surveys might be read as a process of governance in neoliberal cultures, and therefore as involving questions of power.

It is important to note that lifestyle is not a permanent thing. In fact, one of the things we need to remember is that lifestyle-related identity has to have a certain degree of flexibility. Lifestyles have to be unstable. The 'many roles' tag line in Innova advertisements is a precise description of contemporary lifestyle identities. It could be argued that the context for such a fluid lifestyle identity is related to social change. As families get increasingly more nuclearized – often with partners/spouses working in different cities – stable identities within the context of the family are more difficult to acquire. Lifestyle and peer group relationships – the latter is closely aligned to similar lifestyles too – provide a support system. In such a context of social change consumption achieves the same effect, of providing an identity. The identity it provides is *fluid*, *temporary* and *open to change*. The emphasis on 'seasonal' fashions, vacations and 'breaks' (which are bound up with seasons and time) in media and market rhetoric today is indicative of such a shifting lifestyle identity. A fluid lifestyle and consumer identity reflects a fluid social context, and helps, according to some critics, particularly the youth to generate a form of identity (Miles 2000: 157–8). It is through and in constant changes in apparel, gadgets, lifestyles that contemporary youth discover their identity and location.

Lifestyle and Consumer Culture

Consumer culture is about the consumption of goods and services. Critics and social theorists like Mike Featherstone (1991) have argued that contemporary culture in metropolises is driven by the need and desire to consume. Consumer culture has two aspects for Cultural Studies:

i) the cultural dimension of economy: where goods and services are not merely 'utilities' but also have symbolic value
ii) the economic dimension of culture: where even cultural goods, styles and commodities have economic value, and are governed by market principles, monopoly trade practices, competition and labour relations

What this means is:

- Goods have economic value, but also carry symbolic value: of status and prestige. While a price can be placed on a good, symbolic values of prestige cannot be measured in simple economic terms.
- Goods have a certain symbolic value, but they are also part of a larger market/economic process.

- Goods and services are part of a process through which socialization of individuals is achieved, identities built and social cohesion within specific groups is managed.

Activity:

Numerous companies now advertise holidays in exotic places with exotic activities.

Take Club Mahindra for example. It advertises holidays in Simla, Goa, Munnar and other places. These holidays of course have a price attached (Rs. 6000/- per night was the starting price range for the 1 February–30 April period in Goa in 2006–7). This is the economic aspect of the holiday. However, there is another dimension. The other values placed on this holiday are not measurable in economic terms at all. Club Mahindra advertises its holiday thus:

> *Experience hospitality of the highest quality through our One Time Holiday (OTH) packages, designed keeping in mind the essential elements of a memorable holiday – fun, entertainment, adventure, indulgence and relaxation.*

None of the 'values' listed here – fun, entertainment, adventure, indulgence and relaxation – are quantifiable. How does one measure relaxation or adventure in rupees? What is the monetary value of a 'memorable' holiday? These are ***symbolic*** *components: the* ***value*** *of relaxation or adventure.*

Thus the holiday has an economic component but also a symbolic component where emotions, the sense of pleasure and sentiment add a non-economic value to the commodity (the holiday).

A study of consumer culture is therefore interested in both the economic and symbolic aspects of commodity use, circulation and representation.

Advertisements frequently showcase identity. 'Be Yourself', announce ads for various products. 'Develop your self-esteem', announces another. What is important is that 'being oneself' and developing self-esteem – markers of selfhood and identity – are linked to the purchase and use of commodities. Identity therefore gets coded as *objects* of consumption.

In the India after economic liberalization, consumption has been seen as the new marker of identity. According to some critics the 'national' or 'citizen' has been replaced as an identity by 'the consumer' (Breckenridge 1995, Deshpande 2003). That is, the identity of an individual is not as a national citizen located in processes of nation-building (which was the case during the 1950–70 phase). Instead, the very idea of a 'citizen' is modified into a 'citizen who consumes'. What we now have is a new market-driven, consuming citizen who is aware of global trends and has a taste for global products and styles.

And what is now clearly visible, especially in metropolises across India (and the world) is a media-driven, *global consumer culture* (Chip Walker 1996, qtd. in Alden et al 1999: 76–7).

Consumer culture is about the *economic* and *symbolic* value given to commodities and goods where goods have a price tag attached, but they also carry values like pleasure or prestige that are not measurable in terms of money.

What we have learnt so far:

- Lifestyle is about identity-making.
- Lifestyle is about consumption of specific objects/events.
- Consumption is the acquisition of objects and their *symbolic* meanings.
- The act of consumption is governed by the idea of 'taste', as taste becomes a marker of identity and difference.
- 'Taste' is a mode of organizing social behavior (as consumer behavior), and this situates questions of fashion, lifestyle and consumerism within a politics of culture.

The Circuit of Consumption

Consumer culture has as its immediate site the act of shopping. As we have seen lifestyles are acquired through the acquisition of commodities. However, this process is not as simple as its sounds.

Consumption and marketing are said to include 'four Ps': Product, Placement, Promotion and Price (Kotler 1983).

- The right *product* has to be made and on offer.

- It must be *placed* in the right location where, for example, it can catch the eye of the consumer and potential buyer. Notice how chocolates are always placed near the check-out counter at supermarkets, so that the customer, especially the customer's children, will be attracted to them while waiting to be billed.
- The product must be marketed and *promoted* suitably. Promotion is one of the most significant aspects of consumption today, and companies spend billions on promoting their products.
- The *price* of the product should be attractive enough for the consumer to acquire the product.

The 'Four Ps' are aligned with modes of selling, identity- marketing, the rhetoric of use and the spectacle of placements of products. I propose the term 'alignment' here as a mode of reading the circuit of consumption. Alignment suggests an affiliation, an association of objects *and* ideas along a continuum. These can be contestatory affiliations, but they still constitute a temporary relationship. Alignments are temporary, localized and subject to various pressures.

As an example of alignments let us look at the automobile. The car was a status symbol in India until the 1980s. The Maruti revolution changed the urban landscape as nothing else did. Today the choices facing the potential automobile buyer are plenty. An alignment of this particular commodity with lifestyles would be as follows:

> The monopoly of the Hindustan Motors (manufacturers of the Ambassador model) after the 1950s – the opening up of the market to Suzuki tied up with the state-owned Maruti Udyog – the pricing of the small 'family car' – the transformation of the services offered by dealers – the arrival of the credit system and the 'easy finance' schemes – the arrival of other Japanese, Korean companies (Daewoo, Hyundai, Honda, Mitsubishi) – the software boom and the increased liquid assets for the younger generation – the increased spending of this generation – the emphasis on lifestyle and luxury – the boom in luxury cars – the increased linking of function with aesthetic appeal and styling – the erosion of the Ambassador customer base – the publicity around the newer models...

The list is hardly complete. What I am calling 'alignment' is clearly a temporary relationship forged for profit or marketing, but which is based upon and drives consumption patterns, questions of lifestyle, the changing nature of the economy and the profile of companies. These alignments are, of course, sometimes redefined (such as when the Indian government withdrew its share from Maruti Udyog).

'Alignment' is useful because it suggests not only linkage but also a politics. In the case of consumption and consumerism it suggests linkages between production, distribution and rhetoric, and material culture.

Activity:

When you purchase a new laptop, what is the identity you acquire?

The young professional who cannot live without the laptop (and mobile, and iPod, and the internet)? The college-going youngster? The person who works from home?

Does the styling of the laptop matter as much as its functional efficiency?

Representation

We have thus far argued that lifestyle is connected to the consumption of goods. This consumption of commodities begins well before they are purchased and used. Consumption begins before the actual act of shopping: it begins with our consumption of the *signs* of the commodity.

But what exactly do we mean when we say that we consume the sign of the commodity?

A commodity is reduced to a *sign* when abstract qualities are represented as a *product* or *object*. The object comes to *stand in for* particular emotional or social states. That is, a Mercedes-Benz car is not simply a car: it is a status symbol. A hospital is not simply a building: it is a sign of recovery of health. In both these cases the object is treated as a sign of something more abstract unconnected with the object itself. Status is not an intrinsic feature of the car. Recovery of health is not the feature of a hospital building. Both of these are associations. The car and the building therefore become *signs* of something more.

Commodities are now signs of lifestyle and identity. These signs are made through representation, the first stage in the circuit of consumption. How exactly does the media, the shopping centre or the product/commodity project and represent lifestyle? That is, what is the language used in speaking about particular products and lifestyles? (Please note that 'language' here refers to oral, visual and textual forms of representation.) Representational practices are best studied in advertisements – the cultural intermediaries that generate desire for the product. In many cases the cultural intermediaries – media writing, reports, newspapers, publicists, fashion columnists – even suggest models of consumption by representing popular figures (usually from films) as fashion models. Thus 'Festive Chic' in *The Hindu* (Metroplus 23 September 2006: 1) notes how the costumes of characters in *Rang De Basanti*, *Omkara* and *Kabhi Alvida Naa Kehna* 'dominate' the fashion scene. Columnist Mini Anthikad-Chibber noted, in her piece on *The Devil Wears Prada* that 'film and fashion are intrinsically intertwined' (Friday Review, *The Hindu* 15 September 2006: 1).

Let us take two examples, one from a global firm and one from a local company.

An advertisement for Panasonic digital cameras (Metroplus *The Hindu*, 23 September 2006: 1) shows an opened out, digital camera. The scene captured is a set of three flowers, yellow and red roses (there are others, but only three are fully visible) set against a red background. Below this image of the product are its 'specs' (contemporary slang for specifications, or technical features) in small text and three boxed items. What is interesting is the slogan or tag line that is inscribed over the image of the camera: 'Presenting the triple beauty from Panasonic'. The 'triple beauty' refers to the 3 CCD camera system. Nowhere does the ad specify what the 3 CCD camera system is or what it does (or what CCD stands for). That is the technical-technological component of the object. But the camera itself becomes a sign of beauty, represented by the three full-bloom roses. The 'triple beauty' could very well apply to the roses. Therefore, what Panasonic apparently presents is the natural beauty of the flowers. A technical feature – the 3 CCD camera system – becomes a sign of natural beauty. What the ad does is to transform the object's technical attributes into something natural. What the ad achieves is a brilliant act of representation where man-made technology becomes a code for natural beauty. It further suggests that natural beauty can be captured best through such a technological device.

A small award-medal is located at the upper right hand of the camera's image. It declares: 'India's Trusted Brand 2006 ... voted by consumers', with the word 'gold' under it.

And, under the list of tech specifics it lists 'Language Menu (Hindi option also available)'. Finally, before the list of dealers, a boxed item asks the consumer to 'insist on a Panasonic India Warranty Card to avail of a 3-year warranty'.

Notice the things that come together in this ad. It

- links technological advancement to beauty
- naturalizes technology
- suggests that the person who acquires this object might appreciate beauty
- suggests that consumers themselves have voted in its favour
- suggests that it suits Hindi-speaking people too
- suggests that the customer can 'insist' on particular services

Panasonic suggests that beauty can be best captured through this device. The commodity-product enables the owner (who obviously has a certain kind of taste, if s/he wants to photograph flowers) to capture beauty.

The representational mode – we can call it the narrative of the ad – has several features that are significant to Cultural Studies' modes of analysis.

i) The 'meaning' of the object (camera) is achieved through an association with other familiar objects, in this case, flowers. That is, the representation of the camera makes it an object of beauty in and of itself by comparing it with accepted symbols of beauty: flowers. Here the ad notes the *similarity* between the camera and the flowers.
ii) But the ad also marks the object's *difference* from the flowers. By highlighting the technical sophistication of the camera,

the ad suggests that whatever beauty the flowers possess, the camera is better.

So what does this representation do? Here is a commodity that functions as a sign of

- taste
- efficiency
- the technological basis of capturing beauty, and
- vernacularizes non-Indian technology by emphasizing the availability of a Hindi language option in operations

Let us take another ad, this time for ethnic products. This is an ad for clothes, a festival, 'Hasta Kruti', from a line called Second Skin (Metroplus *The Hindu*, 2 September 2006: 1). The visual shows an ornate picture frame inside which is a mannequin, with upper torso and head, wrapped in what looks like a silk sari. Underneath this, written in an innovative font is 'discover the true Indian heritage'. There are two palm-prints beneath, with the inscription 'magical weaves and prints of India'. Beneath this, as the last line of text, we have a box with the name of the company, Second Skin. In smaller lettering below this box is written 'clothing for the contemporary woman'. What does this visual represent?

The commodity – clothes – itself occupies only a small portion of the entire ad. The frame grabs our attention right away – reminiscent of vintage photographs and massive drawing rooms, the ornate nature of the frame ensures that the object inside is well-emphasized. The mannequin has no remarkable features. The text-matter in the ad declares:

> Hasta Kruti is a festival designed to celebrate handspun creations … works that awaken the glory of a legacy gone by … it celebrates the awakening of our enriching culture.

Note the number of things that come together in the ad. It

- emphasizes the *stylish* nature of heritage itself
- suggests that there is one *single* Indian heritage ['the Indian heritage']
- suggests that heritage is worth *emphasizing*

- suggests that a legacy can be *revived*
- suggests that heritage is *relevant* even today

The company promotes its commodity as something that suits the contemporary woman. What it manufactures is ethnic products. Linking the three – ethnic, inherited and contemporary – the ad suggests a continuity between India's past and present.

The same product line's exhibition is advertised later as 'traditional temptations' (Metroplus, *The Hindu*, 9 October 2006: 1)

So what do these representations do? Here is a commodity that functions as a sign of

- tradition
- inheritance
- style
- the continuing relevance of the past

The media advertisements, publicists, credit card companies and banks are cultural intermediaries: they generate the desire for the product, provide services to consumers and ensure that the consumer performs the act of consumption smoothly.

> The theme of lifestyle is inextricably linked to the purchase and consumption of commodities, which acquire certain values and symbolic power (status, interest in heritage, care), where the work of 'coding' the commodity as a sign is the work of representation in the media.

Identity

We have seen in Chapter 1 that the discourse of identity within any cultural process is the subject of cultural analysis. Cultural Studies assumes that representational practices seek to construct an identification between the consumer and the meanings that the object stands for. That is, the task of representation can be seen as

- constructing specific images and meanings of the object
- ensuring that the consumers understand and relate to these meanings

In short: the language of advertisement – representations – seeks to create a relationship (of identification) between the product and the consumer. In order to do so it tries to *project the commodity as a component of an identity we desire.* The commodity is a *sign* of this identity we desire. Therefore we cannot acquire the identity we desire until we acquire the commodity. We acquire not only a commodity but also the *sign* and the *identity* that goes with it.

It is important to recognize that the youth is always surrounded by images of consumables. These representations construct the youth not only as free-to-choose-and-consume individuals but as consumer-citizens.[3] That is, the market's ideologies in the form of representation (from billboards to personalized calls from retailers) often treat youth only as consumers. All other dimensions of youth culture – such as, say, politics or religion – are ignored in favour of their ability and willingness to spend. Even if they are unable to spend, the representation ensures that the desire to spend and consume is inculcated.

Let us return to the ads discussed above to see what identities are constructed through the objects. The Panasonic ad proposes, as we have seen, that the camera is a sign of taste, efficiency and the technological basis of capturing beauty. Four key moments in the discourse of identity are visible in this ad.

First, the ad represents a situation that the consumer would like to be in: photographing beauty. This means, the ad constructs a customer who, once s/he acquires the product (the camera) would go around photographing objects of beauty. We (the consumers) may not, of course, do this. But advertisement works as much at the level of fantasy as it does on real needs and necessities. We would like to be able to photograph beauty some day. What the ad does is to *create* the identity of an aesthete – a person who likes beautiful things. It shows how anybody can become an aesthete, as soon as s/he acquires this sophisticated camera. It also suggests that beautiful things – flowers – must be captured (this is a routine meaning generated in most camera ads), and this demands a good camera.

Second, another identity created by this ad is that of an Indian consumer. By emphasizing the Hindi language option, Panasonic *indigenizes* the technology and the product. Indigenization is an identity here – the Indian consumer can, whatever be the background he or she comes from (those without English, for example), acquire and used this product.

Third, the ad suggests that the customer can 'insist' on a warranty card for extra benefits. This creates the identity of an empowered consumer.

Fourth, the ad links the purchaser of the camera to a larger community of buyers, all of whom have reposed their 'trust' in the product, according to the medallion displayed in the ad. The consumer can buy this product with the knowledge that others have trusted this product. Through this the ad proposes a community of buyers, united in their trust. It creates the identity of a buyer who seeks and obtains assurance (from earlier buyers and users) that this is a good product. It shifts the onus of demonstrating the value and usability of the product from the company to the user/consumer. Other consumers testify to the product, and the consumer would do well to believe them rather than the company's promotional material. Thus the four key identities:

- the aesthete consumer
- the Indian consumer
- the empowered consumer
- the consumer who trusts only other consumer testimonies

Let us look at the print version of the Innova ad, starring Aamir Khan (*The Hindu*, 15 March 2007: 24). Over the visual is the text: 'Everyday. Many Roles. Unlimited Reasons to Celebrate'. The visual shows a quiet street in which the only automobile is the Innova parked by the side. Aamir Khan and a woman walk toward another couple seated at a café table. Khan is informally dressed in a jeans, tees and a jacket. The woman is in a 'dress' (not a salwar-kameez or sari, but an evening gown) and carrying a bunch of flowers. Of the couple seated at the table the man is waving and the woman has turned to watch Khan and the woman walk up to them. On the table are two gift-wrapped objects, suggesting celebrations of some kind.

The street seems to be a quiet residential area, but the café's seating is Paris-like, on the pavement. It is obviously evening because the street lamps – not fluorescent tube lights that are standard fixture on Indian streets but lamps mounted on wrought iron, carved posts suggestive of older streets – are on. There is one other couple in the distance also seated at a table in the café. The street is deserted. The Innova in the visual does not have a registration number, so that the geographical specificity of the city is not available to us. The tag line reads: 'all you desire'.

What is suggested here is a class of people who have the power, occasion and desire to celebrate. The text suggests that there are many reasons – left unspecified. The studied casualness of dress (Khan's, surely the central figure, being the most recognizable face in the ad) and the setting suggests an informal context. The Innova caters to this personality and situation. But this, suggests the text, is only one role that the consumer or the car can play. It suggests personal choice – celebration – and the use of appropriate 'codes' (clothes, setting, car, even the woman, perhaps). The tag line suggests that the car is the cornucopia of all desires: it completes every need and fulfils every desire.

The largest space in the visual is occupied by the vehicle. In fact there is a sense of miniaturization of the human beings, even though the vehicle is spatially situated behind the humans.

What identities are suggested here? First, the ad shows a certain class of people in exclusive settings. This is emphasized in a different way by the statistical details given in the ad, the first of which states that the EMI is Rs. 17,400. The clothes, the evident youth (though by no means can Aamir Khan be considered 'youth') and setting suggest a yuppie generation, confident, full of poise, and who enjoy the good life (Ads using middle-aged characters/celebrities are also increasingly common today. This can be read alongside ads for skin creams and lotions that suggest that even in middle age, romance can be rekindled in relationships through proper skin care).

Second, in this particular ad we see only two users of the car (though other ads of the same product show entire families). We discover, through the text below the visual that it is an 8-seater. Thus, the nuclearization of the user community – where two people travel in a car that can take 8, in a country where automobile fuel is expensive – suggests a well-heeled class, who can afford to do so.

Third, the ad showcases an un-India-like setting, with stone walled buildings, antiquarian lamp posts and street-side cafés. The vehicle, ultra modern, and the costumes of the people are in sharp contrast with the setting.

The Innova ads – on TV and in print media – presents a series of identities: the family man, the businessman who jets around the world, the sporty young man and so on. The ads showcase the many aspects of the character's personality – the tradition-respecting man, the successful go-getter, the romantic and friendly man, among others. These are the identities constructed through the representations, which say: if you want to be all these you need to own an Innova. These are desirable identities, and in order to possess them you also need to possess such a vehicle. The vehicle thus becomes the signifier of these identities.

Take a look at the fashion consumer market, especially its gender constructions. Increasingly these representations project the identity of the career/public woman. In cases where such a woman is the consumer, she is projected as conscious of the colour and styling of her hair, her fitness and health, her skin, but also the level of attractiveness and professionalism. Contemporary ads portray women with a great deal more confidence, aggression and sexuality (John 1998). This is also frequently accentuated by the westernized clothing – from sports gear to the now ubiquitous jeans-t-shirt combine. The identity of the Indian woman is not only more professionalized, it is also more consumerized, where the distinctive identity is constructed not only through her obvious professional role but also through the clothes she wears.

Identities are constructed through representations that invariably link them to commodities. Representations in media suggest how (i) certain identities are desirable (ii) that in order to acquire these desirable identities, it is necessary to own (consume) certain products. Thus consumption of goods is the prerequisite to identity-formation, indeed identities are linked to consumption.

Production

Every product has its own 'culture of production' (a term used by du Guy et al 1997: 43). This includes the way in which a company functions, its organizational structure, the management, perceptions of the company by the world, the social contexts in which the company originated/grew/expanded and the processes of manufacture.

Every company organizes particular identities for itself. For instance, Reliance in the early 1990s did not specify the names of the people – the Ambani family. After the split between Mukesh and Anil Ambani, the Reliance Info company offices and logos carry a tag line: 'Anil Dhirubhai Ambani Group'. This constructs a particular history and identity of the company:

- It is part of the great Ambani *tradition* of industry.
- It gestures at the *family's* patriarch through the use of the full name (Dhirubhai Ambani) of its Chairman (Anil).

We are therefore aware that it is a family company. This ad takes recourse to what is called 'Local Consumer Culture Positioning' where the brand is associated with a local family, consumer cultural habits and tradition.

We are aware that even though the company is moving into very contemporary areas such as communication technologies, it is rooted in the Ambani tradition.

Let us explore the 'culture of production' of the Toyota Innova – a high-priced car in the luxury segment. First: how does the company represent itself, its work culture and its production?

The website of Toyota in India is a good place to start our study (<http://www.toyotabharat.com> 15 March 2007). We discover upon entering the website that Toyota works with the Kirloskar group in India, a fact that is not mentioned anywhere in the publicity/promotional materials for Toyota – and the company's full name in India is Toyota Kirloskar Motor Private Limited. So there is a strong India connection, since Kirloskar is a well-known brand/company in India.

The rhetoric of the home pages is fascinating in the 'culture of production' it showcases.

> TKM, along with its dedicated dealers and suppliers, has adopted the 'Growing Together' philosophy of its parent company TMC to create long-term business growth. In this way, TKM

> aims to further contribute to progress in the Indian automotive industry, realise greater employement [sic] opportunities for local citizens, improve the quality of life of the team members and promote robust economic activity in India.
>
> All Toyota employees are expected to embody these values in their daily work, including environmental protection activities. To 'respect' the environment, we go to the source to identify and analyse problems ('Genchi Genbutsu'), move forward to 'challenge' conventional ideas and old habits, to improve further ('kaizen') through 'teamwork'.

The 'framework' for their work ethic, the website announces, is 'The Toyota Way'. It goes on to speak of Toyota's 'Global Vision 2010' which includes: 'combining consideration for the environment, the benefit to our customers of value-added products and the encouragement of our employees through shared prosperity and social involvement', 'empowering employees', 'respect for people' and 'local community development'.

In its pages on the Toyota Production System the company once again underscores its commitment to *people* ('Toyota has always believed that best way to serve society is to ensure the safety and development of employees'). It has three flashing points on this site, 'kaizen', 'Genchi Genbutsu' and 'jidoka' (the principle of stopping work immediately when problems occur and preventing the production of defective items).

The emphasis here, via the Foreign Consumer Culture Positioning (FCCP) where a brand is explicitly linked to a foreign culture, is on *Japanese* work culture: nowhere is there anything from the Kirloskar (or Indian) side of things. At every point the company's social commitment is emphasized. The image is not of a corporate body, but rather a social organization. The 'Toyota legacy' link declares: 'Toyota's activities are highly appreciated around the world, a result of the company's devotion to customer-oriented activities and social contributions in every market it operates'. Their cars are, it states, 'greener, safer and more fun to drive', thus highlighting its commitment to the environment and passenger safety before 'fun'. Another page deals with Toyota's 'Social Contribution' in which it lists the schools funded and the contributions to the Prime Minister's Relief Fund. It underscores the fact that it funds programmes teaching the Japanese language at Bangalore University. An entire page is devoted to Toyota and the environment. For prospective employees it declares: 'More than your qualifications and experience, we want you for the passion you have for automobiles.' With this the company shifts focus from professional expertise to a more individual state, 'passion'. It relocates success not in expertise but in enthusiasm. It thus moves away from the meritocratic and competitive paradigm to a personal one.

We thus have a specific way of representing the company: a socially committed, generous company whose concerns extend beyond manufacturing automobiles and machinery. It creates the identity of a company with a social dimension and a global (environmental, health, social welfare) interest. What we see on the website is a narrative of public concern, technological innovation, commitment and efficiency. It does not, incidentally, showcase founders and former heads. The narrative emphasis is on the company as a *team/organization* rather than biography of select individuals (there is a mention of Sakichi Toyoda as founder of the Toyota Spinning and Weaving Company) in the 'legacy' section.

As we can see the 'culture of production' for Toyota includes, mainly:

- the image of social commitment
- the image of efficiency and smoother production
- the emphasis on collectivities/team rather than individuals
- the emphasis on Japanese work culture via FCCP

Take, as another example, Reliance Communications. Its write-up on the company's work environment describes the 'setting' this way:

> We are committed to building a non-hierarchical and open work environment and a result-driven meritocracy.
>
> (<http://www.reliancecommunications.co.in/> 2 April 2007)

The emphasis on a non-hierarchic organization suggests a more open, less controlled top-down arrangement. The stress on merit and results suggests a work ethic where your rise in the company is not dependent upon seniority – the standard mode of career advancement in the public sector which (deliberately) ignores questions of result and work produced – but on work done and results achieved. Reliance thus sets out the parameters of its work ethic very clearly.

A more detailed analysis, which I have not undertaken here, is called for in order to understand the 'culture of production'. This would include a study of the marketing strategies, public relations and the general review/opinions about the company.

Consumption

In this chapter, consumption has been linked to questions of identity and lifestyle. Consumption is not, therefore, the simple acquisition of clothes or cars, it is the process through which these commodities acquire significance in social relations. Consumption is the creation of meaning through the use of particular objects. It converts commodities into signs, even as signs (values, meanings such as social status, efficiency, tradition) are symbolized as material objects.

In order to study consumption we need to look at the products themselves, but also the processes through which the products are marketed and purchased. That is, we need to look at what is sold, where, and how. In order to do so this section looks at many different aspects of the culture of consumption and shopping.

Consumption is the

- acquisition and use of objects
- appropriation of value systems and symbolic codes identified with the object

Consumption begins well before the actual acquisition of the object or product. The stages may be roughly described thus:

- the conscious, subconscious or unconscious assimilation of symbols and meanings through the media's representations
- the creation of desire through this assimilation
- the search for particular objects
- the purchase of the objects
- the use of the objects

Clearly the act of consumption is a complex one. We can study consumption at the level of:

- the *product of consumption*: brands sold, customer responses, actual sales of products, the packaging of products
- the *spaces of consumption*: the recent phenomenon of malls

The Product of Consumption

The product of consumption is the object advertised, sold, purchased and used. The product is *not* simply the material object on the shelf. The product in the contemporary era includes and markets particular features:

- novelty
- utility
- brands
- cosmopolitanism

As we have seen you do not purchase a pair of jeans or a mobile phone – you purchase a meaning, a lifestyle. 'Utility' is self-explanatory: you buy a washing machine to wash clothes or a pair of sunglasses to protect your eyes from the sun. In studies of consumption this is perhaps the most obvious. Therefore let us look at the other aspects of the product of consumption. We need to 'read' a product not just in terms of its styling and design but also the packaging and rhetoric that accompany it.

Novelty

Novelty can be defined as anything that disrupts a previous set of individual experiences. It marks a moment of pleasure when it interrupts routine and uniform experiences (Bianchi 1998). Thus novelty is about pleasure through difference and change (but that change or difference should not be too drastic, or else it would not be recognized and might even become a source of threat). Take the case of a coffee-drinker. A regular consumer of coffee has to be persuaded that the new brand is an improved, a novel version of what she consumes every day. The new brand cannot *not* taste like coffee – it cannot be so novel – but should have an additional feature that makes it novel, but remains coffee.

Consumer culture is based on a cult of novelty. The cult of novelty generates a two-pronged rhetoric:

- a rhetoric of pluses,
- a rhetoric of the 'new-now',

Novelty occurs not only when the object is radically new but also when there has been some *delay* between the moment of consumption and the past experience. Take for example, fashion. The return to older styles is based on the fact that the memory of that style is well in the past. Men's trousers are a good example. From the 1960s through the early 1970s there was the famous 'drain-pipe' style: narrow and tapering further. From the 1970s we see the flaring 'bell bottoms'. In the 1990s the tapering form and the flared style are revived. Even jeans, traditionally narrow in form and fitting, now come in loose, 'bell-bottom' styles. The style is not new, as we can now see. It is novel only because the experience of such a style is well in the past – a certain amount of time has passed since we last saw such a style, and hence there is an element of novelty here.

Novelty is bound up with acquisition. Owners of cellphones are tempted with newer models. The newer model generates a sense of novelty through the appeal to acquisition. The search for particular models or features – Do I need a phone with a camera? Do I need to surf the www on my cellphone? – constitute the discourse of novelty because one generally acquires an object that has additional features.

This sense of novelty is what I call the *rhetoric of pluses*. Notice the drive to speak of extras, excess and boundlessness. *The Hindu's* metro feature is called 'Metro*plus*'. The television channel is of course STAR *Plus*. Numerous products advertise their 'extras'. Salt comes with *extra* iodine. The bar of soap has 25 grams *extra*, as does the soft drink. Everything has been *added* to. Novelty is generated through this rhetoric of plus – in a *culture of plus*, actually – because every product seems to offer you more value for the same money. These are not advertisements separated from the product – these are the terms used on the packaging itself. Thus even as you read the name of the brand, you read the rhetoric of pluses.

> Manikchand Mineral Water is 'oxy*rich*', with 300% *more* oxygen
>
> The children's drink Boost is '*New* Boost'.
>
> Another drink, Bournvita, is now 'with *super*chargers'.

Horlicks is also '*super*charged'.

Tata Tea is with a '*New* Rich Taste'.

All Food World products are supposedly '*super* value'.

Garnier Fructis shampoos are now with an '*extra* 25%' free.

Head and Shoulders shampoo is now '*New*'.

Daurala sugar cubes are now '*Double* Refined'.

Revive Starch is now '*Super* Strong'.

Sundrop refined oil is '*new improved* '.

Band-Aid is 'Water Block *Plus*'.

Kellog's Frosties are '*super* charged'.

There are literally dozens of examples to illustrate this rhetoric of pluses. The rhetoric attempts to add novelty by promising something beyond the expected. When you actually expect the 'regular' product the packaging tells you: 'please note, we are giving you something more'.

Then there is the rhetoric of the 'new-now'. Anna Kurian describes the emphasis on novelty, 'newness' *and* immediacy in contemporary culture as the 'new-now' (personal communication). The phrase, I believe, captures the strategy commonly adopted by brands and marketers. Thus the motorcycle Apache from TVS declares it is 'now or never'. Nokia's new model, N 72, is '*now* in gold and black'. Motorazr from Motorola is 'now' available at a reduced price. Air Deccan asks you to 'book *now*'. Lloyd's range of products declares that 'the future's today and brought to you by Lloyd'.

Look at the number of ads that emphasize 'today' and 'now', urging the consumer to perform the act (of buying) right away. 'Hurry', urge many of the ads. Novelty is linked not only to something 'more' ('pluses') but to something more *now*. It is not enough to hold out the promise of something – it has to be on offer, ready for consumption *today*. The rhetoric focuses on the temporal attainment of pleasure, as the rhetoric of 'new-now' indicates.

> Novelty is created in the move between an unconscious *expectation* of the ordinary/regular and the actual *availability* of something new/extra.

Activity:

Take a look at the number of products that promise something more. Please note that the product is inseparable from its advertisements and packaging.

Products these days promise:

- *something free*
- *something extra*
- *something new*
- *something different*

Now ask: what do these offers really do?

What they do is to suggest that for the same money or cost you, the customer, is getting something more. It suggests that you are actually getting more than what you are actually paying for. This is the rhetoric of pluses.

Packaging and Branding

Consumer culture is related to what numerous contemporary thinkers refer to as 'material culture'. Material culture is not only about material objects and things but the *values* assigned to them, the patterns of cultural consumption of particular objects (laptops as a marker of yuppie culture symbolizes the 'alignment' of lifestyle debates, material culture, functionality, aesthetics and expenses). Objects in material culture, as described by Tim Dant (1999), possess the following features:

- as signs of status and ideology
- as vehicles of meaning and equivalence
- as bearers of aesthetic value
- as components of ritual
- as knowledge and ideas
- as indicators of lifestyle and identity

Let us take two objects and their sales/packaging rhetoric to see how material culture operates. The first is an ad for the new Knorr series of Chinese masalas (Metroplus *The Hindu*, 10 March 2007: 1).

The main text reads, in large, bold and black lettering:

Guess who's opening a new Chinese restaurant ?
You.

Below this, after describing the variety available, it states: 'surprise your family with authentic Chinese meals, right at home'. Beneath this, to one corner is:

Restaurant jaisa Chinese Khana, Ghar Pe

The last two words here are in larger lettering.

The visuals include an ethnic hanging lamp, a plate of noodles with chopsticks laid across, a few packets of Knorr with some fruits and vegetables nearby.

The ad showcases the material object – Knorr – in terms of rituals (the formal inauguration of a restaurant), ethnicity (the ethnic lamp, which resembles those made of jute or bamboo), location (home/public space). It underscores the significance of either of two things (the rhetoric leaves it unclear):

(a) being asked to open/inaugurate a new restaurant, suggesting you are a celebrity,
(b) being entrepreneurial enough to open a new restaurant.

The sudden equivocation over the public/private locale – you can recreate the Chinese cuisine in your own home – renders the material object in multiple codes: class, location, culture. It shifts an exotic (Chinese) menu into the home in a process of FCCP. The home is where a multicultural 'event' can take place. Such a meal, the ad suggests, is equivalent to opening a new restaurant. While the reference to a business enterprise gestures at the capitalist mode, it dislocates it by shifting the enterprise *into* the home. The object thus takes on the qualities of:

- a capitalist venture within a domestic setting
- a leisurely trip outside *within* the home
- an exotic element within the familiar
- a profit-making product within the natural-familial

The ad thus mixes codes so cleverly that the Knorr product's actual nature becomes irrelevant. What becomes important is that 'authentic Chinese' can now be localized, indeed intimate. The ideology of intimacy and the family that the ad proposes masks the material object's profit-driven nature under the guise of care (for the family), enthusiasm (experimentation, enterprise) and taste. Everybody can now experience the joys of (capitalist) enterprise if you only try Knorr!

Take as a second example, food products and their packaging rhetoric. Knorr, as we have seen, identifies the *entire family* as consumer. Brooke Bond tea has two main varieties. The Red Label variety has on every package the following tag line: 'warmth for your *family*'. The 3 Roses variety has the following tag line: 'Perfect tea for your *family*'. Maggi Noodles, manufactured by Nestlé India, proposes that there is 'extra health for your family in every pack'. Divya's Chyawanprash uses as its tag line: 'powerful ayurvedic health tonic for family'. The rhetoric of the healthy family is clearly central to food product sales.

Notice how advertisements for cooking oils, food products, refrigerators, hygiene products (like cleaning fluids) invariably focus on the *family as consumer*. The *woman* serves healthy food because she is concerned about the well being of the family. The marketing of clothing and accessories (such as watches), on the other hand, focuses on the *individual as consumer*. Food and eating is more a family ritual where the consumer is embedded within the structure of relationships. Refrigerator advertisements showcase the family, eating healthy food because the refrigerator preserves the taste and good qualities of the food. Dettol hand wash announces that it is 'ideal for everyday use by everyone in your family'.

Clothing, accessories and professional tools (such as laptops, whose advertisements invariably focus on the office space and the individual) are, on the other hand, about the individual. If food products showcase 'success' and/or 'happiness' as derived from a family eating healthy food together, other products in fashion or professional equipment showcase 'success' and/or 'happiness' as derived from an individual's self-esteem, acceptance by peer-group with similar taste in fashion or professional success.

The emphasis on particular groups of consumers is a strategy adopted by many companies. For example, let us look at Coca Cola India's Thums Up brand (originally an Indian brand, bought up by Coca Cola in 1993), as advertised on television (during 2007) and on the website. The key figure here is Akshay Kumar, well known as an 'action star', with spectacular athleticism, youth and machismo. The television ad shows Kumar, dressed in black, leaping from his apartment, negotiating the streets, leaping across buildings, testing every muscle and taking every possible risk – all to acquire a bottle of Thums Up, which he *steals* from a delivery van. The website shows a leather-jacketed Kumar, in sun-glasses, with a two-day stubble, holding a bottle of Thums Up. The write-up reads:

> Thums Up is known for its strong, fizzy taste and its confident, mature and uniquely masculine attitude. This brand clearly seeks to separate the men from the boys.

The key legend is 'Strong Cola Taste, Exciting Personality'.

Beneath this are visuals, much smaller in size, of Chiranjeevi (the action super star from Telugu cinema) in motorcycling leathers and carrying a helmet and a Thums Up bottle, and of Bipasha Basu.

The message is very clear: Thums Up caters to the action-loving male. Machismo and masculinity are written into every section of the television and website ad. The brand sells through this very association.

A certain amount of *mysticism* is also central to product marketing and promotion. Samsung refrigerators announce that they are 'Silver Nano Health System', suggesting the use of state-of-the-art nano-technology. The Philips steam iron apparently uses a 'double active Calc system'. Now neither of these two descriptions makes sense to the non-technical-minded consumer. The product and its functioning are rendered mysterious by deliberately invoking the technology behind it. Since few of the consumers are likely to explore and understand the processes behind the product, the element of mystery and magic is retained.

Such magicality is also invoked more directly. Lay's potato chips, manufactured by Pepsi, has a specific variety, India's '*Magic* Masala'. Several things happen to lend this air of magic to the product. On the package we read:

> These light and crispy potato chips are *more magical* than ever before with a rich medley of Indian spices.

You are invited to 'taste the *magic*'.

In the case of the 'Classic Salted' variety – especially those marketed during the ICC 2007 World Cup (March–April 2007) it states: 'The official global partner of the ICC World Cup 2007', thus linking global manufacturing and consumption to global entertainment (live telecast of the multi-million dollar tournament). It is described as 'the main food for the good mood'. It also has a visual of Saif Ali Khan wearing the Indian cricket team's colours. The 'Caribbean Hot and Sweet Chilli' variety has Saif Ali Khan drumming away. The write-up says:

> These light and crispy potato chips with a playful mix of hot and sweet flavours are a real entertainment for the mouth.

The visual, the description all revolve around the sense of playfulness and fun associated with Caribbean culture and calypso (the television ad for the ICC World Cup 2007 in the Caribbean has as its theme song 'Come Play'. The 'Extra Innings' programme between the live telecasts often focuses on the natural beauties, especially the beaches of the islands. Together they suggest a space of leisure, fun and recreation). Thus a global company sells its food products in indigenized forms, often appropriating local motifs, stereotypes and themes.

There are other aspects to product design and styling. Take, for example, the language of Microsoft Windows. Note the terms commonly used in Windows: 'trash', 'bin', 'desktop' – all common *American* terms. Then, why is it Microsoft '*office*'? Beth Kolko (2006) analysing the design of this product notes how the programme showcases the image of a formal, efficient, American office culture. The technology is geared to office labour, especially of white-collar workers. Other kinds of labour are not recognized at all. Other critics raise the question of the office metaphor. How come the Windows menu/interface uses only 'office' and not (say) the kitchen, the work-bench or the restaurant? (Selfe and Selfe 1994). The point is that product designs often encode particular ideologies and community values. In an age when computer skills and the service economy – operated mostly through computers – are more valued (over physical labour in factories), it is 'natural' that the Windows programme appropriates the office metaphor.

The language of packaging also indicates possible consumers and markets. Most food products use English and Hindi on the package. Everest Masala powders uses English, Hindi and Urdu. Philips uses only English on its steam iron packaging. Kingfisher airlines, from the Mallya group, uses only English. The latter also distinguishes itself from other airlines by emphasizing the personalized service. On its 'welcome pack' (consisting of what it calls 'useful items' – a headset, hand and face wipes, a pen and candy – please note, it is not described as 'chocolate', the common Indian term, but as 'candy', the Euro-American usage) it underscores the *personal* experience of flying the 'good times'.

Brands are a class of goods identified as the products of a *single* firm. Brands (a complex of name, image, slogan. See Frow 2002: 67) became important with the rise of mass production in the nineteenth century when millions of the same car/jeans/domestic appliance were manufactured in factories. Brands indicate

- the identity of the product
- the identity of the company

Thus companies seek to distinguish their product from competing and identical products. Brands give products proper names:

Reliance Mobile
Usha Fans
Godrej furniture

Instead of *generic* products (mobile phones, fans and furniture) we can identify and distinguish between *specific* varieties. This process is branding. Brands and logos are used to lend a mass-produced object a *unique* identity. We buy/consume not the object, but a brand:

Levi's jeans
Coca-Cola drink
Tommy Hilfiger T-shirts
the *Congress* Party

We thus associate the object with something larger – the company and its tradition itself. In each of the above examples the significance is not the object but the *particular company* that creates the object. This is branding. Branding now therefore often includes:

- The *trademark* (a logo, recognizable everywhere by everybody). The logo functions as a guarantee, an assurance that the product is genuine and reliable. Thus logos are meant to evoke familiarity – LIC's famous symbol of the lamp, or Nike's well-known swoosh for example. The logo is thus treasured by the company, and rival companies are sued for misuse of the logo.

- The *date* of first establishment of the company (e.g. Levi's, since...). This is often the heritage of a product, where the older the company the more respectable and reliable its product (apparently) becomes. *Timelessness* is central to the acceptability of a product. Thus Haldiram's tag line of 'the taste of tradition' gestures at the need to retain older values of taste, consumption and food preparation. Even the much smaller brand, the Madras-based Sri Ganeshram's 777 brand masala powders uses as its tag line 'traditionally yours since 1954'.

The brand refers to the products *and* values of the particular company. Branding is about the *recognizability* or *popularity* of a particular company's product. A survey reported in *The Hindu* found that Indian consumers are loyal to brands (9 October 2006: 20). Such a popularity often has to take recourse to traditional and stereotypical themes and icons for ready accessibility. Companies therefore locate themselves in tradition in order to

- create a sense of familiarity
- instil a sense of loyalty among their patrons

ITC's 'Kitchens of India' range of ready-to-eat food does this regularly. The write-up on its 'Chicken Darbari' packet goes as follows:

> The distinctive flavours of Gharana cuisine mirror ancient Indian culinary traditions. The time-honoured methods of choosing only the finest ingredients. The delicate balance of adding every element at its precise, predetermined time. These traditions blend into a work of culinary art that is uniquely Indian. Gharana. An art form kept alive by the master Chefs of ITC Hotels.

ITC is in itself a brand (a private sector company manufacturing cigarettes, apparel, paperboards, and now into information technology). Here the write-up emphasizes tradition constantly. This rhetoric of tradition is reflected in ITC's slogan: 'Enduring Value: For the nation, for the share holder'. The brand and its product therefore link contemporary developments in culinary and food habits – the age of fast foods, ready-to-eats with traditional modes of cooking. It locates postmodern developments within an Indian tradition of cooking, thus suggesting not a break but a *continuity*. The brand, 'not the product', is the experience.

Another, more startling instance of the continuity theme is visible in McDonald's publicity flier distributed ahead of the opening of their first restaurant in Hyderabad city (it opened on 7 July 2006). Printed on glossy, bright red paper, this is what the flier said:

> 1590: Hyderabad was founded
> 1591: Charminar was built
> 1874: Nizam State Railway opens
> 1948: Hyderabad joins the Indian Union
> 2006: McDonald's opens

The flier locates the opening of the multinational giant within the history of the city. It is a part of the city's major moments, with no reference to questions of the foreign brand or MNCs. Indigenous events and constructions occupy the same space as McDonald's.

The brand develops what John Frow calls a 'semantic autonomy' (2002: 64). The meaning of the word/name (such as Xerox or Coke) now is often freed of the object itself. If 'Xerox' has now come to represent the act of photocopying, the name 'coke' refers less to Coca Cola than to carbonated drinks (you can consume 'coke' even as you drink Pepsi). The brand acquires a life of its own, *separated* from the product that carries the name.

The new Coca Cola advertisement starring Aamir Khan declares 'sabka thanda ek – Coca Cola' and seeks to project a set of diverse Indian community on the train (one can recognize yuppies, a traditional north Indian family, an executive, a fez-wearing Muslim gentleman) homogenized as consumers of the drink. It clearly plays on the very old (and very clichéd) 'unity in diversity' theme: The difference being: the unity is now achieved through a controversial MNC drink. We have an MNC brand that appropriates a postcolonial Indian slogan for its promotion. India's consumer-globalization is disguised as a unifying ethos. It marks a shift in paradigms – from a political culture and sloganeering to consumer-globalization.[4] The use of traditional slogans to sell an MNC product constitutes this shift of paradigms.

At this point it is useful to look at what the presence of a best-selling and recognizable face like Aamir Khan's achieves. In order to understand this we need to move beyond the mere issue of brands to that of signatures and endorsements. The brand, John Frow (2002) has demonstrated, is a quasi-signature, for it belongs not to a singular person (a signature is a particular individual's and that individual's *alone*) but to a corporate. The Aamir Khan 'starrer' here is not part of the cultural or entertainment industry – it is a part of the manufacturing industry. Thus the signature of Aamir Khan on coke or Sachin Tendulkar on Boost is the *convergence* of two things:

- of the *signature* – that of the individual star
- of the *brand* – that of the product/company

This convergence is also significant because it relies on a convergence of the qualities embodied in the endorser which the product claims for itself: Dravid and his renowned reliability and Anchor lights, Dhoni's flair in batting and his flamboyant hairstyle which the gel apparently enables, Amitabh Bachchan and his reputation of being the best (hence 'bond with the best', for Reid and Taylor). It is also interesting that Coca Cola's newest ad uses a *Muslim* film star – known for his nationalist ideology in films like *Lagaan, Mangal Pandey* and *Rang De Basanti*, with a marked change in *Fanaa*) to speak of Indian unity: apparently coke cuts across religious, ethnic, linguistic and class distinctions.

The brand and its endorsement are located somewhere between

- the *aesthetic* realm of images and icons and
- the *market* of products and sales

The brand endorsement is thus a convergence of

- the cultural or sporting industry
- the manufacturing industry

Such convergences are now increasingly common, bringing together celebrity culture (film and sports stars endorsing products) and manufacturing/industry culture. The brand image here includes not only the image of the product but also the person endorsing it.

Twinings is a well-known London tea company, specializing in distinctive flavoured teas. It advertises itself as 'Twinings of London'. Established in London in 1706, and reputed to have introduced tea drinking to English people, the name is associated with English culture. The products are now available in India. The product has been indigenized cleverly. The tea-bags come in a packet that announces, just above the label, 'By Appointment to Her Majesty Queen Elizabeth II'. The location of the product/ brand in English culture is firmly established through this connection with the monarch. On the side we have in the lemon flavoured tea variety the following legend: 'a unique blend of Indian teas delicately scented with natural lemon flavour'. An *English* company, associated with the monarch of *England*, no less, now promotes distinctive *Indian* teas. Adjacent to this legend is a visual, a map that depicts a section of the Indian subcontinent showing Kolkata, the river Ganges, the Bay of Bengal. Slightly to one side, in the Bay, is a ship. The ship is clearly an old model, with a large mast and sails. Two themes figure in this visual rhetoric. First, Kolkata recalls the first English Presidency and fort: Fort William, Calcutta, established towards the end of the seventeenth century. Second, the old model of the ship recalls the ships of the English East India Company: Bengal was the chief port of trade for these ships. Thus the rhetoric of the packaging invokes not only a history of consumption (of tea in England and India) but also a history of international trade and colonization. Tea represents a major commodity of international trade, and now of global consumer culture. Even though it promotes an Indian flavour of tea, the product remains firmly located in the history of colonial trade.

Activity:

Take the sudden flurry of Dhoni advertisements for things as wide-ranging as motorcycles to hair gel.

Ask the following questions:

What are the qualities that Dhoni is known for?

Does the product seek to present these same qualities?

In addition to the convergence of the signature and the brand another kind of convergence must be noted in the case of branding. The brand is also copyrighted – there are *legal* restrictions on the use of particular logos and images (one hears of McDonald's copyright cases against the use of 'Mc' by others). So we can now expand the above convergence into the following, as characteristics of brands:

- of the *personalized* signature of the star endorser
- of the *brand* of the product/company
- of the *legal* rights and responsibilities of the company's trademark

So we have the industrial, cultural and legal discourses coming together in brands and their endorsements.

Products and brands use particular forms of rhetoric, and rely on ideologies of family, age, economy, utility or patriotism even as they project particular images of the manufacturer and buyer, often mediated through endorsements by particular celebrities that link the cultural industry with the manufacturing one.

It is not enough to package and brand a product. The shape, style and feel of a product are central to its circulation and popularity. Product design is therefore a major area of research and intense innovation in any industry.

Think of the early clunky desktop PC. The convergence of technologies has enabled the product to grow smaller and integrate more and more functions. Laptops grow lighter and sleeker with each new model. Television sets incorporate more and more features. The PC doubles as a television set.

Clearly, 'design' is crucial to the brand and product (we shall return to the question of design in the chapter on 'cultures of communication'). Technology caters increasingly to specific groups and kinds of customers: the business-woman, the sports fan, the housewife, the college kid, the traveller. Nokia's Concept Store in major cities even projects *future* technologies and products so that you can be prepared for revolutions in models and designs.

Cosmopolitanism

Notice how many labels and brands advertise their other-nation origins and affiliation. Eclecticism also includes mixing of codes and cultural vocabularies. Thus Indian ethnic costumes and cultural codes mix with European styles. Hindi film tunes are downloadable onto Nokia phones, and Pizza Hut provides Indian toppings such as Chettinad Chicken. The bilingual nature of ads and displays for most brands suggests mixed cultural vocabularies and codes. Contemporary consumer culture represents the landscape of global cultural 'flows'.

One of the most conspicuous features of contemporary consumption is its irreducible cosmopolitanism, especially in the case of clothing and food products.

Zodiac Shirts announces its European spirit. Opel Astra cars announce their German technological expertise. Every brand now available is a multi-national or other-national one. In one mall you consume Italian pizza, speak on a (Finnish) Nokia cellphone, listen to music on a (Japanese) Sony machine, drink an (American) Coke (spilling some on your made-in-Taiwan but marketed-by-Levi's of the USA T-shirt), and enquire about the price of a (Korean) LG microwave before driving off in your (German) Opel Astra. After getting home, to recover from the drive, you might consume a soothing (Ceylon) tea, Dilmah, imported into and marketed in India by the global Heinz India Limited and nourish yourself with Lay's potato chips from Pepsico India, and advertised as 'the World's No. 1 Potato Chip' (there are also global varieties such as '*American* Style' and '*Spanish* Tomato Tango', in contrast to the *non-geographic* 'classic salted').

This is the paradox at the heart of global consumer culture: the desire to be unique and exclusive (markers of lifestyle and identity) is troubled by the increasing standardization of consumption and lifestyle products. What you believe you own as a unique cultural/ consumer product is actually a standard. It is therefore important to note that the global consumer culture scene is divided between

- global labels and brands (obtainable almost in every metropolis) and
- the boutique proudly labelled 'exclusive'.

Lifestyle is caught between these two poles.

At home you might want to try Chinese food. Noodles, especially by Maggi, revolutionized eating habits. Maggi indigenizes noodles. One variety is 'vegetable atta noodles'. The linguistic merger between Indian ('atta') and Chinese (noodles) suggests a multicultural cuisine, or rather an indigenized one that retains its exoticism while catering to local tastes. Likewise, McDonald's advertises its McAloo Tikki, an Indianized product.[5]

And now there are many varieties of 'authentic' *Chinese* noodles manufactured in India. Indo Nissin manufactures and sells Top Ramen noodles. Capital Foods (Nasik) markets one under the brand name 'Ching's Secret', with its tag line 'Real Chinese, Tasty Chinese'. The Food World chain has its own range of Egg Noodles.

There is also the culinary multiculturalism of Chinese food in India. Chinese dishes are now standard fare even in traditional hotels. The vendor and small eateries serving 'Chinese fast food' (often spelt in very interesting ways) are ubiquitous in cities today. In the American contexts, as studies have shown, Chinese American dishes enable cross-cultural interaction and survived hospitality towards immigrants, especially in the first half of the twentieth century. Chinese restaurants, in fact, became agents of cultural *change* (Barbas 2003). Food multiculturalism is now a central feature of globalization and global consumerism. In a sense, as Marylouise Caldwell et al argue (2006), global consumer culture facilitates individual self-development by enabling her/him to move beyond the (familiar) local and the regional to other cultures, food habits and fashions.

Anzac cookies were manufactured during World War I by wives and mothers of the Australian and New Zealander soldiers to raise the latters' morale. Later they were sold to raise funds for veterans – all this information is printed on the package itself, so we get a sense of the product's history. For some strange reason the logo is inscribed with this legend: 'Australia's favourite cookie'. It drops New Zealand from the mark. And now Anzac cookies are available in India, manufactured by Unibic biscuits. The legend on the package reads: 'Supporting India's jawans'. Beneath this it states: Unibic donates 3 per cent of sales for the support of Indian Jawans. Notice how in the globalized world the contexts are sought to be replicated. The biscuits were first produced for a particular purpose, in a particular context. Several decades later the original aim of the biscuit making has been transferred to Indian soldiers and their welfare. In the globalized world transference of cuisine and manufacturing techniques also apparently includes a transfer of symbolic meaning. The world is also apparently linked by a common ideology – of caring for its soldiers.

In addition, foreign firms set out to capture the Indian palates and markets by manufacturing things that are clearly Indian. An example would be Pepsi's Lehar line of food products manufactures the traditional Indian savoury, aloo bhujia. The reverse is also true. ITC's Sunfeast range, for instance, manufactures (Italian) pasta.[6]

Other global products now available include the more recent Minute Maid (marketed in India by Coca Cola) and Tropicana fruit juices (it is significant that Microsoft Word converts the 't' in Tropicana to caps instantly, as a recognized proper noun identified even by software), Pringles chips, the omniscient (and controversial) carbonated drinks from Pepsi and Coca Cola, Kellog's corn flakes, Mars chocolate bars ... the list is almost endless.[7]

You have just been globalized.

Global brands are now available – even manufactured – in India, as consumerism takes on global dimensions, even as global products get indigenized for Indian users.

The Spaces of Consumption I: The Mall

India is going through a phase of mall culture. A study by the *Images* fashion magazine (reported in *Xinhua*, the Chinese newspaper, and archived at www.englishpeople.com.cn. Updated 22 September 2005) stated that the number of shopping malls in India is set to reach 358 by the end of 2007. It went on to say:

> Droves of middle-class Indians have broken off their love of traditional stand-alone stores that have no air-conditioning, organized parking and other public amenities.
>
> (<http://www.englishpeople.com.cn> 15 March 2007)

Spectacle

The mall marks a radical departure from the usual retail store. In the case of the retail store one asks for the things one needs, and the shopkeeper supplies those.

In the case of the mall the shopper gazes on a whole range of goods and products – many of which s/he may not need – before selection. The mall is therefore a space of display, where goods are arranged for maximum visual appeal. In other words, the arrangement of goods has to be attractive enough to instil desire for particular products so that the shopper will purchase the same. Spectacle, attention-holding and desire are thus central elements of the shopping experience in the mall.

The mall can be read

- primarily, as a site of gazing and the spectacle
- secondarily, as a site of shopping

Walkways, views and prospects inside a mall

People who come into malls are mainly *looking* (it is no coincidence that Rachel Bowlby's first book on shopping is called *Just Looking*), and hence the significance of visual appeal in the structure of the mall.[8]

The presence of models and posters constitute the *spectacle of fantasy*. The images of models in shop windows in a mall exceed in number and dimension what you would find on a shopping street. Indeed in a mall one is surrounded by such images of attractive men and women, cosy families and energetic youth. The mall itself is a fantasy world, into which you enter and experience the illusion of acquiring perfection as embodied in these images. The shop windows and their displays suggest *possibilities*, and are always future-directed: you can also look like this (if you acquire this particular object). The trying-on of clothing and accessories ensures that the spectacle of the fantasy – what Sharon Zukin terms 'Disneyfication' (1998) – extends a step further: immersion in the fantasy world in corporeal terms. You adorn yourself, robe yourself, redesign yourself for a time. Strategically placed mirrors and images ask you to compare your 'new look' with what is possible. The mall asks for participation in the fantasy: you can *become* whatever you want.

Spectacle is not simply about the fantasy of a future possibility. It is a *performance* that the customer-consumer can initiate and participate in. So it is not simply a spectacle that one 'sees', it is something that one 'performs' and 'enacts'. You handle the objects, touch them, examine them and, even try them on (e.g. clothes). It is thus a theatrical performance that is interactive. It is a spectacle that comes alive with the visitor/potential consumer. The staged nature of malls evokes an other world.

The display of consumption – showing people eating, wearing and using is aligned with the spectacle too. What we now have in the mass media representation of consumer culture is the display of consumption itself, even as the spectator consumes the display. The ads *represent* the act of consumption, and the spectator consumes (as in experiences, perceives) the ad. What this means is that the spectacle is almost entirely of signs. Consumption is coded as a sign, which we in turn consume.

Prospect view and spectacle inside a mall. The mirror reflecting the other shops and stair (to the left of the picture) adds to the depth and hyperreal nature of the spectacle.

The spectacle effect is also achieved through the *vistas* that open out at every level within the mall. Balconies and viewing points at every floor enable one to *survey* large sections of the store. We therefore have a *prospect* (incidentally the 'prospect' was a form of painting popular in eighteenth and nineteenth century Europe and England, in which a land lord's property was represented as spread out for his viewing pleasure) of shopping unveiled before us. The view is part of the spectacle – where one has to take in the view (prospect) as part of the pleasure of the shopping experience. It suggests a sense of choice too – where to go, what to buy.

Closely aligned with the theme of spectacle is that of *eclecticism*. One of the central features of conventional shopping areas and stores has been their uni-dimensionality: you go to one place for handlooms, another for glass-ware, and yet another for fashion. The mall centres all this. Contemporary consumer culture is the culture of the world.

This makes the experience of the mall a wonderfully *cosmopolitan* one: the world under one roof. Eclecticism and the mixing of products, styles and traditions are a central feature of the mall and consumer culture.

Organization

Sat Garg writing about the altered shopping culture of India states:

> After more than 150 years of unorganised retailing, the Indian retail industry has finally taken vital steps towards modernisation, systemisation and consolidation.
>
> (<http://www.imagesfashion.com> 17 March 2007)

Garg summarizes the three main dimensions of mall culture: modernization, systematization and consolidation. These three could be discussed under one basic heading: 'organization'.

The mall is an intensified experience of city life, but with some crucial differences. Reading the mall as a text, one can decipher particular meanings and codes.

It *extends* the city into the shopping area. The mall is an *enclosed* street, roofed and walled in (Backes 1997). That is, the street which once had a row of stores (as in any market area), has been taken *into* the mall. One used to stroll down and go to the shops one wanted. Now the strolling is in the space of the mall. The mall thus combines the stroll with the shopping: you walk down alleys and lanes in this controlled space and look in through shop windows before deciding on a visit. The shopper is what critics have called a *flâneur*: a stroller (Mona Abaza 2001. Abaza points out, following Zygmut Bauman, that malls were originally spaces for *strolling*).

It is a *sanitized* city – free of dirt, pollution, bad weather, vehicular noise, chaotic traffic, but also, significantly, of beggars, street people and vendors. It is different from the city because it is more organized – with marked pathways to walk on, sit and sell. Designated places for rest, leisure and entertainment are in sharp contrast to the chaos of the Indian street, where any organization has very little effect.

Sign inside a mall-indicating a secured space

It is a *secured* city space. The entrances are guarded and undesirable elements are kept out. The mall's security directs traffic and parking. Unlike an Indian street where traffic, pedestrians and vendors mix messily and in unregulated fashion, the space of the mall is tightly monitored. Security personnel, in uniform or in civilian clothes, security cameras and floor managers monitor the traffic inside the mall. Signs posted announce 'this complex is under electronic surveillance' add (notionally at least) to the customer's sense of security.

The mall is an *escape*, separated from the rest of the city (indeed, from the world). It is a stand-alone space set apart from the city's chaos and traffic. One critic, Jerry Jacobs, even titled his work *The Mall: An Attempted Escape from Everyday Life* (1984). It becomes an escape because one can go to the mall to 'hang out', for want of anything better to do. It is an end in itself. It is important to note here that while in most 'First World' countries the malls are located outside and away from the main town, Indian cities seem to want malls in the city centre. This makes the notion of escape even more exciting and tempting.

It is a *hyperreal* space. The hyperreal is the creation through illusion (or, to use the term from postmodern critical theory, simulation) of what has never existed before. Paths that do not lead to destinations but to more images and paths would be a good example of the hyperreal. Even as one heads for the exit, another display or sign leads us astray. You move from display to display, object to object rather than from display to exit or object to exit. The mall is a universe in itself, with windows into many worlds.

The numerous glass fronts and mirror surfaces – glass is the central element in all malls – reflect other stores *endlessly*, creating a fantasy world of products and objects of desire in a *mise en abyme* – a fragmented, miniaturized repetition of products, stores, looks – of consumption. Thus while you are looking into or out of a shop you encounter another in the form of a reflection. It adds to the sense of the hyperreal because it seems to create a world of endless stores and objects – a kind of fantasy-utopia of never ending consumer choices and consumption.[9] The hyperreal is also accentuated by the fluid designs often adopted for walls and floors.

Time, the seasons, the weather do not matter here. The lighting, arrangement of spectacles and the controlled environment (air conditioning, for example) renders it more real. It is a clean city where the most common everyday elements have been incorporated but in a modified, upgraded and purified version. The hyperreal is the 'mixed reality' of the mall: the illusion merges with the real, the illusion is made real and experienced by actual flesh-and-blood bodies. The space of the mall and its controlled environment are given solidity because of the presence of people who, for that period of time, experience it as their only reality. Mixed reality is the interpenetration of the artificial (the spectacle, the cinematic effect of the displays) with the bodily. The space of the mall is activated and transformed as the user negotiates that space. The mall is labyrinthine, and intentionally so. Paths do not always lead to exits, but to more stores. The arrangement of shop windows and stores, entertainment points and décor ensure that one's path to the exit is not always smooth or clear. Each path is a scene, and leads one to more scenes (clothes, accessories, luggage, electronics, food, movies, play stations) rather than to the exit. The

Hyperreal reflections inside a mall. The mirror on the left adds to our visual field of the other section of the mall as various spaces and shops merge.

route one takes can be, at least theoretically, random. Directions are painted on the floor, and markers displayed at regular intervals, and constitute the mall's equivalent of a city's traffic signals.

Adding to the sense of the hyperreal is the *ahistorical* nature of the mall. While the streets of any city carry markers of its history (old buildings, broken down objects, faded name boards, and even the user's prior knowledge or the place's history and culture) the mall lives exclusively in the present. It is beyond historical time and outside history. Plastic, glass, PVC and fibre, synthetic wood and mass-manufactured flowers in pristine settings render the space of the mall a garden that has just been invented. Time collapses inside a mall not only because changes in the weather or the time of the day (morning, afternoon, night are the same inside the heavily lighted mall) are irrelevant but because history does not matter here.

The mall is also a *postmodern secular* space. Freed of the spaces of religion, caste, class (except the class of consumers) the mall is a substitute for the secure spaces of religion and social grouping. The free-floating nature of the mall – as opposed to say, the neighbourhood park where the people who gather every day are more or less familiar to each other – makes it postmodern and in a state of constant flux. From the local park with familiar faces and the familiar retailer who knows your entire family (sometimes even more about your family than you realize!) the scene has shifted to a non-identitarian (by which I mean an identity that is free-floating, where you are only a number or a consumer) mall. It is a scene that reinvents itself every day precisely because it is so bland and has nothing unique about it. In a sense, the mall is the very antithesis of individualism (represented by retail shopping or the community park) in its anonymity and secular spaces.

Some malls occasionally have local cultures and native lines included in their spectacle. But overwhelmingly, malls in India are about *cosmopolitan* fashion and brands. McDonald's apparently, is the one sure 'store' in any mall. A 'candy cart' – the ubiquitous American phenomenon of not-so-long ago – finds its odd place in one complex! Conventional food items are more uncommon, though one could easily pick up brownies, Australian cookies, pizzas, burgers and Georgia coffee at most of the malls. Fast food seems to be the mainstay of the culinary component of the mall/super store shopping experience. Yet it is also the increasing privatization

Candy cart inside a mall. The American candy cart lends a cosmopolitan air to the Indian mall.

of public space where corporate bodies control what used to be public space when more and more of the street is taken into the mall (Zukin 1998).

The cosmopolitanism is also evident in the kinds of brands and products available. John Players, Allen Solly, Spykar, Lee, Wrangler and dozens of cosmopolitan/global brands are concentrated in the space of the mall. Native and local products are difficult to find. Is the mall then the outlet for global trends and brands?

Critics have argued that the mall is a *feminine* space (Bowlby 1985; Backes 1997; Abaza 2001). The city and other public spaces, in most cultures, have traditionally been hostile to women (who are relegated to the space of the home). Or, if women were allowed into the public space, it was in the accompaniment of males, or through mechanisms of regulation such as a designated 'woman's day'. The mall on the other hand sets out to *attract* the woman shopper-stroller (strolling is an integral element of the mall-shopping experience). Enhanced security, for instance, is meant to ensure that women strollers feel more comfortable here.

The mall marks a *pedestrianization of* space. Even as you enter floor plans tell you about the organization of the complex. 'Kids', 'women', 'food' are often marked on the walls or in the form of panels so that you can opt for particular areas within the complex. Instructions – 'elevator', 'stairs', 'please pay here', 'alterations', 'restrooms' – are prominently displayed, once again organizing your experience for you. The mall, while giving you the illusion of freedom, does control the route of movement.

You move between floors by escalators, elevators or stairs, but most of the time you walk. It is a walk through a series of spectacles. In hybrid malls you do not quite know when the brand-section or even the product line has ended.[10] Since there are no differentiating walls, one tends to move from men's shoes to children's shoes in the space of a few steps. Most malls therefore allocate sufficient space for walking, and walkways run across the entire complex. The crowded aisle – a feature of superstores – is a rarity. Some malls have seating at every level, a few even marked prominently, 'For Senior Citizens'.

An interesting feature of contemporary shopping in malls and superstores is the emphasis on *cleanliness*. The ethos of security, freedom to walk without being obstructed, accosted or having to dodge vehicles is heightened by the sense of hygiene, safety (fire extinguishers for example) and cleanliness. This marks the mall and the superstore as distinct from the market area of the city.

The mall erases or collapses the merging of the natural and the human that marks the traditional city (trees and buildings, animals and humans). The controlled environs of the mall secure it from stray animals (a common feature of the Indian street). Plant life is strictly limited to specific areas, and there are a few examples of the potted fern or small plant. But by and large it is clear of any botanical or zoological elements.

The mall is a good example of the *globalization of culture*. Products and brands from various places, cultures and communities are under one (large) roof.[11] In an earlier age vendors would wander around with products they had themselves made. This gave way to the retail store that stocked products from a few companies. In a mall the company itself has an outlet. The mall also represents globalization through another mechanism. Local festivals and events are given special importance within the world of the mall. Festivals become the occasion, in fact, for greater consumption. Celebrations of festivals are linked to consumption and fashion ('trendy'). We see special offers, decorations, even traditional décor (lamps and lighting) for Diwali in most malls. It is a space of paradox where McDonald's or Reebok offers Diwali specials, a token gesture of global firms at assimilating local cultures into their sales fabric. Indianization of global products and the globalization of an Indian festival/event is the central paradox of the shopping mall.

However, such a discourse of festivals and consumption often highlights the tensions between tradition and globalizing/consumerist modernity. *The Hindu* asked its readers to respond to the question 'Are festivals all about lavish spending?' Readers writing in were unanimous in stating that festivals were about 'preserv[ing] customs', 'upliftment of society' while mourning the materialist culture of the present day (Metroplus *The Hindu*, 9 October 2006: 3). Clearly the dilemma between consumer globalization and tradition weighs on people.

This globalization of culture defines the *reshaping of public space* in the city. The new cosmopolitan lifestyles, represented in the cosmopolitan commodity culture, now demand new kinds of spaces that reflect global diversity, product range and cultures. Uncle Sam stares out from American brands and posters, even as advertisements use both (global/globalizing) English and the local languages. The mix of local architecture with the global chrome-and-glass one suggests such a redefining of public space. Shop assistants greet you in both traditional Indian style (with a 'namaste') as well as in the American mode ('how may I help you?').[12]

The mall is also hybrid in another sense: it is a space of/for shopping and of social interaction. It is not uncommon to see the mall's spaces transformed into spaces of youth culture, with youngsters meeting friends for an evening (popularly, 'hanging out'). The space of the mall, apparently dedicated to shopping, is a space of leisure and entertainment. They become the equivalent of the parks and other public spaces. Thus Hyderabad Central's tag line is 'eat, shop, celebrate'. The last has little to do with shopping per se. The very act of cruising the mall is a celebration of leisure. Play areas for kids, movie screens and 'games zones' are common features of the mall, built on the assumption that people may visit not necessarily to shop but to relax.

Hybridity here has spatial equivalents. The mall is a space where various spaces are collapsed:

- the picnic spot
- the romantic spot
- the public park
- the shopping area
- the relaxation/leisure space

This mixture of spaces – of which, it must be reiterated, consumption is only one space – is what makes the shopping mall unique. As Meaghan Morris has pointed out, it is not shopping that defines the mall, but the unique sense of place that it generates (Morris 2004).

The mall is a *uniformly hybrid* space where the mixes of registers and structures is the same everywhere. Glass surfaces, vinyl and wood, well-maintained floors and walls, seating arrangements, entry and exit points, horticultural arrangements, music and announcements (of special offers, location of specific stores or products), carefully located art works and vibrant colours are common features of most malls. It is also uniform in another sense: the mall, especially in India, is basically a space of multinational products and commodities. A website www.mallhimall.com provides information about shopping malls/plazas in India. It lists the following: AEZ Vaishali (Ghaziabad), Ansal Plaza (New Delhi), The Centrestage Mall (Noida), East Delhi Mall (Ghaziabad), Shipra Mall (Ghaziabad) and Supertech Shoprix (Noida). The stores common to these malls are: Barista, Café Coffee Day, McDonald's, Pizza Hut (or Pizza Corner). In addition, Music World, Adidas, Lee Cooper, Reebok are stores in most malls.

Leisure and Recreation

The mall is a space of leisure and recreation, while also being a shopping area. In fact it could be argued that shopping is only one of the several purposes of a mall, and leisure is central to its very structure, style and organization.

Leisure shopping, as some social studies have termed it, is about 'pleasure shopping for nonessentials' (Horner and Swarbooke 2005: 250). A stroll through the mall, which might lead to actual purchases, is about the pleasure of the stroll, of spectacle and secure environment. Leisure shopping often includes the following elements:

- the trip to the mall
- the company of friends (sometimes family)
- visual pleasures (of displays)
- a meal
- a movie or games

Leisure shopping areas thus offer not only branded clothes but also restaurants, movie houses, games and entertainment areas in a seamless manner. The constant piped music is part of the superstore/mall's attempts to ensure that we see it as a space of relaxation and leisure. Game zones, kids' play areas and entertainment are all accounted for, so that the space becomes an area of leisure.

One of the best examples of leisure shopping is the airport mall. Places like Dubai generate vast profits not only from airline operations but from leisure shopping (it had a turnover of $590 million in 2005, with 35,600 transactions per day). Almost every airport in the world offers a shopping area integrated into the infrastructure. Large airports like Houston International (Houston, Texas) are less like airports than shopping areas, with wide, sweeping paths connecting shops – and designated areas and entry points into boarding zones – and entertainment spots. Bahrain airport, like others, has many levels of shopping. Passengers waiting for connections can combine travel with leisure shopping. This is non-utility shopping: no one makes a trip to the airport to shop, you shop at the airport when you have time to kill between flights. This form of leisure shopping is a key aspect of contemporary shopping culture, even though India is only now opening up to the idea. In fact, according to Nupur Chakraborty and others, airport retailing in India is about to expand, with an eye on the 2010 Commonwealth Games (<http://www.imagesretail.com/cover_story_dec06.htm> 15 March 2007).

> The mall is a hyperreal, ahistorical, secure, postmodern-secular, uniform space of escape that takes the streets of the city into itself in a tightly controlled environment where time, weather, season do not matter and where the 'natural' is made through artificial lighting and horticulture, and ensuring that this public space resembles the city but offers more security and choice.

The Other Side of the Mall

However, it is not that the mall is exclusively a producer's 'design'. Undoubtedly, the organization of consumption for profits is the key structural and ideological feature (we can even call it 'intention') of the mall. And yet the space of the mall is modified and appropriated by the shoppers-strollers for purposes other than what the mall may have intended. For example, the mall could be very well a place used for youths' romantic trysts that have nothing to do with shopping. While the trysts may enable the consumption of entertainment (the cinema) and food (the restaurant) they may not be about acquisition of products and goods. Then, older people may respond to malls as places to relax in and watch people rather than as shopping sites. That is, for the older people the controlled environments and safety present a world with fewer dangers than the public space of the city.

Hybridity is also a paradox where contradictory elements negotiate. In the case of consumption and consumerism in India, one is struck by the discourses of modernity (coded as Westernization) and tradition. Tradition, as we saw in the case of clothing and food products above, is posited as a counter to modernity and fast foods. What is interesting is the way in which tradition and traditional forms of cooking itself becomes 'modernized' and made available as ITC's Kitchens of India. This characterizes much of the circuit of consumption, where globalization and westernization are to be contested through a revival of traditional forms, even as traditional forms themselves try and get globalized.

Arvind Singhal in an essay on rediff.com, dated 17 March 2005, points out several disconcerting and less-glamorous features of India's mall culture. Tenants (those who have purchased floor space and set up shops in malls) complain that people do not actually buy. Local retailer tenants who have moved from the high street of the town do not find it easy to corner customer loyalty. A central problem of the mall, according to Singhal, is the very nature of the mall. Most people visit malls for food and a movie (malls integrated into multiplexes are common now). Thus shopping is *not* central to the mall visit. The uniformity of the mall means that the retailer has to create a distinctive identity for himself/herself.

What we have learnt so far:

- The circuit of consumption includes representation, identity, production and consumption.
- The act of consumption cannot be separated from the packaging, branding and media representations of the product.
- Consumption also includes the spaces where products are displayed and sold.
- Malls are sites of spectacle and illusion, secure places organized around maximizing conditions for consumption.

The culture of consumption is thus a complex negotiation between the discourses generated by brands, consumer studies and builds on the imagined happiness to be achieved through consumption. The discourses and narratives also organize the experience of consumption through the space of the mall.

Spaces of Consumption II: Online Shopping

The first set of things one notes about online consumption includes:

- The emphasis is on *easy* buying processes (at one click, using your app);
- The emphasis is on *easy*-returns (on most products), with door-pick up of the product you wish to return;
- The loss of the *tactile* component to shopping, since you cannot handle the product before you buy it, and the consequent dominance of the visual component.

Online shopping, as Amazon offers it, is a 'convenient, fast and secure way' to 'search, browse, compare offers and shop online quickly and easily, at anytime from anywhere.

Three notable aspects of online shopping deserve attention:

- The organization of choice
- The organization of easy-ness
- The organization of risk

The Organization of Choice

Myntra declares: '2,00,000+ styles and 1000+ bestselling brands'. Amazon describes itself as a 'customer centric company', a 'place where people can come to find and discover virtually anything they want to buy online'.

Online shopping and its option of examining comparative pricing and offers remains one of its key attractions. 'Choice' now is not simply the choice of styles and brands but the price range, delivery time and ease of shopping offered by the various portals.

The organization of choice is marked by two specific features in online shopping:

(a) Decisional interference, wherein the predictive nature of Amazon or any portal tells us what we could *possibly* be seeking by finishing our query for us and thus determines our choices. For example, when I start typing in 'Green' in the search box on Amazon, I have the following options to complete the search query:

   Green tea in All Departments
   Green tea in Gourmet and Speciality Foods
   Green tea in Health and Personal Care
   Green tea in Kitchen and Home
   Green tea for weight loss
   Green tea bags
   Green tea coffee bean extract
   Green tea maker
   Green screen

   (www.amazon.in/?tag+googhydrabk-21&ref_=pd_mn_ABKror1112)

   The data unfolding in the box and the dropdown menu is the organization of my choices and more importantly of my desires because I am given these options even before I had decided what I might want. These are also not necessarily the choices I wish to make, but the choices others have made, and are now being offered to me.

(b) The appropriation of data from my searches and purchases in order to
   i) Offer the same to other online buyers
   ii) Offer it to me the *next* time I go online because the system has now begun shortlisting my preferences and tastes

The Organization of Easy-ness

Given the rise of app-cultures whether in hiring taxi services or purchasing products, the key feature of online shopping might be said to be the organization of easy-ness.

Several aspects of the easy-ness of online shopping draw our attention:

- The absence of physical movement in terms of *going* to a mall and *walking* through rows of shops
- The absence of tactility: no 'trying-on' or handling of the product one is considering buying
- Home delivery mechanisms ensure that you never have to leave the comfort of your home in order to shop
- No discussions with the sales-person about the pros and cons of the product
- No waiting in queues to pay: just one click would do, especially if you are a registered user-consumer on say Amazon.
- The customization and personalization of searches online.

Online shopping is projected more as a matter of play than a chore, an easy, relaxing process that does not involve waiting in queues, looking for trial rooms, rude salespersons, among others.

The sense of play and simplification is central to online shopping.

It also alters the scope of social interaction that has traditionally been the locus of shopping. This includes:

- The absence of discussions with the sales person about your tastes or preferences, unless one chooses to phone in

- The absence of bargaining with the sales persons
- The absence of advice-seeking at the place of the sale

What we notice, therefore, is the privatization of a previously social process of shopping.

> Online shopping converts the physical and social process of shopping into a personal and private process, even as it replaces the tactile component with the visual component.

The Organization of Risk

Online shopping entails some risk, and all online portals draw our attention, as a result to, the returns policy ('Hassle-free 30 day returns and exchanges', says Myntra). The risk elements include the probability of losing money, the probability of the product not performing satisfactorily, and the product might be harmful to you (Wann-Yih Wu and Ching-Ching Ke 2015).

The organization of this sense of risk requires several measures on the part of online dealers:

- Secure servers for financial transactions
- A clear commitment to returns policy
- The development of trust.

Brand-building is no different in the online world and the above three factors remain the cornerstone of the shopping experience with particular brands such as Amazon or Myntra.

But the organization of risk also entails the organization of feedback mechanisms, advice, the community of sellers and buyers and a careful regulation of the rhetoric of sellers and buyers. Discussion boards on eBay offer user-feedback on products and sellers listed on the portal. Site policies ensure that offensive materials are not posted in order to lure some consumers. eBay for example, prohibits listing of

- items bearing symbols of the Nazis, the SS, or the KKK, including authentic German WWII memorabilia such as Olympic medals that bear such marks
- Music or films that promote hatred and racial supremacy
- Holocaust denial books

- Crime scene photographs
- Morgue shots
- Letters and artworks from notorious murderers
- Electric chairs and related capital punishment items

  (http://pages.ebay.in/help/policies/offensive.html)[13]

Here, eBay seeks to organize risk and feedback mechanisms in ways that prevent social unhappiness over matters like race and the Holocaust.

> Online shopping portals even as they emphasize easy-ness have to develop the same, if not greater, levels of trust in the consumers. This means putting in place mechanisms to regulate the possible risk factors that consumers notice about the process but also to prevent social ill-will in terms of racist representations.

---

1. Discourses of branding, lifestyle, social mobility and class are common to the culture of the mall and tele-shopping, as Judi Cook demonstrates (2000).
2. However, there has also been a resistance to the burgeoning of malls. For example, gopetition.com, an online petition forum has a petition (created by Madhu Ahuja, 3 June 2006) titled 'No more shopping malls in India'. It states that with increased costs of living, education, medical and maintenance require more money for households. Public amenities and agricultural reforms are more needed than malls. One can sign the petition at this site (<http://www.gopetition.com/no-more-shopping-malls-in-India.html>).
3. John Urry writing on the tourist argues that to be 'in attendance at the "court of commodities"' is to assert one's existence and to be recognized as a citizen in contemporary society – as a consumer (1990: 149).
4. It has been argued that any cultural-anthropological study of consumption has to account for globalization *and* vice versa (Appadurai 1996).
5. For a study of such indigenization of a transnational product within local contexts see Paige MacDougall's fascinating essay 'Transnational Commodities as Local Cultural Icons: Barbie Dolls in Mexico', *Journal of Popular Culture* 37.2 (2003): 257–75.
6. An interesting phenomenon has been observed in the USA. Indian immigrants try to assimilate into their new culture by adopting American style clothing and consumer culture. They spend far less on Indian ethnic wear, for instance. Later, as their confidence and stability increases they spend more on Indian ethnic products and clothes. For a study see Rajagopalan (2005).

7. Globally informed patterns of consumption are also, incidentally, problematically linked with nationalist concerns and ideologies. Frequently the debates about Western fashion and leisure are centred around the woman – who is constructed as the marker of 'Indian' tradition, and whose adoption of Western clothing and practices (like pub visits or discos) is seen as a betrayal of India itself. Witness the frequent right-wing outbursts against Western apparel fashions among women. For a localized study of the gendered debates about consumption in the age of globalization see Lukose (2005) .
8. Critics have pointed out that the spectacle of the mall had its origins in the visual culture of the panoramas of the nineteenth century (Gibian 1997).
9. Meaghan Morris does use the term 'utopian' to describe the world of the mall (2004).
10. Hybrid malls are a mix of a mall and a multi-brand super store on the higher levels.
11. Global forces, Peter Jackson (2004) suggests in what is a highly questionable argument, are 'domesticated' by local cultures through contests over consumption.
12. The truly hybrid nature of the speech registers, commodities displayed, architecture and discourses is, incidentally, located in a parallel discourse the world over – and India is no exception – about purity and tradition often raised by right-wing and reactionary forces.
13. Michele White has noted eBay's heteronormative stance, and its attempt to excise gay representations on its site (2010).

5

Cultures of Memory

Central to Cultural Studies' examination of everyday life, the links between culture and power, questions of identity and representation is the role of memory in the making of meaning for individuals, communities and cultures as a whole. This chapter studies cultures of memory using one case study, the Indian Memory Project.

Memory studies probes the modes of memory-making, at individual and social/collective levels. After the work of Maurice Halbwachs (1995), we know that what and how any individual remembers is dependent upon the culture and environment of that individual. Personal and collective memories intersect, in other words.

Memory studies tells us that memory, individual and collective, relies on representation. Cultural Studies is interested in memory as cultural practice and involves examining

- representation in memorial projects,
- the controls asserted over materials of memory,
- the modes of archivisation (principles of collection, selection, editing, sequencing, for instance),
- the access, retrieval and modes of/rights of/authority over interpretation,
- memory as a social communicative device that links people together.

All of these may be subsumed under the large category, 'the politics of memory'.

Sites, Terms and Conditions

All memory requires a narrative and therefore language. For memories to be recognized as memory it requires the putting into language of some kind, even when we are recalling our own experiences. Needless to say, much of this language of memory that even the individual needs and uses, comes from the social milieu.

Memory is *constructed* out of personal experience and a language in which that experience might be made available to us. It is here that CS makes its crucial political intervention. If memory is constructed for consumption at a later date, then we need to examine the ways in which the past and the experiences from that past are being represented. CS assumes that some experiences are marginalized in favour of others.

Memory is mediated by the modes of archiving, technologies of representation and the modes of recall.

i) Public memorials and cenotaphs, audio tapes and CDs, oral materials (interviews), folk and popular culture practices like songs, official history texts are devices that construct memory.
ii) Personal diaries, individual memories and family albums also constitute a different, perhaps more subjective, form of memory-making.

For CS the intersection of this latter with more 'objective' memory materials like in (i) are worthy of examination.

In terms of public memory, we remember, for example, the events of the Freedom Struggle through the patriotic songs, the annual 15 August/26 January celebrations, the Republic day floats, among others, all of which are public devices of recall. Annual memorial exercises recalling dead leaders constitute another mode. Statues of heroes, leaders and significant historical figures make icons of the dead and constitute a material mode of memory-making. For CS the politics behind the choice of particular figures – in recent times we have had debates around Veer Savarkar and Vallabhbhai Patel, the remains of Bahadur Shah Zafar – is less about the figures themselves than their appropriation into public and national memory that needs to be studied.

Memory is a construction, and involves the use of representation to capture and communicate a past experience.

Theorists of memory examine the complex connections between memory and history, often treating the former as a counter to the sweeping, 'macro' tendencies of history writing. Thus the memory of a family house in a village might actually offer a counter to the larger history of the village, or offer insights that the sweep of historical narrative might omit.

Conditions of production and consumption of memory are known as 'regimes of memory' (Radstone and Hodgkin 2003). The regimes of memory would include the conditions of access to and circulation of say a family history and its relationship with History. In other cases, studies of regimes of memory would pay attention to the values placed upon specific groups of people and their experiences. For instance, in the case of the collective memory of India's freedom struggle, an entire school of historians – the Subaltern Studies collective of the 1990s – argued that histories (a form of memory-making) had

- Focused on upper caste/upper class experiences of the movement
- Ignored the tribal and peasant rebellions

Only certain kinds of resistance were represented in the memorialization of the past (in school textbooks, museums, histories of the movement). This means, very simply, the experiences of tribal groups or peasant groups in their engagement with the anti-colonial struggle were not deemed worthy of remembering. Memorials built for 'freedom fighters' were forms of representation that made some people heroes and icons. The process of memorialization erased from public/collective memory the valour and stories of, say, Birsa Munda, Jhalkaribai and the Santal rebellions in favour of Gandhi, Rani Lakshmibai and the Congress party.

For CS memory studies enables the field to ask the following questions:

- How does the community or nation's past come to us?
- How is a memory sequence of events organized so that some events get highlighted?
- What uses are these memories put to in the present?
- Are personal records and family albums equally valid as sources of memory as official documents?
- Are oral histories (an important source of memory) recorded and edited to suit the purpose of the interviewer?
- Does a community own its memories as 'ethnic property'?
- Does individual and subjective memory run counter to 'official' memory?

As should be obvious what CS is interested in is the present political and ideological contexts in which the past is *represented* and *consumed*. Conditions of memorializing and recall are both equally important for CS.

Memory can be hegemonic when some aspects of the past become dominant in the public mind while others are marginalized.

One only has to look at the debates over school textbooks to understand this: should Muslims be represented as invaders? Should tribals be represented as the original inhabitants? Should equal space be given to Dalit and upper-caste freedom fighters? Is Gandhi's train journey in Africa that led to his determination to fight racism to be given more importance than Ambedkar's train journey wherein the future Constitution-maker understood the need to be silent about his caste identity?

What we have learnt so far:

- Memory requires representation.
- Memory is about conditions of production of memory and conditions of reception of that memory, or what is called 'regimes of memory'.
- Memory can be hegemonic where some experiences of the past are less remembered (or not at all) and others constantly remembered.
- The control over memory is what every community, nation and culture fights over: it is as much the content of memory as the systems of production.

In 2010, Anusha Yadav, a photographer, book designer and archivist trained at the National Institute of Design, Ahmedabad, founded the Indian Memory Project, or IMP, an 'online, curated, visual and oral-history based archive that traces a personal history of the Indian Subcontinent, its people, cultures, professions, cities, development, traditions, circumstances and their consequences'.[1] It archives family and school photographs, letters, records and such, donated by individuals and families. The works are available in open access. The archives contain fascinating material of public personalities as well as complete unknowns. Thus, we have a portrait, by a family member, of Gyan Singh, the first Indian to lead an expedition to Mount Everest, or personal recollections from individuals such as Radha Nair's account of her parents. There are photographs of the pre-Independence era, from families now in Pakistan.[2]

IMP offers us many opportunities to examine the regimes of memory in contemporary times.

The Production of Memory

As noted earlier, memory projects often make use of personal memory to generate, add to or subvert 'official' or collective memory. IMP offers us the personal as a supplement to the official History we know, but does so in interesting ways.

That photographs are powerful visual means of evoking memory is not something we need to examine – since it is now a truism. But there are aspects of IMP's artefacts that bear investigation.

Sense or Affective Memory

The photographs in IMP are all personal artefacts, having remained within the family's possessions for years and therefore, by definition, unexposed to the public gaze.

These photographs function as modes of affective memory. For members of the family these photographs generate a sensation of their past. Take the case of Veena Sajnani as documented in the IMP, uploaded by her niece. The visual shows Veena in a swimsuit and as a contestant (eventual winner) of the 1970 Miss India contest. Under the photograph is the caption:

> My aunt, Veena Sajnani, winner of the Miss India Crown, Bombay, Maharashtra 1970.

Further below the photograph there is the following introductory statement preceding the story of Veena Sajnani:

> The following text is the story my Bua, (father's sister) Veena Sajnani, narrated to me while flipping through her photo albums.

There is a striking paragraph in the subsequent text:

> Before the day of the pageant, we were asked to come to the *Times of India* office terrace (parent company of *Femina*) with

> a swim-suit and be photographed in it, because in those days, judges looked at pictures instead of the actual girls in swim-suits; and we were saved the embarrassment of coming out on stage in swim-suits. Instead, during the interval, the judges came backstage to check us out and since it was dark they had flashlights and our photos in their hands! Yes, it was very funny indeed. We all giggled through the ordeal but in retrospect it was better than walking out half naked under full lights- a very scary prospect to say the least.

The staged *photograph*, the visual component of the Sajnani artefact, of the swimsuit-clad Sajnani is evocative in the sense of it being a seductive photograph, even titillating. But the text running underneath it generates a different 'sense' of the visual.

I propose that the visual + text combine generates more than a common memory.[3] The visual + text offers up

- a *historical* moment/event: the caption under the photograph gives us date, place, event.
- a *personal* affective or sense memory of Sajnani herself recalling the momentous occasion, the embarrassment and the anxieties of the event.

Sense memory is affective memory, and is more than just the representations of the events: it brings back into the present the very sense and emotional aspects of that event.

The visual and its caption by placing a temporal limit (1970, Bombay, etc.) imposes a distance from the present and perhaps a toning down of the affective effects of the moment. This toning down and distancing is what the text under the photograph seeks to balance. The aunt says:

> And I will always remember them [Persis Khambatta and Meher Mistry] fondly for this adventure.

What is being foregrounded is not thought memory but sense and affective memory here. Jill Bennet writing about traumatic memory says: 'The art of sense memory, then, does not make a claim to represent originary trauma – the cause of the feeling – but to enact the state or experience of posttraumatic memory' (35).

I extend Bennett's formulation to propose that even joyous moments recalled, as in the case of Sajnani, bring back *affective* and not common memory. She recalls the embarrassment and anxiety of appearing in a swimsuit (in the text) which, when juxtaposed with the visual, forces us to concede that the staged nature of the photograph is a reminder not only of her triumph but also of a certain *sensation* of embarrassment, of a *sense* of awkwardness and a sensation of triumph. What links Sajnani now with this past of hers is a recall of the *embodied* embarassments and thrills.

The memory here is sense and affective memory that supplements the official account of the 1970 Miss India contest whose 'history' will simply capture the winners and losers, but not the emotions of any of the participants. The photograph and the caption constitute this official memory of the event, but Sajnani's 'story-behind-the-photograph' offers us the sensations of walking the ramp before the judges, the anxiety of knowing the rankings, the embarrassment of wearing certain costumes, the gratitude for specific kindnesses and the thrill of victory.

Sense memory here enables us to witness, via the visual + verbal text, the events of the 1970 beauty pageant. We are, however, invited to not only *see* Sajnani and the event but to *feel* her sensations and affective state. We are invited to be moved by the artefact.

In the case of the IMP's personal memory projects, therefore, we can see how the production of affective and sense memories of the Partition (from which several photographs, letters and accounts are uploaded on the IMP website) constitute the individuals for us not only as protagonists of a historical event or age but also as individuals who *felt*. The return to affective and sense memories that IMP highlights cautions us against the 'dryness' of official history. It also serves as a 'smaller' history of the Miss India event, one where we have individuals with feelings rather than mere 'participants', 'losers' and 'winners'.

The regime of memory that IMP utilizes is one of sense or affective memory rather than official and objective ones. It foregrounds the subjectivity (defined here as the sense of selfhood, the sense of being a human, and most importantly of being embodied) of individuals, and tells us that history can also be viewed and recalled in terms of what subjects *felt* at that time. The regime of personal sense memory here resists incorporation into the regime of official and objective memory. It is not the final triumph that Sajnani records but the process, fraught with dramatic tension and deep anxieties.

What we have learnt so far:

- Representations of some events prove inadequate to memory.
- Sense or affective memory seeks to evoke the sensations and emotions (whether traumatic or triumphant) of the events.
- Personal memory projects such as the ones IMP archives are essentially projects about sense memory.
- Sense memory as generated by these projects offer a different, sometimes alternate and even subversive, history from the official History by showing us thinking and feeling individuals.
- Such a personal history and subjective regime of memory can thus be used to resist incorporation into official History.

The Materiality of Memory

As should be clear from the IMP archives, all artefacts are coded for the digital domain.

What is also important to note in these new cultures of memory is that the digital domain allows a whole new shareable and transmissible *materiality* to memories. Family photographs, facsimiles of historical records, but also oral traditions and stories that IMP archives constitute a process of mobile memories where the digital format enables materiality to be shared and transmitted across zones, people, and national borders.

This suggests a transcultural memory itself, made possible by the digital domain. Memory theorist Astrid Erll (2011) has proposed that such a wandering of carriers, media, contents, forms and practices of memory constitutes a transcultural memory but one that is made possible through the *travels* of memory across spaces. Individuals who possess these memories in the IMP constitute embodiments of memories. When they move into the digital domain in the form of 'my grandfather's photograph' or 'our family's home' we can treat the individuals or families as carriers of memory, where the carrying is *not* restricted to the corporeality. In other words, I am proposing here that the carriers of memory that Erll sees as central to memory work are corporeal entities but also *virtual*.

Memory travels through carriers such as people, media, content, forms and practices that include people, the specific medium, letter or diary or photograph (as form) and practices such as annual memorial days.

Travelling memories involve the use of multiple media formats in the digital domain. Sound and visual texts remain the cornerstone of the IMP archives. Without the provision of transcoding (the process of shifting data from one form into another – such as the analog to the digital) carriers of memory would not acquire the reach we see here.

Yet, what is interesting in these new cultures of memory is that digitization calls attention to the *materiality of memories* when the IMP archive shows us scanned originals of letters, passports, photographs and such. The materiality of memory draws our attention to

- the mortality of the protagonists in the story.
- the mediated nature (paper, photographs, sound records) of the memory of the people.
- the fragility of the medium through which the memory is made available to us.

The production of memory therefore is also about the *modes* of producing and reinforcing memories: the medium of the memory is crucial to how it can be transmitted and shared.

It is brought home to us in the virtual that somewhere the fragile, musty and brittle material paper actually exists. I therefore do not see the new cultures of memory exemplified in IMP as doing away with the material but rather as emphasizing the materiality, especially the mortality of materiality. It is in the interstices of the faded, dog-eared, blurred and yellowed photographs or papers that I recognize the *mortality* of both, the people therein 'captured', and the material that seeks to immortalize them.[4]

What we have learnt so far:

- Personal memory projects also require a medium.
- The nature of the medium determines the degree of transmissibility of memory.
- The arrival of the digital has enabled a greater dissemination of memory.
- Ironically, in the virtual domain we are made aware of the materiality of memory and the mortality of the protagonists of the story being memorialized in the form of frayed paper and faded photographs.

Personal Memory and Knowledge

The IMP insists that the guardian or owner of the artefact has some measure of knowledge about the people in the photograph. The terms and conditions of submission state:

- Please do ensure you *know* of the people in the photograph, their professions, about their lives, the location, the approximate year, even if not exact. Asking relatives, family and friends always offers new information. Photographs could be of your home, a personal contribution to society, your parents, relatives, friends, associates, extended family, grandparents and/or higher in ancestry.
- Please caption the visuals carefully with as much accuracy as possible.
- FOR PHOTOGRAPHS Names, Approximate/Exact year the image was taken, location in picture, profession, alternate professions, religion (if not obvious) and whatever other history/and details of their lives you'd like to add.
- FOR LETTERS/DOCUMENTS Names, Approximate/Exact year the letter was written, other history/and details of their lives you'd like to add. For letters, it is mandatory to know of the sender and the receiver.
- The Photographs/Letters can be from anywhere in the world, as long as it has a connection to the people and/or places in South Asian Indian Subcontinent.

- **Narratives/Stories about the photographs and letters are mandatory.**

(emphasis in original)

The guidelines, as we can see, insist on historical record being supplied with each artefact. The onus on providing 'accurate' knowledge is that of the owner. Further, the instructions make it mandatory to offer a narrative along with the artefact. In other words the owner of the artefact has to produce

- an original story.
- an explanation and explication of the incident/event documented in the artefact.

This is the production of a regime of memory as well, one where the owner of the artefact contextualizes the artefact, giving it a history, location and cause-effect sequence.

Memory, as commentators inform us, constitute us as *subjects*. Our identities are embedded in what we recall *of* ourselves. Thus, our knowledge of ourselves is also founded, at least partially, on the memories we possess, and share.

What IMP proposes is to offer memory as a way of knowledge-making on a larger (that is more than the personal scale). Individual stories, it suggests, contribute to our *knowledge* of the historical past in some way or other. In this IMP shifts the focus away from History as objective knowledge or commentary toward the anecdote as

- constitutive of individual subjects.
- enabling a knowledge of a larger History.

Memory projects constitute us as subjects.

In the next section I address the question of a collective sense of subjectivity or identity as a result of projects such as the IMP.

What we have learnt so far:

- Artefacts of personal memory in the digital medium are linked with other such artefacts.
- These artefacts with their narratives offer a source of knowledge.
- Memory constitutes us as subjects, offering us a sense of our personal and collective history

The Consumption of Memory

The IMP homepage warns us:

- Copyright belongs to the guardian of the photograph
- Pictures & Letters CANNOT be used for any reason whatsoever, without prior permission.
- Any unauthorised use will lead to prompt legal action.

It should be clear that the right to the artefact is with the (oddly named) 'guardian', one who is, we may safely assume, a family member or trustee. Under the 'terms and conditions' the project states: 'The "Uploader"/"Sender" must be the guardian/owner of the photograph and letters'. Yet, the circulation of the digital version of the artefact does more than offer us glimpses of the past. The question of 'ownership' of memory here offers interesting prospects for analysis.

From Personal to Cultural and Collective Memory

The visuals and voices on IMP not only become 'public', they transform the way we as individuals come to our 'own' family or personal history when we see these responses. People writing in with more photographs and links, information and recollections that link with our own means that we view our grandparents' photographs and lives differently – not simply as 'my' grandparents alone but as people who shared lives, spaces and belief systems with several *others*. It suddenly strikes me that the person I saw only in terms of 'my' or at the most 'my family' is one of many, located amongst others. This shifts, I propose, the very nature of our perceptions of these individuals. The multiple formats of the digital domain mediate my experience of these people in the archive. To phrase it differently, our minds actualize the memories we see on IMP.

IMP enables a shift of our memory and perception of our grandparents or older members of the family as having been a part of a larger community. They cease to be simply, 'my grandfather' and instead becomes 'my grandfather' as a representative of a generation.

Mnemonic forms – symbols, icons – that enable repetition across contexts constitute an important aspect of travelling memory (Erll). What IMP does is to offer the space of the digital as the space of such repetition across multiple contexts. With no border restrictions, passports or territoriality, the digital archive of memories is at once untethered and local, global and personal. Icons such as the freedom movement or school buildings (which seem to be a particular favourite among IMP contributors) are repeated from Old Delhi to nineteenth century Madras, from pre-Independence days to the present. Ferguson College, Madras Christian College, Victoria Terminus and other such icons serve as mnemonic forms for digital recall on the IMP.

All personal memory morphs into cultural memory. Cultural memory, as Marita Sturken defines it, is a

> field of cultural negotiation through which different stories vie for a place in history ... a field of contested meanings in which [people] interact with cultural elements to produce concepts of the nation, particularly in events of trauma, where both the structures and the fractures of a culture are exposed. (1997: 1–3)

Cultural memory is usually associated with cultural objects that exist outside formal – official, governmental, corporatized – historical accounts and histories, mainly within private collections and objects. Experiences of schooling, growing up, clothing trends that we see shared in the IMP collections means that these experiences, although not always the same or even remembered the same way, now contribute to our overall sense of a period, fashion, belief, practice or custom. This is the intertwining of individual and collective memory that we see in IMP's archives. We imagine eras and belief systems that exist outside our immediate perceptions or practices through these collections, drawing links, noting parallels and forging alliances.

In IMP the individual postcard or photograph refuses to remain within the bounds of a family's story. Instead

- it situates the family's or individual's story within other stories,
- it calls for and provides links to other stories.
- it offers personalized but shared accounts of historical events.
- it enlarges the sense of the events as something several people experienced *and* recall.

This is how a collective memory is generated: through the *sharing* of personal stories and memories of the historical event.

Cultural memory is a collection of individual/personal memories and stories that often deliver different perceptions of the same event(s), thus bringing home to us the fact that our sense of the past can always conflict with or contest somebody else's sense of the same.

In doing so, it is possible that we are able to glimpse 'other' stories of the past. Thus, for families from the pre-Independence days the Raj meant something very different, and these memories (which we can see in several photographs from IMP) might be at odds with the official narrative of racial suppression and subjugation. What an online archive like IMP does is to make these conflicting narratives part of a wide open database of possible interpretations. History after SPARROW and IMP must always be seen as a set of contested and multiple interpretations to which – and this is important – all of us can contribute minus official sanction. A miniscule amount of agency and freedom thus comes to the common reader through such digital projects as IMP. I see IMP and its contributors as people who are not mere consumers of knowledge handed down but as producers of knowledge. They contribute to a more open, less censored, knowledge base. In the new cultures of memory this act of archiving memories produces a whole new ethos, belonging and identity, and the regime of memory has moved away from the personal to the collective and cultural.

Cultural memory such as that generated by the IMP offers us counter-histories, different perceptions of the events of the past, so that the meanings of the past are constantly under scrutiny, and need to be negotiated.

What we have learnt so far:

- The dissemination and additions to the memory of an individual *story* slowly coalesces into a community's shared memory, what might be thought of as cultural memory.
- Cultural memory resists official History, and even within itself can offer us different versions of the events as individuals remember them.
- Cultural memory of historical events that then are used to generate a sense of *collective identity* has to be negotiated – this is the politics of memory.

Memory Citizenship

Michael Rothberg and Yasemin Yildiz (2011) propose that memory has often functioned as 'ethnic property'. Migrant archives of memory, argue Rothberg and Yildiz, are multidirectional, where the migrants engage with the past and with a history and memory of which they are ostensibly *not* a part of. The archive of trauma is read from different vantage points, especially by those who are 'migrants', such as second-generation family members but also general visitors to the IMP website such as myself, to that archive. IMP makes it possible for all and sundry to become migrants to the memories of say pre-Independence India.

Memory citizenship is a process by which people and communities who are not direct recipients of a memory from their families might still participate in the act of memorialization and thus acquire a sense of citizenship.

To participate in a memory project such as the IMP from different corners of the world is to effect a community belonging. Thus Radha Nair's account of her family is situated, in this digital space, alongside that of Laxmi Murty, Anupam Mukerji, Sawant Singh, Raj Rajendra Singh, Paritosh Pathak, and others. These contributors are geographically diffused in terms of current location: Pune, Bengaluru, Mumbai, the USA, among others. It is in the space of the digital archive that a new geography of affinity is forged, linked by the theme of 'education' (this is the tag for a whole bunch of photographic records in this database).

IMP is cultural work that enables a sense of cultural insiderness to emerge through the sharing of individual memories.

IMP pulls individuals into the archive and we can, if we wish, become cultural insiders, because we are contributors, to local, community or national history. Since much of the online world of this kind (Flickr, Instagram for example) thrives on non-commercial sharing and participation we can envisage an entire community of 'Indian historians' represented in IMP. Communities of interest such as those represented in IMP are built through a sharing of virtual territory (recalling the territorial roots of community) but also through the cultural *work* we see embodied in the amount of information people collate and put online.

What I am suggesting as 'cultural work' is the 'work' of compilation and uploading enabled by digital technologies. It has three main features. It is

- recreational.
- non-commercial.
- participatory.

It is labour, but of the 'immaterial' kind (i.e., wageless) and is founded on a belief in sharing and networking. Payment is not expected except in terms of 'likes' and feedback. Communities of interest that we see in the huge responses and participation in IMP constitute a 'fun-way' of doing history where my grandpa's photograph connects me to your family and, in incremental fashion, enables both me and you to come to a shared understanding of the times they lived in. It is participatory because it is entirely 'crowd-sourced' with little or no official intervention.

The instructions on submission I have already quoted from the IMP website suggestions tell us not only about how the cultural work is to be undertaken but also about the making of histories, as already noted.

The onus here is on the significance of the particular letter or visual to the family and by extension to other participants in the project. Thus the IMP shifts the writing of history *away* from the historically significant incident or event to personally significant events and people. 'Small histories' as we can think of these materials on the IMP database is the historicizing of local and personal stories.

As already noted, many of the materials are accompanied by emotional and personal write-ups, a far cry, as we know, from the dry-as-dust History we read in books and official records. This, I suggest, is a major shift in the conceptualization of history itself: history is made of emotionally significant events and people who perhaps do not contribute to or appear in 'national histories', but have informed lives somewhere.

IMP does not suggest this writing of emotionally relevant histories that then accrete into a larger history as work. Cultural work is the *participatory* work performed by those who find meaning outside the frames of reference of standard history writing (which involves research, peer review, acceptance, publication, etc).

The cultural insiderness that this sharing produces offers a whole new way of perceiving each other, and ourselves. Cultural insiderness is the making of a *contributory history of ourselves*, sharing borders, lives and belief systems with a larger community of interest. When IMP places a condition for the selection of contributions it gestures at precisely this cultural insiderness. To quote once again a crucial point on the linkage across artefacts:

> The Photographs/Letters can be from anywhere in the world, as long as it has a connection to the people and/or places in South Asian Indian Subcontinent.

This tenuous linkage to the South Asian Indian Subcontinent offers us a map of connections outside the national histories of people, families and communities. The connection itself is often nebulous, vague and primarily personal since the materials, as noted above, are sent in because they hold emotional significance for the contributors. Cultural insiderness is the forging of such connections of memory-work.

With the cultural insiderness of the participants as they bring to IMP their personal records and data, there is a whole new sense of belonging that develops. I have already suggested that communities of interest constitute a new geography. I now want to propose that participants in the IMP are engaged in 'memory citizenship' (Michael Rothberg and Yasmin Yildiz). Performances of memory are also acts of citizenship, acts that are beyond the norms of citizenship and regardless of formal citizenship status. They define new ways of belonging. In a globalized world, to participate in a project such as IMP is to simultaneously be disaggregated from roots and origins in the physical sense but belong in the affective, mnemomic and virtual sense.

Memory citizenship is the sense of belonging emerging from this sense of emotional recall of, and emotional response to, such materials as we have discussed above. The memory citizenship of IMP is not merely tokenist or nominal. The memories produce emotions, as we can see from the responses on the website, and these make memories *material*. Memory citizenship undeniably offers a sense of belonging and attachment. Whether these are Non Resident Indians or resident ones, it is memory citizenship that brings them together in their very acts of remembering. Acts of remembering, in my reading, transform into acts of solidarity.

The Indian Memory Project enables a process of remembering so that the ordinary individual who shares personal memories is involved in generating cultural memory. New cultures of memory are new ways of belonging.

What we have learnt so far:

- The cultural work of memory-making and sharing enables a certain cultural insiderness among the viewers and uploaders.
- This is participatory work.
- When we participate in the cultural work of memory making we are also drawn into the structures of recall and hence of belonging.
- The cultural work of recall here, individually and collectively, generates a memory citizenship.

The Politics of Memory

Having examined the production and consumption of memory and noting how each has its own specific aims, processes and politics, it is now time to narrow the focus to a very particular kind of politics: of those memories that do not find a presence in the global circuits.

All studies of trauma, mourning and memory in the twentieth century have been overdetermined by the Holocaust, globally, and the Partition, locally for us in India. The Hollywoodization of the Holocaust has provided an idiom, a register and a set of words that are used globally to signify genocide.

The Holocaust has offered the world of literary-critical, psychoanalytic analysis, the basic structures of thinking about genocides in the form of trauma studies.

It is imperative that we pay attention to the films, survivor-accounts, comics, oral narratives, critical studies, museums that have showcased the Holocaust as the great genocide of the 20th century. In other words our interest lies in examining the structures of media, language, representational strategies that have ensured that the Holocaust becomes the singular noun from which *all* studies of trauma and massacre *must* begin.

On 12 April 2015 Pope Francis called the massacre of Armenians (most of them Christians) in Turkey 'genocide', exactly 100 years after the events. Turkey withdrew its Ambassador to the Vatican and immediately contested the use of the term 'genocide'. *The Hindu* (25 April 2015: 14) wrote about the commemorative gathering in the Armenian capital Yerevan:

> The patchy list of foreign dignitaries attending commemorations in Yerevan highlights the lack of international consensus over Armenia's bid to get the massacres recognised internationally as a genocide.

We have noted in the preceding sections that memories, such as of the Holocaust, in the late 20th and early decades of the 21st century are constitutive of cultural identities – and the Jews exemplify this trauma-linked identity more than any other race on earth. For us in Literary and Cultural Studies the following questions arise:

- So what of the cultural identity of those who have also experienced genocide, like the Armenians, the Tutsis or the Romanis, but whose memories are *not* part of a global memorialization project, except for a few films like *Hotel Rwanda*?
- Is the global memory project we see embodied in museums, rituals of media-hyped mourning and continued interest in particular genocides structurally iniquitous towards others?

> If memories are integral to the making of cultural identities and even citizenship of particular ethnic groups in the global comity of nations, then the proscription and exclusion of their traumatic memories of genocide automatically marginalizes them.

Assuming that an ethical turn in Literary and Cultural Studies is long overdue, in the remainder of this section we shall see how a global memory project focused on genocide and trauma might be essential to the reinvention of the Humanities itself.

Local and Embodied Genocide Memory

Memorialization begins at the local and embodied levels. Cultural traumatic memory of any tribe, ethnic group or collective requires 'carriers' (Erll 2011: 12). It requires the transition and transmission from autobiographical memory, from *embodied* memory (of surviving, starvation, pain), to its *performance* in the form of texts, icons, symbols. In short, cultural memory demands that survivors generate a language in which their pain, embodied inside them, is given a *representation*.

Individual, local and cultural memory all rely on representation (visual, verbal, oral), which begins at the level of the vernacular, the local and the particular by survivors and first generation descendants.

One of the major anxieties that ought to inform our 'sense' of Armenia and Hiroshima-Nagasaki – and to some extent Rwanda, already several decades old – whose survivors have begun to die out is precisely the impossibility of this transition being ever effected. On the other hand, we note that third generation Holocaust survivors have taken to tattooing their grandparents' concentration camp numbers on their own arms to indicate their legacy. With a hundred years gone by how many of such carriers of the Armenian massacres are alive now? This means all memory is embodied at one stage and is then mediated into performance by the carriers when they testify, write their memoirs, give interviews, etc. This transition or performance from embodied and subjective to the documentary and 'outside opens up a problem: of authenticity and authority. Mediation is always a risky act, for it determines the shape of memories that will be consumed later, well after the mediator or carrier, is dead. This poses a problem of interpretation for us, readers, if we are to see these 'texts' as direct and transparent access to historical 'facts'. As readers we have to be, of course, responsible for reading the text, but we should also be aware that we are looking at forms of narrativizing subjective memories. That is, we need to be aware of forms of memory-making, how it is produced and preserved. Given the fact that memorialization is different in different parts of the world – notice the vast gulf between 9/11 memorialization and Hiroshima's – it becomes our task to not subsume all memorialization or memory-texts under one head and instead seek differences between memory cultures. This is especially important because these memory texts are *mourning-texts* and mourning is a localized, culture-specific performance and we would be perpetuating violence when we seek to homogenize different performances of mourning under the rubric of, say, the Holocaust. This entails an examination of the various forms and contexts of technologies of media production and their reception within social structures.

However, this might end up as *localizing* cultural trauma by rooting it solely within its forms of local production and consumption. While genocide memory-making might begin at the level of the local, and if only selective genocide memories are globalized (like the Holocaust) *and* if we wish to rethink the world, we need to give the space to many such memories, taking them from the level of local and embodied to the level of the global.

> Cultures of memory, in the case of genocides, are cultures of mourning, and for any memory project this has to be accounted for at the local level – because cultures of mourning and memory are different across the world – but cannot be retained at the local level if we are to think in terms of global memory projects in which all victims must find a place.

Global Memory Projects

Even before setting out to archive global genocide memories, we need an ethics that brings the several genocides to the fore, each different, with each life grievable and recognizing the separate contexts of their deaths, while also recognizing the shared precarity of all humans. This ethics of difference, but a difference that needs to be treated as though every different life matters equally at least in the representations, demands the making of common principles of vulnerability.

Judith Butler (2004) suggests that we begin with the assumption that all humans are vulnerable. This should lead us to ask questions of the frame which helps, or hinders, us from understanding the loss of somebody else's life, even the life of the distant Other. By 'frame' I am thinking in terms of the cultural/discursive public sphere – manifest in the media, popular culture and literary texts – wherein representations initiate debates and arguments about loss, mourning and values. Butler notes that, 'there are no obituaries for the war casualties that the United States inflicts, and there cannot be' (34). If we consider the obituary as a component of the cultural/discursive public sphere in which American lives are valued higher than any other lives in the world, then it becomes incumbent to find ways and means of reconstituting this public sphere at the global level. I am proposing an ethical culturalization of the global public sphere of mourning, remembrance and grievability which can at least begin to present us other genocides and genocide memories.

> The role of media in keeping the memory of genocide is a crucial one, even when the media itself is corporatized, and its representations need to be read alongside popular cultural texts such as films, cartoons, comics and songs.

Such a culturalization around mourning and memory demands a massive shift in the Humanities. It demands that we showcase art works, literary texts and autobiographies that emerge from societies and cultures whose lives we have taken to be, thanks to the valorization of white (read: American) lives, less valuable. We can recognize that other lives, embedded in conditions of precarity greater than our own (that is, subject to starvation, torture, deprivation, death) – assuming, after Butler, that all lives share a precarity, but this precarity is differential – are precarious because of political formations of the state, economic injustice and world indifference. This also means being alert to the mediated nature of differentially valued lives and 'ways of dying' (as Rosi Braidotti put it). For example, in the heavily mediated coverage of Islamic State's beheadings or flogging in Saudi Arabia, what is lost is the operations of the material reality of Euro-American interventions in particular ways and the USA's own racialized apparatuses of civilian bombings, tortures and massacres. Since the reality of war can no longer be separated from the representations of war – thanks to embedded journalism, live coverage, etc. – American deaths rank way higher than African or Asian ones. Alongside the iconic visuals of 9/11 or the concentration camps of Nazi Germany, for example, why not also include Picasso's *Guernica* (1937), arguably the most stunning representation of the horrors of war after Francisco Goya's *The Disasters of War* (1810–1820) and the visual evidence from Abu Ghraib?

> Multimedia works of art depicting genocides from around the world, incorporated into teaching and textbooks, ensure first the visibility needed for these ethnic groups and their memories.

Susan Sontag asks in *Regarding the Pain of Others*: 'which atrocities from the incurable past do we think we are obliged to remember?' (2004: 93). Sontag catalogues in her work, the bombing of Dresden, Rwanda, Hiroshima-Nagasaki, all instances of genocidal attacks and feats of exceptional horror inflicted on civilian populations. What the Humanities demands then is a global history of trauma and hells on earth. In terms of pedagogy we need a curriculum that expands the chest of horrors documenting the ways of dying and the structures producing those ways. It requires considered critical work in the Humanities on archives of mourning from Rwanda, Armenia, Nellie, Nanking, Hiroshima-Nagasaki and Dresden. Holocaust studies cannot remain the only domain of investigation.

Having said that about an awareness of differential precarity and mediated representations of war and genocide around the world, it is also now incumbent to think in terms of the work of cultural memory. Cultural memory of trauma, has three components (adapting Jeffrey Alexander, 2004, on cultural trauma):

- the nature of pain,
- the nature of the victim, and
- the attribution of responsibility.

While it is important to understand the singularity of every life and every death what perhaps is essential is to see how their shared precarity slips into *structural helplessness* induced by political formations. African lives might be singular in each case, but what they share is structural helplessness brought on by banana republics, economic crises, socially discriminatory policies and – this is a key factor – the world's indifference (the Rwandan genocide is an excellent paradigmatic instance of this last). That is, we move from the recognition of a condition of vulnerability we all share to a condition of helplessness that is induced for some people due to human factors such as those outlined above. It is not the vulnerability and precarity we need to focus on – it is now a truism – but those structures that convert these lives into helpless lives. The Nigerian government's apparent inability to find and rescue the Boko Haram kidnapped girls would be a recent example. The nature of the victim and the nature of the pain then must be identified before we move on to the next stage: the attribution of responsibility. What a cosmopolitanization of genocide memory needs to pay attention to is the set of social, political and economic factors that enabled extermination.

> An ethical position from which to read, in CS courses, cultural texts of genocide from around the world would be the sense of shared *precarity* of all humans, followed closely by the social and economic conditions that consign some of these humans in different parts of the world to structural *helplessness*.

Christine Gerlach's massive study, *Extremely Violent Societies* (2010) while accepting the crucial role of the state in perpetrating genocides, also makes the important point that genocides are 'multi-causal' (3). Gerlach argues that without mass support, without the participation and collusion of actors from every level of society, genocides cannot be explained. Diverse social groups, for various reasons, participate, and the state is only one such formation: 'it is mass participation which often gives modern mass violence its ghastly pace and thrust and which makes [state] policies of destruction actually materialize' (3). Thus, 'governments ... devise and modify policies according to perceived public pressure and opinion' (4). Gerlach calls for attribution of responsibility for genocide to social groups and not just the state. Whether in Rwanda or Nazi Germany, if we believe Gerlach, the genocide was made possible because of the social base: the active participation of diverse social groups and formations. To take one instance of how history erases the complicity of diverse social groups in favour of state-sponsored violence, Urther Rwafa studying filmic representation of the Rwanda massacre, notes that even otherwise sensitive films like *Hotel Rwanda* fail to point to the church as one of the epicentres of the genocide, essentially therefore shying away from attributing responsibility (2010: 396). However, Rwafa agrees that the international organizations and regimes are, correctly, held accountable in the film for their indifference that exacerbated the magnitude of the massacres. One mode by which some social groups work to seek dominance over others is within national cultures of mourning, celebration and remembrance.

A global genocide memory project would include the study of

- popular cultural forms,
- art,
- survivor accounts
- critical ethnographic studies

from all over the world, brought into the CS classrooms to examine the forms of representation, the forms of media used and the power relations embodied in the cultural production of, say, a Hollywood film like *Hotel Rwanda*.

If the nation-state, as memory theorist Astrid Erll puts it, is a 'social framework of remembrance' (2011: 7) then we need to ask if remembering atrocities is a part of our social framework. If we do not include 'other' memories in national remembrance projects – from Republic Day to Martin Luther King Day – we run the risk of denying some people their memories, and consequently their presence in national archives of mourning/celebration and by extension citizenship itself. If memory theorists are right, cultural memory is inextricable from cultural identity: to deny one is to deny the other as well. If a national history refuses to produce museums of atrocities against particular groups then it not only erases its own darker history it also forces the groups to lose some part of what they are. A museum devoted to the history of its many exploitations might of course be deemed unpatriotic or anti-national but is essential as an ethical commitment to that nation's many citizens, many of whom belong to beleaguered groups. From this erasure of memory to the erasure of their cultural identity and eventually their marginalization as citizens itself, I propose perhaps provocatively, is a step: your memories are not valuable enough to be part of the national memory project because your contributions are not significant enough, and therefore you are not significant enough.

> How is the hierarchy of victims organized across the world? This question needs to be asked of slaves, Dalits, women, prisoners of war, Jews, Armenians, gypsies and others, so as to look at the forms of representation that denied these only *some* of these already oppressed groups the right to self-representation and ensured that their memories did not form part of the circuit of memory.

Alertness to shifts in social conditions – in India we can think in terms of attitudes towards migrants and minorities, for example, that might then drive state policies – is what is called for.

It is not the state policies that are the origins of genocides but the social order, and watching this order is precisely what the Humanities needs to do. The job of the Humanities in particular is to memorialize, observe and comment on – and thus call attention to – changing attitudes that could potentially become contexts for the structural helplessness of some groups. In the emergent global public sphere, as members of a global witnessing public, we move from the local to the global, reading one within the frame of the other. This means, despite and with due respect for local conditions, we frame the question of minorities, foreigners, Others, strangers in India within a history of such questions. A global genocide memory project would tell us that minoritization – the process of rendering some people into minorities, into strangers, foreigners and Others – in the world was the social context that enabled state-sponsored genocide. Now, if the nation-state is a 'social framework of remembrance' then can we envisage the world as a larger framework of remembering atrocity? Transcultural memory, writes Astrid Erll, is the refusal to bind memory to the frame of a place, a region, a social group, a religious community, or a nation (2011: 10). My term, the cosmopolitanization of genocide memory, is a part of the process Erll outlines, with the additional feature of an ethics of responding to the memory of Others.

This requires aligning memory with reflection. Remembering, claims Sontag, is an 'ethical act' (115). If this is so, then the question of compiling genocide memories opens up the ethics of memorialization. The work of *The Legacy Project* (www.legacy-project.org) and other initiatives is to open up the space for such an ethics, to provide a global history of genocide, each unique and yet all similar for the affective and reflective response they demand from us. Should genocide memory be the ethnic property of survivors and denied to others? Michael Rothberg and Yasemin Yildiz propose a memory citizenship where people can be migrants to memories of the Holocaust (2011). This means the possibility of responding to other genocide memories exists even if we have no relation to the survivors. We can become global witness citizens by migrating to the memories of Others' atrocities and histories of suffering. The larger point being made here is that a relation can always be made to come into being, if our affective, pedagogic and interpretive frames are enlarged to look beyond local genocides and discover that, like global warming, a certain universalism of trauma can also be studied.

If vulnerability is the constituent condition of all of us, genocide memories ought to be also a constituent interpretive practice in the Humanities because we are able to see erasure of memories and shifts in social order – which then produced genocide – elsewhere as potentially our conditions too. Watching the appropriation of some memories and state-sponsored but socially approved erasure of other memories need to be read as the preface to larger material effects – as a perusal of comparative histories of trauma and genocide will tell us. The Humanities needs genocide memories so that we understand the ways of dying of some humans, ways that have been produced in social contexts and in cultural discourses of demonization. To respect the genocide memory of the Other is to migrate to that memory as well, in some small way.

What we have learnt so far:

- Genocide memories need to be incorporated into CS projects so as to examine the mediated nature of these representations and cultural productions like films or biographies.
- Genocide memories are integral to the ethnic identities of communities and when we deny them these, we deny a significant aspect of how they perceive themselves.
- Genocide memories begin at local level but need to be taken into the worldwide circuit so that one event – the Holocaust – does not dominate the paradigm of analysis.
- As we account for these memories, we need to develop an ethical standpoint, of shared vulnerability, to read these films or comics.
- We need to undertake projects whereby, as we document these atrocities, we pay attention to the social conditions specific to *each* genocide even as we cast them in universal terms of suffering.

---

1. For more details, see http://www.indianmemoryproject.com/about/.
2. There are of course other such archives. One of the best known is SPARROW (acronym for Sound and Picture Archives for Research on Women), run by the Mumbai-based Tamizh short story writer, C.S. Lakshmi (pen name: Ambai), and which documents women's history in India. Sparrow's motto is 'different ways of seeing, different ways of remembering, different ways of writing history'. For more details, see http://www.sparrowonline.org/.
3. This is defined by Jill Bennett as 'not simply a form of narrative memory inherent in the individual subject but the language that enables such memory to be transmitted and easily understood' (2003: 29).

6

Cultures of Impression Management

This chapter examines the newest trend in the era of rapid digital communications: the selfie. Barack Obama, Narendra Modi, Ellen DeGeneres, the Pope, and astronaut Rich Mastracchio have all given selfies that have achieved a million+hits. But the selfie revolution is really the work of the ordinary person on the street, armed with a cellphone camera and of course a face. Driving to work, Monday morning blues, sick states, happy day, funerals and even 'chemo-states' are the subjects of selfies.[1] The phenomenon has been so successful that the *Oxford Dictionary* listed it as the 'word of the year'.

We focus here on the processes through which an individual or a group organizes the world's perception of themselves.

- The chapter does not seek to explore all the dimensions of the phenomenon of impression management, but only the selfie. Impression Management also includes status messages, FB updates, the Instagram post, Tumblr, etc.
- It treats impression management as a cultural practice.
- It examines the production and consumption of the self in the selfie.

Sites, Terms and Conditions

Why would Cultural Studies be interested in the selfie? The answer should be obvious: the selfie is now part of the everyday, it is integral to what I have elsewhere termed the 'museumization of the quotidian' (2012: 51–3), and participates in a social project.

The selfie offers us an excellent domain for a Cultural Studies reading because

i) It can be read within multiple cultures – communications, body performances, and consumption.
ii) It calls attention to formal and aesthetic practices.
iii) It fits into a contemporary culture of surveillance.
iv) It is an integral component of the techno-sociality of the present age, and thus feeds into questions around the role of community, representation and mediated socialities.

v) Finally, it forces us to address questions of *identity*, *agency* and *self-representation* – for a long time, the concerns of Cultural Studies work.

The Everyday

With the advent of the digital and numerous platforms for sharing, the everyday has become the site of archiving, memorialization and museumization. Earlier the photograph celebrated a special event or occasion or a significant person: weddings, births, deaths, graduation, a triumph, a tragedy, a celebrity. With blogging, Flickr, Instagram and now, in a different way, Twitter and selfies, the everyday gets recorded, archived and circulated. The everyday with its irritations, pleasures and distractions is deemed worthy of documentation because it is *my* everyday.

What this means is the aura of the photograph has been 'deauratized' even as the everyday itself has been upgraded into a photo-op and aura-worthy event. For example, we are used to seeing celebs fully made-up, poised and smartly turned out. But the selfie has altered that as celebs tweet or circulate selfies of their unmade-up, acne-ridden and ordinary faces for us to consume. As Jessica Bennett pointed out, in such cases where celebs own up to their 'imperfections' like their flawed skins, it promotes a whole new form of empowerment that says, women are not afraid to show their flaws (2014). While I shall return to this form of self-fashioning and agency later in the chapter, for now I simply wish to draw attention to the fact that the everyday in the life of the celeb is a part of their celebrityhood, and they reveal themselves as/for what they are, minus the appurtenances of fame.

The selfie is a form that makes the everyday a part of *social memory* when it is disseminated and validated by the community. Thus, the everyday of an individual slides into the public's

i) cognition
ii) memory
iii) archives

when it circulates in the form of selfie updates. The everyday of one individual is shared across spaces and people thus building an archive via diffused audiences. The diffused audience however does not passively consume the self in the selfie: by liking, forwarding or cross-posting, it participates in the process of the individual's self-fashioning.

For Cultural Studies this is an important development because the individual now directly intervenes in social memory processes, documenting something as banal as traffic congestion, an accident or a violation. Moving away from auratic photographs, corporate media profiles and official (that is, state) processes of memory-making, selfie culture encourages individual participation in the social memory project, very often offering a citizen archive of the city on its everyday basis. A history of the city or region is thus built up when individuals do the selfies at odd, unplanned locations – as opposed to hagiographic chronicles of the city.

Techno-sociality

Before we move on to a discussion of the culture of selfies, a rehearsal of some of the arguments made on contemporary techno-sociality are in order, mainly by way of contextualization.

According to one report a million selfies are taken everyday (Tiller 2014). The selfie embodies a cultural shift where to showcase the self online, via instant updates and posts, is increasingly a 'natural' state of affairs facilitated by the cellphone camera, 3 and 4G phones, free and easy-to-use sites and portals for uploads. The ready and quick affirmation by the world – okay, online community – in the form of likes and responses is what drives the stream of selfies. A global techno-sociality is made possible due to the new technologies, and the self-representation is no longer restricted to the immediate location: rather the immediate location is delocalized and globalized.

All sociality is based on exchange and sharing – of information, personal details, likes and dislikes, etc. In earlier eras this was done, mainly, face-to-face. The digital era has amplified and altered the processes of exchange making it practically instantaneous. Our modes of exchanging information and personal details are not through face-to-face interactions but through our *profiles*, or mediated presences on screen. While it remains unchanged that we present our 'best selves' to the world – essentially implying that we are careful to regulate the kind of image we present for the world to see – the mode of doing so has changed.

The selfie is one more mode of self-representation, and in its exchange of information for social currency, it resembles older forms of profile management, albeit in the digital medium.

Self-Fashioning, Agency, Community

For Cultural Studies, the emphasis lies in examining the codes through which an individual presents a self to the world to consume. What are the modes of self-representation used? Does the individual have a measure of control over the self-image s/he seeks to circulate? What are the norms of self-representation across various platforms?

For Cultural Studies, the selfie is, like consumption, a definite mode of identity construction, of self-fashioning. It involves the presentation of the body's materiality, the choice asserted in terms of appearance, the willing exhibitionism it demands, the unabashed attention-seeking process that it really is. As such it involves

- the production of a self,
- a certain regime of representation (text, image),
- circuits of dissemination and sharing (groups, networks) and
- consumption (reception, leading to redistribution).

Self-fashioning or identity construction is an act of agency involving a set of processes through which an individual first fashions and then declares her/his identity to the world, but an identity that draws upon her/his location and influences the environment (community) around the self as well.

As should be clear from the above statement, the selfie is at once a project of the self and of fitting in into a community, norms and aesthetic practices. The presentation of the self requires validation in the form of the community's acceptance, 'liking' and participation (forwarding, linking).

We shall return to several of these ideas for greater elaboration in the course of the chapter.

What we have learnt so far:
The selfie

- is a *self-fashioning* of the individual in supposedly individualistic ways, by portraying her/him as user of certain products and possessing certain attitudes ('I don't mind being seen without my make-up', as numerous Hollywood celebs have done).
- is a mode of *sociality* where this individual via this techno-mediated self-representation inserts him/herself into the community by sharing a personal detail (the selfie is a combination of image, story and the anecdote).
- contributes to the social memory of a town or community.

The Production of the Self

In this section we shall study how the selfie is produced, its ramifications and cultural role. What is the nature of the self, the identity, that emerges in a selfie? The answer to this question might be organized around several sections, which together constitute the 'production of the self'.

Narrating as Self-fashioning

The selfie marks an important cultural moment because we are now in charge of the narratives we want the world to consume. Thus we are the subjects of our own narratives, and can fashion it the way we want it to be. I insert my story alongside that of others' on social media sites. The selfie is a practice that enables one to be the subject of a story or narrative and not just its object. The selfie enables us to script our own story, complete with facial expressions, exclamations and tags. But even as we shoot ourselves for the world to consume we also see ourselves shooting ourselves. To break down this formulation, we can say that the process of narrating the self in a selfie has two components:

- Being the *subject* of the narration: *I* tell my story.
- Being the *object* narrated: I tell *my* story.

In the case of a photograph we are the object of somebody else's story, the object in a text (the photograph is a text). In a selfie I tell my own story and I watch myself as I tell this story. The selfie is a reflective medium in more ways than one because:

i) It reflects us back to ourselves on the camera screen as we shoot ourselves. We register our selves when we take our picture. Our sense of selfhood emerges from the moment of cognition and recognition: this, on the screen, is me.
ii) It allows the time to reflect on the nature of the self portrayed *before* we forward/upload it.

This is an important aspect of the culture of impression-management because our identity or subjectivity is *not* fixed for good (as in a photograph) but can be edited, morphed or deleted almost at the instant the picture is taken. I propose therefore that we see the subjectivity or sense of selfhood that we obtain when we see our own selfie as soon as it is taken as a 'provisional subjectivity', open to alteration before we send it into the world.

The selfie is an instance of the individual telling the story of her/himself to the world, in the form of images.

There is another aspect to this self-fashioning narrative. People who do selfies also *follow* others' selfies. Hence it exposes the individual to different scripts of the self, done by others. The repertoire of ideas about self-fashioning has grown exponentially in the age of the digital and the selfie is one instance of this domain of possibilities. It is therefore possible for an individual to choose among a repertoire of self-images to mimic and then send out. Self-fashioning here is thus the agency to choose what kind of image of the self the individual wants to 'own'.

The selfie takes the power to represent oneself and hands it back to the individual. Since the cultures of impression management are inextricable from the cultures of communication, the individual's control over the kind of image of her/him that circulates in digital space becomes an important way of branding the self for the world to see. The power of self-representation is the starting (and staring!) point for the circulation of the self in the digital world.

What we have learnt so far:
The selfie serves self-fashioning

- by making the individual the narrator and subject of the story being narrated.
- by also making the individual the object of the story being narrated.
- by giving the individual the freedom to alter the self-image or representation as soon as the selfie is taken.

The Body Returns

The selfie as a part of the public project of the self has two crucial *corporeal* aspects:

- The selfie foregrounds the body as the seat of human identity.
- The selfie asserts the primacy of the material body in an age where every single aspect of the human self, identity and personhood is mathematized and converted into data.

In an age dominated by the online, electronic and text-based social interaction and fragmented identities, the selfie brings the body back into the picture, literally. Embodiment, that foundation of subjectivity, is firmly reasserted with the selfie's focus on bodily expressions and posturings (even erotic and sexualised ones). But the cultural shift we need to take cognizance of is this: embodiment is technologized and technology itself is materially embodied. It is not uncommon to see selfies with the face plastered to or lips smashed against the camera lens, thus bringing the corporeal self into immediate (and even violent) contact with the medium. Even the sick body is now the subject of a selfie and, as recently reported, one can post a 'sick selfie' to prove to your boss you cannot go to work, or continuously update the world on the progress of your cancer.

Amelia Jones writing about the self-representations using contemporary technology says: 'the screen is embodied and the flesh takes its texture and materiality from the monitor' (2006). There is a haptic and tactile immediacy to the selfie that tells us the body is never obsolete, even when it is mediated because the medium can only be accessed via a body. But what is crucial is, unlike text-based communication, the selfie reveals the singularity of the body: *my* face, *my* body.

The selfie focuses primarily on the body.

In the selfie the body lends materiality to the technology, even as the technology mediates our self in the world.

Self-therapy and Empowering Exhibitionism

If the body is reinstated as the seat of identity, as argued above, then the selfie also enables the individual to acquire knowledge of her/his self, starting with 'this is what I look like'. A heightened awareness of the body, its appearance and expressions, is facilitated by the selfie's demand that one be conscious of the self.

This kind of self-reflectivity might have, on occasion, been the source of individual dissatisfaction. Contemporary commentators however claim that the selfie arose at a time where self-therapy was an accepted form of functioning. For cultural critics the selfie has been a major development as a means of self-therapy because it offers a 'body-positive' image of one's self (Tiidenberg 2014). By putting one's 'natural', that is unscripted, self out there for the world to see, one has willingly subjected oneself to the surveillance of the world. In an important argument about Jennicam (Jennifer Ringley was the first 'webcam girl', who recorded her life for the world to see), Rachel Dubrofsky makes the point that this publicizing of the self, or the willing subjection to the global eye, suggests 'the idea of being content with the self – not changing the self' (Dubrofsky 2007). This affirmation of the self – the 'body-positive' of Tiidenberg – functions, argues Dubrofsky, in a therapeutic capacity': 'this *is* me'.

The nature of the selfie suggests that one asserts (critics would say 'flaunts') one's corporeal identity, even when it does not subscribe to the current mainstream norms of sexy or appealing or even interesting.[2] People whose bodies do not fit these norms and who have otherwise found it difficult to gain social acceptance (except in negative ways) have particularly benefitted from the 'body-positive' advantage of the selfie, studies show. In such interpretations, the selfie is seen as a significant instrument of self-assertion, confidence – and morale-building exercises and psychological wellbeing (maybe a case of selfie-esteem?).

Controlling how one looks on the selfie posted online offers an individual a sense of empowerment.

In terms of the production of the self then, the selfie functions as a means of

- affirming the self.
- publicizing the self.

Together these two processes constitute a therapeutic function where the individual comes to terms with her/his body and appearance. It also, in terms of cultural contexts, offers variants to the established norms of 'good looking' and sex appeal. But there are other dimensions to the selfie as self-therapy.

The selfie might be read as an instance of 'empowering exhibitionism' (Koskela 2004). It is empowering because one controls the representations of the self, of the body, out there by transmitting one's pictures. It suggests a certain measure of control over one's life and story when we actively pursue a visual narrative of one's day or week or work through uploads/updates, scraps and posts. The selfie therefore is an important mode of telling one's story in the way one chooses to, and should be seen as a mode of interacting with the world, of 'putting on a face' one *wants* the world to see. It is an act of *agency*: to determine the nature of one's profile in the world, and to determine who sees it ('close friends' or 'all' on social networking sites). The selfie is a mode of inserting oneself into the social circuit driving communications, but it is one that allows the individual the freedom to choose how s/he might be perceived in the online social spaces.

The selfie represents the continuity of lived experience with spectacle. The spectacle is not 'out there', but here, with me, in my cellphone, in my everyday moments. Capturing the day as it proceeds ensures a documentation – museumization – of the ordinary, and translating it into a spectacle. The spectacle, previously associated with the spectacular, is now that of the ordinary. The monitor is where I (too) see my life being lived, as it is being lived, when I click and upload my selfies. Thus, the selfie represents the move to make the lived experience participate in the process of visual spectacle that is the digital world.

It inserts and projects everyday life in/onto screens so that everyday life becomes a part of the information flow that makes up the world today. The materiality of bodies is part of the material of spectacle now. The body, says Sarah Graham, is a 'commodity in the economies of attention' (Sarah Graham, cited in Vasey 2013: 7). The difference is that we have a measure of control over the self to which attention might be drawn. But the question of 'economies of attention' requires sustained examination in a later section.

When the selfie seeks an insertion of the body into the economies of attention, the individual also takes care to ensure that the body appears in a certain way so as to obtain the attention s/he seeks. Katrin Tiidenberg's empirical research has shown how individuals began to develop an interest in composition and techniques of photography, even as they begin to experiment with how *else* the body can be displayed. In other words, empowering exhibitionism enables the individual to constantly *reinvent* the body in order to receive, or sustain, the attention in the streaming spectacle that is the digital world.

The selfie converts the self, its everyday life, emotions and events, into a public spectacle.

What we have learnt so far:

The selfie

- reasserts the primacy of the body as the seat of personhood and identity.
- enables the individual to have a body-positive image when s/he broadcasts it to a set of people, and thus is akin to self-therapy.
- is an instance of empowering exhibitionism by allowing the individual to control the visual narrative of the self being sent out into the world.
- offers the individual the opportunity to reinvent the self-image s/he wishes to project.

Participatory Surveillance

The selfie represents a parallel surveillance culture to the organized surveillance by the state corporate entities because it subjects itself to the public gaze. If the CCTV can generate a story about me, then I would rather generate the story I *want* the world to see. It is also important that the very acting of selfshooting implies the presence of a community of watchers/viewers with whom the selfie is to be shared.

The selfie might be read here as performing two things:

- Surveilling it-self
- Visibilizing it-self

What the selfie represents then is an on-camera *performance* of the self for the world we know will see it. The individual inserts himself or herself into the larger social project of surveillance *voluntarily* with the selfie, and this is no different from the non-official (that is, non-state) forms of surveillance we see in the form of loyalty and membership cards or frequent flier coupons we collect and for which we share personal information to a manufacturer or supplier in exchange for benefits and deals.

The selfie voluntarily participates in the project of surveillance that is now ubiquitous, but hopes to do so on the individual's terms.

If empowering exhibitionism enabled the individual to fashion and *refashion* the self for consumption, it also enables an agential participation in the body cultures of the digital world. This participation in surveillance cultures is in fact conducive to a critical awareness of the norms of surveillance (who might be surveilled, what might be the response?) and of the community of viewers. Yet again this implies a sense of the world rather than an escape from it into cyberspace. The selfie by being part of the flow of information seeks to create a community of people who respond positively to one's looks, attitude and lifestyle. Participatory surveillance therefore needs to be seen as a way of exchanging the kind of information that solicits a certain kind of response.

Continuums and Punctum

The selfie represents a new regime of the self-in-the-world. This regime is made of continuous and consistent visibility enabled by technology. The self-in-the-world is necessarily now the visible self, so we can think of the regime of visibility that drives the selfie, and the self. The digital is a world and culture of high-speed distributability and mutability. I suggest that it is precisely these contexts that invite selfies.

In a world given over to perpetual morphing and flexibility (flexi-work, flexi-pay, flexi-timings) the selfie presents a *continuum* – my *self* through the day, week, year, relationships, workplace, activities, as documented by the person closest to me, myself. It offers a sense of continuity in a world of transmission, streaming, flows, speed and mutation, because the selfie from yesterday and the one from today, both self-shot, are the same *me*. Yet it also gives the individual the necessary flexibility of altering appearances to their taste. In other words, the selfie marks the taking of control over one's image in the digital world. This also means those who study autobiography and lifewriting need to address this new medium in which the self is written. Finally, the selfie is the *punctum* (the sharp point, singularity, also root of the word 'punctuation') in the general pursuit and flow of information about and around me ('pursuit' is linked to 'studium', which means 'to study', 'to scan', an etymology that serves as an apt metaphor for the age of flows today). If we see the self as unique or singular then we can consider the selfie as an attempt to establish this singularity in the field of images pursuing each other and being pursued.

The selfie is an attempt to establish a sense of continuity so that the flow of information does not overwhelm the self, but instead serves the purpose of maintaining the self, and its public image, across a period of time.

The selfie is at once the *singularity* of the self the individual asserts by claiming authenticity for the self expressed/caught in the selfie, and the insertion of this singularity into a flow and pursuit of images that will be scrutinised (studied), morphed and circulated. The selfie interrupts – punctuates – the flow and scansion of lines about me when I consciously, as a free agent, insert this self(ie) into the torrent (okay, an intentional pun there).

The Consumption of the Self

I propose from an entirely different context (Nayar 2015), that the selfie can be made to function as

- contributing to social memory.
- offering a chance to operate as a form of 'dissident surveillance'.

The selfie is a mode of social interaction to adapt van Dijck's argument about blogging (2008), as noted earlier. The empowered exhibitionism of the selfie also gathers around itself a community of 'likes' as the clip-culture of the Whatsapp age forwards the selfies around the users. A parallel 'community narrative' of those people who do not fit the corporeal or 'attractiveness' norms begins to emerge. It is possible to see the selfie as providing the cornerstone of a mode of social memory-making. 'Friends' who forward and post links function as mediators in the process that takes the personal selfie into the world and the public space. Indeed one needs to perhaps see the friends and 'hangout groups' as co-producing an individual's public persona when the latter sends out a selfie and they simply forward it.

The personal photograph and the selfie now are increasingly incorporated into the social memory of a community. This social memory is non-official, unscripted (usually), user-generated and random. Birthday parties, local hang-outs and other events that constitute the routine of everyday lives become the moments of selfies and groupies, and their circulation the foundation for social memory. New norms of looks, fashion, recreational activities might emerge from such selfie-circulation in a community.[3] As a means of social relations, the selfie presents the self to the community, seeks approval and endorsement through sharing – and this is no different from the various modes of impression-management that we regularly and routinely practice for social relations. The selfie serves as the digital business-card, the personal information bulletin, even the personal souvenir (what Erving Goffman, 1959, called 'expressive equipment').

The selfie functions as an *embedded witness* to the location, the event and the people, and a certain 'I-was-thereness' quality marks the selfie. The selfie is one form of the 'witness video' (Wilson and

Serisier 2010). Selfies at awkward and odd moments not only place the centre of authority at a disadvantage they also locate the selfie-taker as a witness. In a sense then the selfie functions as a parallel surveillance project where the routinely watched ordinary person becomes a watcher.

The common discourses around the widespread use of self-representation in the digital world are therapeutic – as we noted in the case of self-therapy and selfies above – and democratic (Thumim 2013). But even the assumption that these are unmediated self-representations is problematic, and this is something Cultural Studies is concerned with. Thumim's work shows how all self-representations, even in the digital world are *mediated* – by institutions, by textual processes and cultural frames. We use particular forms of self-storying or representation that are accessible (and will be liked by) people. Our content and form are both determined by the institutional processes of the portal, site or service provider used. Studies show that the individuals' perception of the personal information control offered by the site/portal features such as 'profile picture, display name, about you, or basic personal information' determines how they offer information about their self (Kuo et al 2013: 639).

The selfie is often mediated by technologies and cultural systems, and users need to find these suitable and safe enough for them to use: hence selfies are as mediated as other forms of social expression.

Thus, to summarize, involves:

- The policies of the portal/site
- The technological processes that insist on particular formats and even sometimes content

Following Thumim, this means that we have to examine the contexts of production of selfies, the people who engage in this activity, the cultural factors that allow them to do so and the reception of the selfies that then encourages more of them.

The selfie makes use of strategies of representation that will receive a positive feedback because by definition a selfie posted online is a selfie-for-the-*world*. Selfies are texts that use the kind of symbolic forms and language in anticipation of the reception, like all systems of communication and presentation.[4] To adapt Erving Goffman, controlling personal information and impression management is important for people to (i) create and (ii) preserve their *best* self, which means, the self that is most likely to find particular kinds of reception. Online self-representations, especially since these are the 'best' faces we put out there, have been known to affect individual's perceptions of themselves as well (a phenomenon called 'identity shift') (Gonzales and Hancock 2011: 80). The selfie however resists the 'best self' only project, instead offering a more realistic presentation of the self.

The selfie, like all self-representations, influences the individual sense of self too.

Like much of online cultures the selfie blurs the distinction between private and public. Indeed the publicizing of the private *in order to* attain a public image is what the selfies might be said to facilitate. The *performance* of the private, the intimate and the personal online is indeed what makes up the *public world of online networks*.

What we have learnt so far:

- Selfies are examples of embedded witnessing and have the potential to be dissident witnesses.
- They contribute to social memory.
- Selfies use strategies of self-representation so as to attain viewership and therefore are forms of social interaction.
- Selfies blur the line between private and public.
- Selfies, like all self-representations, are also mediated and users are conscious of privacy and information controls.

1. Lisa Adams inaugurated this last type of selfie when she tweeted updates about her Stage IV breast cancer treatment procedures.
2. This is especially true of gender roles in self-representation. For feminist Cultural Studies the issue would be whether the self-representations challenge dominant models of femininity.
3. Feminist activists and academics have objected to selfie culture as objectification of women by themselves so as to score higher in the dating-mating game by emphasising their appearance. (Murphy 2013). In April 2014 Time.com

reported the story of a woman who underwent cosmetic surgery so she could look better in her selfies (Chayka 2014).

4. Media theorist Nick Couldry (2004) suggests that online interactions are as ritualistic as real-life ones. These rituals frame our production of texts – such as the selfies – and the reception of the texts by partaking of similar values and belief systems.

Bibliography

Abaza, Mona. 'Shopping Malls, Consumer Culture and the Reshaping of Public Space in Egypt', *Theory, Culture & Society* 18.5 (2001): 97–122.

Alden, Dana L., Jan-Benedict E.M. Steenkamp, Rajeev Batra. 'Brand Positioning through Advertising in Asia, North America, and Europe: The Role of Global Consumer Culture', *Journal of Marketing* 63.1 (1999): 75–87.

Alexander, Jeffrey C. 'Toward a Theory of Cultural Trauma', in RonEyerman, Jeffrey C. Alexander, Bernard Giesen, Neil Smelser and Piotr Sztompka (eds) *Cultural Trauma and Collective Identity.*

Althusser, Louis. *Lenin and Philosophy and Other Essays.* Tr. Ben Brewster. New York: Monthly Review P, 1971.

Amin, Ash and Nigel Thrift. *Cities: Reimagining the Urban.* London: Polity, 2002.

Appadurai, Arjun. 'Disjuncture and Difference in the Global Cultural Economy'. In John Benyon and David Dunkerley (eds) *Globalization.* London: Athlone, 2000 (1990). 92–104.

_______. *Modernity at Large: The Cultural Dimensions of Globalization.* Delhi: Oxford University Press, 1997.

_______. 'Grassroots Globalization and the Research Imagination', *Public Culture* 12.1 (2000): 1–19.

Backes, Nancy. 'Reading the Shopping Mall City', *Journal of Popular Culture* 31.3 (1997): 1–17.

Barbas, Samantha. '"I'll Take Chop Suey": Restaurants as Agents of Culinary and Cultural Change', *Journal of Popular Culture* 36.4 (2003): 669–86.

Barthes, Roland. 'Towards a Psychosociology of Contemporary Food Consumption'. In R. Forster and O. Ranum (eds) *Food and Drink in History*. Baltimore, Md: Johns Hopkins, 1979. 166–73.

Barthes, Roland. *Mythologies*. London: Jonathan Cape, 1972.

Baudrillard, Jean. 'The Masses: The Implosion of the Social in the Media'. In Paul Marris and Sue Thornham (eds) *Media Studies: A Reader*. New York: New York UP, 2000 (1985). 99–108.

_______. *Simulations*. Tr. Paul Foss et al. New York: Semiotext(e), 1983.

Beck, Ulrich. *Risk Society: Towards a New Modernity*. Tr. Mark Ritter. London: Sage, 1992.

Bell, Daniel. *The Coming of Post-Industrial Society: A Venture in Social Forecasting*. Harmondsworth: Penguin, 1973.

Bennett, Jessica. 'Our Bodies, Our Selfies: The Feminist Photo Revolution', Time.com 13 August 2014.

Bennett, Jill. 'The Aesthetics of Sense-Memory: Theorising Trauma through the Visual Arts', in Susannah Radstone and Kathryn Hodgkin (eds) *Regimes of Memory*. London and New York: Routledge, 2003.

Bennett, Tony. 'Stored Virtue: Memory, the body and the evolutionary museum', in Susannah Radstone and Kathryn Hodgkin (eds) *Regimes of Memory*. London and New York: Routledge, 2003.

Berkeley and London: U of California P, 2004. 1-30.

Bhabha, Homi K. *The Location of Culture*. London and New York: Routledge, 1995.

Bharucha, Rustom. *The Politics of Cultural Practice: Thinking through Theatre in an Age of Globalization*. Delhi: Oxford UP, 2001.

Bianchi, Marina. 'Consuming Novelty: Strategies for Producing Novelty in Consumption', *Journal of Medieval and Early Modern Studies* 28.2 (1998): 3–18.

Bourdieu, Pierre. *Distinction: A Social Critique of the Judgement of Taste*. Tr. Richard Nice. London: Routledge, 1999 (1989).

Bower, Anne L. 'Romanced by Cookbooks', *Gastronomica* 4.2 (2004): 35–42.

Bowlby, Rachel. *Just Looking*. London: Methuen, 1985.

_______. *Carried Away: The Invention of Modern Shopping*. NY: Columbia UP, 2002 (New ed.).

Brabazon, Tara. 'Buff Puffing an Empire: The Body Shop and Colonization by Other Means', *Continuum* 15.2 (2001): 187–200.

Braidotti, Rosi. 'The Politics of "Life Itself" and New Ways of Dying', in Diane Coole and Samantha Frost (eds) *New Materialisms: Ontology, Agency, and Politics*. Durham and London: Duke University Press, 2010. 201–20.

Breckenridge, Carol. Ed. *Consuming Modernity: Public Culture in a South Asian World*. Minneapolis: U of Minnesota P, 1995.

Brown, Karen McCarthy. 'Fundamentalism and the Control of Women'. In John Stratton Hawley (ed.) *Fundamentalism and Gender*. New York and Oxford: Oxford UP, 1994. 175–201.

Bruce, Steve. *Fundamentalism*. Cambridge: Polity, 2000.

Bryden, Inga. '"There is no Outer without Inner Space": Constructing the *Haveli* as Home', *Cultural Geographies* 11 (2004): 26–41.

Burgess, Adam. *Cellular Phones, Public Fears, and a Culture of Precaution*. Cambridge: Cambridge UP, 2004.

Butcher, Melissa. *Transnational Television, Cultural Identity and Change: When STAR Came to India*. New Delhi: Sage, 2003.

Butler, Judith. *Gender Trouble: Feminism and the Subversion of Identity*. New York and London: Routledge, 1990.

_______. *Precarious Life: The Powers of Mourning and Violence*. London: Verso, 2004.

Caldwell, Marylouise, Kristen Blackwell and Kirsty Tulloch. 'Cosmopolitanism as a Consumer Orientation: Replicating and Extending Prior Research', *Qualitative Market Research* 9.2 (2006): 126–39.

Castells, Manuel. *The Rise of the Network Society*. Oxford: Blackwell, 1996.

Chakrabarty, Dipesh. 'Postcolonial Studies and the Challenge of Climate Change', *New Literary History* 43.1 (2012): 1–18.

Chayka, K. 'Woman Gets Plastic Surgery So She Can Look Better in Selfies', Time.com, 24 April. http://time.com/75610/woman-gets-plastic-surgery-so-she-can-look-better-inselfies/. 24 July 2014.

Cheung, Sidney C.H. and Eric K.W. Ma. 'Advertising Modernity: Home, Space and Privacy', *Visual Anthropology* 18 (2005): 65–80.

Clark, David. *Urban World/Global City*. London and New York: Routledge, 1996.

Clover, Carol J. 'Her Body, Himself: Gender in the Slasher Film'. In Stephen Prince (ed.) *Screening Violence*. London: Athlone, 2000 (1987): 125–74.

Cook, Judi Puritz. 'Consumer Culture and Television Home Shopping Programming: An Examination of the Sales Discourse', *Mass Communication and Society* 3.4 (2000): 373–91.

Couldry, Nick. 'Theorising Media as Practice', *Social Semiotics* 14.2 (2004).

Dant, Tim. *Material Culture in the Social World*. Buckingham: Open UP, 1999.

De Certeau, Michel. *The Practice of Everyday Life*. Tr. Randall Johnson. Berkeley and London: U of California P, 1988.

Deleuze, Gilles. *Foucault*. London: Athlone, 1986.

Derrida, Jacques. *Of Grammatology*. Tr. Gayatri Chakravorty Spivak. Baltimore and London: Johns Hokpins UP, 1976.

Deshpande, Satish. *Contemporary India: A Sociological View*. Delhi: Penguin, 2003.

Döring, Nicola and Sandra Pöschl. 'Images of Men and Women in Mobile Phone Advertisements: A Content Analysis of Advertisements for Mobile Communications Systems in Selected Popular Magazines', *Sex Roles* 55 (2006): 173–85.

Dredge, 'Mobile Gaming – The Troubled Teenaged Years'. *Receiver* 17 (2006). www.receiver.vodafone.com. 20 April 2007.

Du Gay, Paul, Stuart Hall, Linda Janes, Hugh Mackay and Keith Negus. *Doing Cultural Studies: The Story of the Sony Walkman.* London: Sage, 1997.

Dubrofsky, Rachel. 'Therapeutics of the Self: Surveillance in the Service of the Therapeutic', *Television and New Media* 8.4 (2007): 263–284.

During, Simon. 'Postcolonialism and Globalization: Towards a Historicization of their Inter-Relation', *Cultural Studies* 14. 3–4 (2000): 385–404.

Dürrschmidt, Jörg. 'The Delinking of Locale and Milieu: On the Situatedness of Extended Milieux in a Global Environment'. In John Eade (ed.) *Living the Global City: Globalization as a Local Process.* London and New York: Routledge, 1997. 56–72.

_______. *Everyday Lives in the Global City: The Delinking of Locale and Milieu.* London and New York: Routledge, 2000.

Easthope, Anthony. *Literary Into Cultural Studies.* London: Routledge, 1991.

Erll, Astrid. 'Whither Memory Studies?', Parallax 17.4 (2011): 4–18.

Falk, Pasi and Colin Campbell. Ed. *The Shopping Experience.* London: Sage, 1997.

Falk, Pasi. *The Consuming Body.* London: Sage, 1997 (1994).

Featherstone, Mike. *Consumer Culture and Postmodernism.* London: Sage, 1991.

_______. *Undoing Culture: Globalization, Postmodernism and Identity.* London: Sage, 1995.

Fiske, John. *Reading the Popular.* Boston: Unwin Hyman, 1989.

_______. 'Down Under Cultural Studies', *Cultural Studies* 10.2 (1996): 369–74.

Foley, Carmel, Caryn Holzman and Stephen Wearing. 'Moving Beyond Conspicuous Leisure Consumption: Adolescent Women,

Mobile Phones and Public Space', *Leisure Studies* 26.2 (2007): 179–92.

Foucault, Michel. *The Birth of the Clinic. An Archaeology of Medical Perception*: Tr. A.M. Sheridan-Smith London: Tavistock, 1973.

_______. *Discipline and Punish: The Birth of the Prison*. Tr. Alan Sheridan. London: Allen Lane, 1977.

_______. *Power/Knowledge: Selected Interviews and Other Writings*. Ed. Colin Gordon. Tr. Colin Gordon et al. New York: Pantheon, 1980.

Franklin, Bridget J. 'Constructing a Service: Context and Discourse in Housing Management', *Housing Studies* 13.2 (1998): 201–16.

Frow, John. 'Signature and Brand'. In Jim Collins (ed.) *High-Pop: Making Culture into Popular Entertainment*. MA, Mass.: Blackwell, 2002. 56–74.

Gant, Diana. and S. Kiesler. 'Blurring the Boundaries: Cell Phones, Mobility and the Line Between Work and Personal Life'. In Barry Brown, Nicola Green and Harper (eds) *Wireless World: Social and Interactional Aspects of the Mobile Age*. Godalming and Heidelberg: Springer Verlag, 2001. 131–41.

Gerlach, Christine. *Extremely Violent Societies: Mass Violence in the Twentieth-century World*. Cambridge: Cambridge UP, 2010.

Gibian, Peter. 'The Art of Being Off-Center: Shopping Center Spaces and the Spectacles of Consumer Culture'. In Peter Gibian (ed.) *Mass Culture and Everyday Life*. London and New York: Routledge, 1997. 238–91.

Goffman, Erving. *The Presentation of Self in Everyday Life*. Anchor, New York, 1959.

Gonzales, Amy L. and Jeffrey T. Hancock. 'Mirror, Mirror on my Facebook Wall: Effects of Exposure to Facebook on Self-Esteem', *Cyberpsychology, Behavior, and Social Networking* 14.1-2 (2011): 79-83.

Goyal, Suresh, Sanjay S. Upasani and Dhiren Patel. 'Designing Best-in-Class Impact-Tolerant Cellular Phones and Other Portable Products', *Bell Labs Technical Journal* 3.3 (1998): 159–74.

Gramsci, Antonio. *Selections from the Prison Notebooks*. Ed. and Tr. Quintin Hoare and Geoffrey Nowell-Smith. London: Lawrence and Wishart, 1971.

Gray, Ann. *Research Practice for Cultural Studies*. London: Sage, 2003.

Green, Nicola. 'On the Move: Technology, Mobility, and the Mediation of Social Time and Space', *Information Society* 18 (2002): 281–92.

Gupta, Dipankar. 'Secularization and Minoritization: The Limits of Heroic Thought'. In D.L. Sheth and Gurpreet Mahajan (eds) *Minority Identities and the Nation-State*. Delhi: Oxford UP, 1999. 38–58.

Habermas, Jürgen. *The Postnational Constellation: Political Essays*. Tr. and Ed. Max Pinsky. Cambridge: Polity, 2001.

Hall, Stuart. 'Cultural Studies: Two Paradigms', *Media, Culture and Society* 2.1 (1980): 57–72.

———. 'Encoding/Decoding'. In Paul Marris and Sue Thornham (eds) *Media Studies: A Reader*. New York: New York UP, 2000 (1985). 51–61.

———. 'The Question of Cultural Identity'. In Stuart Hall, David Held and Tony McGrew (eds) *Modernity and its Futures*. Cambridge: Polity/Open University, 1999 (1992). 273–325.

Hall, Stuart and Tony Jefferson. Eds. *Resistance through Rituals: Youth Subcultures in Post-War Britain*. London: Hutchinson, 1976.

Hand, Martin and Elizabeth Shove. 'Orchestrating Concepts: Kitchen Dynamics and Regime Change in *Good Housekeeping* and *Ideal Home*, 1922–2002', *Home Cultures* 1.3 (2004): 235–56.

Harpham, Geoffrey Galt. *Shadows of Ethics: Criticism and the Just Society*. Durham and London: Duke UP, 1999.

Harvey, David. *The Condition of Postmodernity*. Oxford: Blackwell, 1989 (1980).

Hebdige, Dick. *Subculture: The Meaning of Style*. New York: Methuen, 1979.

Heitzman, James. *Network City: Planning the Information Society in Bangalore*. Delhi: Oxford UP, 2004.

Held, David et al. Eds. *Global Transformations: Politics, Economics and Culture.* Cambridge: Polity, 1999.

Heldke, Lisa. '"Let's Eat Chinese!" Reflections on Cultural Food Colonialism', *Gastronomica* (2001): 76–79.

Hickey, Hannah. 'Mobile Phones Facilitate Romance in Modern India'. 12 February 2007. University of Washington. www.uwnews.org. 20 April 2007.

Hjorth, Larissa. 'Odours of Mobility: Mobile Phones and Japanese Cute Culture in the Asia-Pacific', *Journal of Intercultural Studies* 26.1–2 (2005): 39–55.

Horner, Susan and John Swarbrooke. *Leisure Marketing: A Global Perspective.* Amsterdam: Elsevier, 2005.

Hyderabad Airport Development Authority. *Report on the Draft Master Plan for the Hyderabad Airport Development Area – 2021.* Hyderabad: Hyderabad Airport Development Authority and Hyderabad Urban Development Authority, 2003.

Ilaiah, Kancha. 'Productive Labour, Consciousness and History: The Dalitbahujan Alternative'. In Shahid Amin and Dipesh Chakrabarty (eds) *Subaltern Studies IX.* Delhi: Oxford UP, 1996. 165–200.

Ito, Mizuko, Daisuke Okabe and Misa Matsuda. Eds. *Personal, Portable, Pedestrian: Mobile Phones in Japanese Life.* Cambridge, MA: MIT, 2005.

Ivison, Duncan. *Postcolonial Liberalism.* Cambridge: Cambridge UP, 2002.

Jackson, Peter. 'Local Consumption Cultures in a Globalizing World', *Transactions of the Institute of British Geographers* New Series 29 (2004): 165–78.

Jenisch, Markus, Harald Orlamünder, Nina Köstering and Torsten Brügge. 'My Personal Mobile City Information', *Wireless Personal Communication* 33 (2005): 271–179.

John, Mary. 'Globalization, Sexuality, and the Visual Field: Issues and Non-Issues for a Cultural Critique'. In Mary John and Janaki Nair (eds) *A Question of Silence? The Sexual Economies of Modern India* (1998).

Jones, Amelia. *Self/Image: Technology, Representation and the Contemporary Subject*. Routledge, New York and London, 2006.

Jones, Owain, Morris Williams and Constance Fleuroit. '"A New Sense of Place": Mobile "Wearable" Information and Communications Technology Devices and the Geographies of Urban Childhood', *Children's Geographies* 1.2 (2003): 165–80.

Kakoudaki, Despina. 'Spectacles of History: Race Relations, Melodrama, and the Science Fiction/Disaster Film', *Camera Obscura* 17.2 (2002): 109–53.

Katju, Manjari. *Vishva Hindu Parishad and Indian Politics*. Hyderabad: Orient Longman, 2003.

Katz, James E. 'Mobile Communication and the Transformation of Everyday Life: The Next Phase of Research on Mobiles', *Knowledge, Technology, and Policy* 19.1 (2006): 62–71.

Katz, James E. and Mark A. Aakhus. 'Conclusion: Making Meaning of Mobiles – A Theory of *Apparatgeist*'. In James E. Katz and Mark A. Aakhus (eds) *Perpetual Contact: Mobile Communication, Private Talk, Public Performance*. Cambridge: Cambridge UP, 2002. 301–18.

Kaur, Raminder and Ajay J. Sinha. 'Bollyworld: An Introduction to Popular Indian Cinema through a Transnational Lens'. In Raminder Kaur and Ajay J. Sinha (eds) *Bollyworld: Popular Indian Cinema through a Transnational Lens*. New Delhi: Sage, 2005. 11–32.

Kellner, Douglas. *Media Culture: Cultural Studies, Identity and Politics between the Modern and the Postmodern*. London and New York: Routledge, 1995.

Kesseler, Angela and Alexander Bergs. 'Literacy and the New Media: *Vita brevis, lingua brevis*'. In Jean Aitchinson and Diana M. Lewis (eds) *New Media Language*. London and New York: Routledge, 2003. 75–84.

Kolko, Beth. 'Cultural Considerations in Internet Policy and Design'. In David Silver and Adrienne Massanari (eds) *Critical Cyberculture Studies*. New York: New York University Press, 2006. 119–28.

Kopomaa, Timo. 'Speaking Mobile: Intensified Everyday Life, Condensed City'. In Stephen Graham (ed.) *The Cybercities Reader*. London and New York: Routledge, 2004. 267–72.

Koskela, H. 'Webcams, TV Shows and Mobile Phones: Empowering Exhibitionism', *Surveillance and Society* 2 (2004): 199–215.

Kotler, Philip. *Marketing Management*. Englewood Cliffs, NJ: Prentice-Hall, 1983. 6 edn.

Kunzel, Regina. 'Situating Sex: Prison Sexual Culture in Mid-Twentieth-Century United States', *GLQ* 8.3 (2002): 253–70.

Kuo, Feng-Yang, Chih-Yi Tseng, Fan-Chuan Tseng, Cathy S. Lin. 'A Study of Social Information Control Affordances and Gender Difference in Facebook Self-Presentation', *Cyberpsychology, Behavior, And Social Networking* 16.9 (2013): 635-343.

Larson, Reed W. 'Globalization, Societal Change, and New Technologies: What They Mean for the Future of Adolescence', *Journal of Research on Adolescence* 12.1 (2002): 1–30.

Lefebvre, Henri. *The Production of Space*. Tr. Donald Nicholson-Smith. Oxford: Blackwell, 2000 (1991).

Lemish, Dafna and Akiba A. Cohen. 'On the Gendered Nature of Mobile Phone Culture in Israel', *Sex Roles* 52.7–8 (2005): 511–21.

Lipscomb, Thomas J., Jeff W. Totten, Roy A. Cook and William Lesch. 'Cellular Phone Etiquette among College Students'. *International Journal of Consumer Studies* 31 (2007): 46–56.

Lowenthal, David. *The Past Is a Foreign Country*. Cambridge: Cambridge UP, 1985.

Lukose, Ritty. 'Consuming Globalization: Youth and Gender in Kerala, India', *Journal of Social History* 38.4 (2005): 915–35.

Lyon, David. *The Electronic Eye: The Rise of the Surveillance Society*. London: Sage, 1994.

Lyotard, Jean-François. *The Postmodern Condition: A Report on Knowledge*. Tr. Geoff Bennington and Brian Massumi. Minneapolis: U of Minnesota P, 1984.

MacDougall, J. Paige. 'Transnational Commodities as Local Cultural Icons: Barbie Dolls in Mexico', *Journal of Popular Culture* 37.2 (2003): 257–75.

Mackay, Hugh with Wendy Maples and Paul Reynolds. *Investigating the Information Society*. London: Routledge, 2001.

Madan, T.N. *Modern Myths, Locked Minds: Secularism and Fundamentalism in India*. Delhi: Oxford UP, 1997.

Madanipour, Ali. *Public and Private Spaces of the City*. London: Routledge, 2003.

Manovich, Lev. 'Interaction as an Aesthetic Event'. *Receiver* 17 (2006). www.receiver.vodafone.com. 20 April 2007.

Manuel, Peter. *Cassette Culture: Popular Music and Technology in North India*. Delhi: Oxford UP, 2001.

Martens, Lydia and Sue Scott. 'Under the Kitchen Surface: Dometsic Products and Conflicting Constructions of Home', *Home Cultures* 3.1 (2006): 39–62.

Massey, Doreen. *Space, Place and Gender*. London: Polity, 1994.

McCarthy, John D and Mayer N. Zald. 2003. 'Social Movement Organizations'. In Jeff Goodwin and James M. Jasper (eds) *The Social Movements Reader*. Oxford: Blackwell, 2003. 169–86.

McRobbie, Angela. 'The Politics of Feminist Research: Between Talk, Text and Action', *Feminist Review* 12 (1982): 46–57.

Melchionne, Kevin. 'Living in Glass Houses: Domesticity, Interior Decoration, and Environmental Aesthetics', *Journal of Aesthetics and Art Criticism* 56.2 (1998): 191–200.

Miles, Steven. *Youth Lifestyles in a Changing World*. Buckingham: Open University Press, 2000.

Millett, Kate. *Sexual Politics*. New York: Avon, 1971.

Mitchell, William J. *Me++: The Cyborg Self and the Networked City*. Cambridge, MA.: MIT, 2003.

Miyata, Kakuto, Jeffrey Boase, Barry Wellman and Ken'ichi Ikeda. 'The Mobil-izing Japanese: Connecting to the Internet by PC and Webphone in Yamanashi'. In Mizuko Ito, Daisuke Okabe and Misa Matsuda (eds) *Personal, Portable, Pedestrian: Mobile Phones in Japanese Life*. Cambridge, MA: MIT, 2005. 143–64.

Morley, David. *The Nationwide Audience*. London: British Film Institute, 1980.

Morris, Meaghan. 'Things to Do With Shopping Centres'. In Simon During (ed) *The Cultural Studies Reader*. London: Routledge, 2004 2nd ed. 391–409.

Moyal, A. 'The Feminine Culture of the Telephone', *Prometheus* 7.1 (1989): 5–31.

Murphy, M. 'Putting Selfies under a Feminist Lens', Straight.com, http://www.straight.com/life/368086/puttingselfies-under-feminist-lens. 24 July 2014.

Nandy, Ashis. 'A New Cosmopolitanism: Toward a Dialogue of Asian Civilizations'. In Kuan-Hsing Chen (ed.) *Trajectories*. London and New York: Routledge, 1998. 142–9.

Nayar, Pramod K. *Digital Cool: Life in the Age of New Media*. Hyderabad: Orient BlackSwan, 2012.

Nayar. *Citizenship and Identity in the Age of Surveillance*. Cambridge: Cambridge UP, 2015.

Pachter, B. and S. Magee. *The Jerk with the Cell Phone: A Survival Guide for the Rest of Us*. New York: Marlowe and Company, 2004.

Pain, Rachel, Sue Grundy and Sally Gill with Elizabeth Towner, Geoff Sparks and Kate Hughes. '"So Long as I Take my Mobile": Mobile Phones, Urban Life and Geographies of Young People's Safety', *International Journal of Urban and Regional Research* 29.4 (2005): 814–30.

Palen, Leysia and Amanda Hughes. 'When Home Base is not a Place: Parents' Use of Mobile Telephones'. *Personal and Ubiquitous Computing*.

Parker, Simon. *Urban Theory and Urban Experience: Encountering the City*. London: Routledge, 2004.

Penders, Jacques. 'Privacy in (Mobile) Telecommunications Services', *Ethics and Information Technology* 6 (2004): 247–60.

Pile, Steve. *The Body and the City: Psychoanalysis, Space and Subjectivity*. London: Routledge, 1996.

Radstone, Susannah and Kathryn Hodgkin. Ed *Regimes of Memory*. London and New York: Routledge, 2003.

Rajagopalan, Ramya. 'Ethnicity and Consumer Choice: A Study of Consumer Levels of Involvement in Indian Ethnic Apparel an Contemporary American Clothing', *Journal of Fashion Marketing and Management* 9.1 (2005): 83–105.

Rakow, L. and V. Navarro. 'Remote Mothering and the Parallel Shift: Women Meet the Cellular Phone', *Critical Studies in Mass Communication* 20.3 (1993): 144–57.

Rawafa, Urther. 'Film Representations of the Rwandan Genocide', *AfricanIdentities* 8.4 (2010): 389–408.

Rich, Adrienne. *Blood, Bread and Poetry: Selected Prose, 1979–1985*. New York and London: WW Norton, 1986.

Robertson, Roland. 'Glocalization: Time-Space and Homogeneity-Heterogeneity'. In Mike Featherstone, Scott Lash and Roland Robertson (eds) *Global Modernities*. London: Sage, 1995. 25–44.

Rothberg, Michael and Yasmin Yildiz. 'Memory Citizenship: Migrant Archives of Holocaust Remembrance in Contemporary Germany', *Parallax* 17.4 (2011): 32-48.

Samarajiva, Rohan. 'Surveillance by Design: Public Networks and the Control of Consumption'. In Robin Mansell and Roger Silverstone (eds) *Communication by Design: The Politics of Information and Communication Technologies*. Oxford: Oxford UP, 1996. 129–56.

Selfe, Cynthia and Richard Selfe. 'The Politics of Interface: Power and Its Exercise in Electronic Contact Zones', *College Composition and Communication* 45.4 (1994): 480–504.

Showalter, Elaine. *A Literature of their Own: British Women Novelists from Brontë to Lessing*. Princeton: Princeton UP, 1977.

Silverstone, Roger and Leslie Haddon. 'Design and the Domestication of Information and Communication Technologies: Technical Change and Everyday Life'. In Robin Mansell and Roger Silverstone (eds) *Communication by Design: The Politics of Information and Communication Technologies*. Oxford: Oxford UP, 1996. 44–74.

Simpson, David. 9/11: *The Culture of Commemoration*. Chicago and London: Chicago University Press, 2006.

Singhal, Arvind. 'Shopping Malls: Myths and Realities'. 17 March 2005. www.rediff.com. 15 March 2007.

Smith, Michael Peter. *Transnational Urbanism: Locating Globalization*. Oxford: Blackwell, 2001.

Smith, Neil. *The New Urban Frontier: Gentrification and the Revanchist City*. London and New York: Routledge, 1996.

Sontag, Susan. *Regarding the Pain of Others*. New York: Picador, 2004.

Spivak, Gayatri Chakravorty. *In Other Worlds: Essays in Cultural Politics*. London: Methuen, 1987.

Srivastava, Lara. 'Mobile Mania, Mobile Manners', *Knowledge, Technology, and Policy* 19.2 (2006): 7–16.

Strom, Georg. 'Mobile Devices as Props in Daily Role Playing', *Personal and Ubiquitous Computing* 6 (2002): 307–10.

Storey, John. *Inventing Popular Culture*. Oxford: Blackwell, 2003.

Sturken, Marita. *Tangled Memories: The Vietnam War, the AIDS Epidemic, and the Politics of Remembering*. Berkeley, CA: U of California P, 1997.

Subramaniam, Radhika. 'Urban Physiognomies'. In *Sarai Reader 02: The Cities of Everyday Life*. Delhi/Amsterdam: New Media Initiative and Society for Old and New Media, 2002. 8–13.

Taylor, Alex S. and Richard Harper. 'The Gift of the *Gab*? A Design Oriented Sociology of Young People's Use of Mobiles', *Computer Supported Cooperative Work* 12 (2003): 267–96.

Telecom Regulatory Authority of India. *Consultation Paper on Issues Pertaining to Next Generation Networks.* Consultation Paper No. 2/2006. 12 January 2006.

Telecom Regulatory Authority of India. *Performance Indicators October-December 2005*. 10 April 2006.

Telecom Regulatory Authority of India. *Recommendations on Allocation and Pricing of Spectrum for 3G and Broadband Wireless Access Services.* New Delhi: TRAI House, September 2006.

Telecom Regulatory Authority of India. *Recommendations on Issues Pertaining to Next Generation Networks*. 20 March 2006.

Telecom Regulatory Authority of India. *Supplement to the Indian Telecom Services Performance Indicator Report for the Quarter ending September 2005*.

Thrift, Nigel. *Spatial Formations*. London: Sage, 1996.

Thumim, Nancy. *Self-representation and Digital Culture*. New York, NY: Palgrave-Macmillan, 2012.

Tiidenberg, Katrin. 'Bringing Sexy Back: Reclaiming the Body Aesthetic via Self-shooting', *Cyberpsychology: Journal of Psychosocial Research on Cyberspace* 8.1 (2014): 1–15.

Tillery, Alisha. 'Selfie Nation', *Essence September* 2014, 5.

Torchin, Leshu. *Creating the Witness: Documenting Genocide on Film, Video, and the Internet*. Minneapolis and London: U of Minnesota P, 2012.

Urry, John. *The Tourist Gaze*. London: Sage, 1990.

Valkenburg P, Peter J, Schouten A. 'Friend networking sites and their relationship to adolescents' well-being and social self-esteem', *Cyber Psychology & Behavior* 9 (2006): 584–590.

Van Dijck, J. 'Digital photography: Communication, identity, memory', *Visual Communication* 7 (2008): 57–76.

Van Loon, Joost. *Risk and Technological Culture: Towards a Sociology of Virulence*. London: Routledge, 2002.

Vasey, George. 'Self2Selfie', *Art Monthly* 371 (2013): 5–8.

Virilio, Paul. *Pure War*. Tr. Mark Polizotti. New York: Semiotext(e), 1997 (Revised ed).

Wajcman, Judy. *Feminism Confronts Technology*. Cambridge: Polity, 1991.

Webster, Frank. *Theories of the Information Society*. London and New York: Routledge, 1995.

Wei, Carolyn Y. 'Mobile Hybridity: Supporting Personal and Romantic Relationship with Mobile Phones in Digitally Convergent Spaces'. Diss. U of Washington, 2007. http://scarlethamiter.com/research/dissertation.html (28 March 2007).

White, Michele. 'Listing eBay Masculinity: Erotic Exchanges and Regulation in "Gay" and "Gay Interest" Underwear and Swimwear', *Journal of Gender Studies* 19.1 (2010): 43–58.

Williams, Raymond. *Keywords: A Vocabulary of Culture and Society*. London: Fontana, 1983 (1976).

_______. *The Long Revolution*. Harmondsworth: Penguin, 1961.

_______. *Culture*. London: Collins, 1981.

Willis, Paul. *Profane Culture*. London: Routledge and Kegan Paul, 1978.

Wilska, Terhi-Anna. 'Mobile Phone Use as Part of Young People's Consumption Styles', *Journal of Consumer Policy* 26 (2003): 441–63.

Wilson, Dean and Tanya Serisier. 'Video Activism and the Ambiguities of Counter-Surveillance', *Surveillance & Society* 8.2 (2010): 166–80.

Wood, Rod C. *The Sociology of the Meal*. Edinburgh: Edinburgh UP, 1995.

Wu, Wann-Yih and Ching-ChingKe. 'An Online Shopping Behavior Model Integrating Personality Traits, Perceived Risk, and Technology Acceptance', *Social Behavior and Personality* 43.1 (2015): 85–98.

Zeirold, Martin. 'Memory and Media Cultures', in Astrid Erll, AnsgarNünning (eds) Cultural Memory Studies: An International and Interdisciplinary Handbook. Berlin, New York: Walter de Gruyter, 2008. 399–407.

Zukin, Sharon. 'Urban Lifestyles: Diversity and Standardisation in Spaces of Consumption', *Urban Studies* 35.5–6 (1998): 825–39.